The James Burton Coffman Commentaries
THE HISTORICAL BOOKS, Vol. VIII

COMMENTARY ON

Ezra, Nehemia
and Esther

By

James Burton and Thelma B. Coffman

1993

A·C·U PRESS
Abilene Christian University
Abilene, Texas

DEDICATION

Sissy (Thelma) and I wish to dedicate this eighth and final commentary on the Historical Books of the Old Testament to:

Dr. Frank Todd Barfield
and his wife
Shirley Lou Barfield
of
Columbus, Texas

These precious Christian friends have blessed us in many ways. Doctor Barfield is a very distinguished ophthalmologist, whose professional skill, with God's blessing, has enabled our work on the commentaries for years, by maintaining my sufficient eyesight, in spite of disease and congenital weakness of my eyes.

Doctor Barfield is an Elder of the Church, a member of the Board of Trustees of Abilene Christian University; and both he and his wife are universally loved and appreciated by their fellow citizens of Columbus, where they are recognized as civic and community leaders. Patients come to Doctor Barfield from throughout Texas and surrounding states as far as Georgia.

---James Burton and Thelma B. Coffman

PREFACE

This is the thirty-fourth volume of our Bible Commentaries, including sixty-one of the sixty-six books in the Bible. We praise the Lord for his blessing us throughout more than a quarter of a century required by these labors. Blessed be the name of the Lord!

Deo volente (God willing), we shall continue to work toward the conclusion of this project; but the calendar reminds us that we cannot be very far from life's *terminus ad quem*. We earnestly pray the Father that, if it be His will, we may live and retain sufficient health and strength to complete our research and commentaries upon the remaining five books of the Holy Bible. We also prayerfully request that great host of friends who have purchased our books and encouraged us through many years to join us in this prayer.

What an incredibly blessed privilege it has been to pursue these sacred studies in God's word!

---James Burton and Thelma B. Coffman

ABBEVIATIONS

AAOT = Archeology and the Old Testament
AB = Albert Barnes or F. C. Cook
AC = Adam Clarke
A. D. = *Anno Domini,* Year of Our Lord
AMOB = *All the Men of the Bible* by Herbert Lockyer
AnBi = Anchor Bible
ANF = Ante-Nicene Fathers
ASP = Arthur S. Peake's Commentary
ASV = American Standard Version
AV = Authorized Version (King James Bible)

BBC = Broadman Bible Commentary, Vol. 3.
BC = Before Christ
BWLD = Britannica World Language Dictionary

c. = about
ca. = about
cf. = compare
ch. = chapter
chs. = chapters
CFK = C. F. Keil (Keil-Delitzsch OT Commentary)
CRB = Cross-reference Bible

DV = Douay Version of OT

EnBr = Encyclopaedia Britannica
EOTB = *Everyone in the Bible* by Wm. F. Baker

f = verse following
FCC = same as AB
ff = verses following
FHR = Fleming H. Revell Company
FWF = F. W. Farrar in Expositor's Bible

GDH = George DeHoff Commentary

GNB = Good News Bible

HHH = *Handbook of the Bible* by Henry H. Halley
HIST = Historical Books

IB = Interpreter's Bible
ICC = International Critical Commentary
ISBE = International Standard Bible Encyclopedia
JBC = James Burton Coffman
JFB = Jamieson, Fauset and Brown Commentary
JOSA = Flavius Josephus, Antiquities
JRD = J. R. Dummelow Commentary

LBC = Layman's Bible Commentary
Ltd. = English equivalent of incorporated
LXX = The Septuagint Version of the OT

MAPR = Major Prophets
MIPR = Minor Prophets
MH = Matthew Henry Commentary

NBCR = New Bible Commentary Revised
NBD = New Bible Dictionary
NEB = New English Bible
NIV = New International Version
NLBC = New Layman's Bible Commentary
No. = number
NT = New Testament
op. cit. = *opere citato* (work cited above)

p. = page
PBD = Peloubet's Bible Dictionary
pp. - pages
PENT = Pentateuch
PC = Pulpit Commentary
PHC = Preacher's Homiletic Commentary

RSV = Revised Standard Version

TBAA = The Bible and Archaeology
TBC = Teacher's Bible Commentary

vv. = verses
Vol. = volume
WBC = *Word Bible Commentary* , *Vol. 16* by H. G. M. Williamson
WBE = Wycliffe Bible Encyclopedia
WW = Wilson's Word Studies in the OT
WYC = Wycliffe OT Commentary

YACOB = Young's Analytical Concordance of the Bible

Special Abbreviatioins in this Volume
1C = First Chronicles
2C = Second Chronicles
1K = First Kings
2K = Second Kings
1S = First Samuel
2S = Second Samuel

Commentaries by JBC...

NT Vol. 1 = Matthew
NT Vol. 2 = Mark
NT Vol. 3 = Luke
NT Vol. 4 = John
NT Vol. 5 = Acts
NT Vol. 6 = Romans
NT Vol. 7 = 1 & 2 Corinthians
NT Vol. 8 = Galatians - Philippians
NT Vol. 9 = Thessalonians - Philemon
NT Vol. 10 = Hebrews   ...
NT Vol. 11 = James - Jude ...
NT Vol. 12 = Revelation   ...

PENT Vol. 1 = Genesis
PENT Vol. 2 = Exodus
PENT Vol. 3 = Leviticus/Numbers
PENT Vol. 4 = Deuteronomy

HIST Vol. 1 = Joshua
HIST Vol. 2 = Judges & Ruth
HIST Vol. 3 = I Samuel
HIST Vol. 4 = 2 Samuel
HIST Vol. 5 = 1 Kings
HIST Vol. 6 = 2 Kings
HIST Vol. 7 = IC & 2 C
HIST Vol. 8 = Ezra, Nehemiah, Esther

MAPR Vol. 1 = Isaiah
MAPR Vol. 2 = Jeremiah
MAPR Vol. 3 = Ezekiel
MAPR Vol. 4 = Daniel

MIPR Vol. 1 = Joel, Amos, Jonah
MIPR Vol. 2 = Hosea, Obadiah, Micah
MIPR Vol. 3 = Nahum, Habakkuk, Zephaniah, Haggai
MIPR Vol. 4 = Zechariah, Malachi

Ps. 1 = Psalms 1 - 72
Ps. 2 = Psalms 73 - 150

MYS = The Mystery of Redemption

TABLE OF CONTENTS

Commentary on Ezra

INTRODUCTION

The various introductions to this book vary in size from half a column to 22 pages, the latter being that of Williamson in his Word Biblical Commentary. We feel that, "The Book of Ezra is a work of so simple a character as scarcely to require an introduction."[1]

Any detailed investigation of the alleged 'sources' of the author, accompanied by the assignment of the several sections of the book to various authors, and many other scholarly speculations should be questioned and rejected, because such views, "Spring from over-refinement, and they assume a keenness of critical discernment which cannot be claimed without arrogance."[2]

A, *Ezra a Separate Book.* A favorite theory among many current scholars is that the books of Chronicles, Ezra, and Nehemiah are all parts of a larger composition including all three.[3] However, the very able scholars who wrote the Keil-Delitzsch OT Commentary declare that, "The reasons assigned as the basis of the opinion that Ezra is merely a fragment of such a larger work, upon closer examination, prove too

---

[1] PC, Vol. 7, p. i.
[2] Ibid., p. ii.
[3] NLBC, p. 524.

weak to confirm that view."[4]

The position assumed in this commentary is that Ezra is a completely separate work, even from Nehemiah, with which it is combined as a single book in the Hebrew Bible and so listed in the works of Josephus. This is easily explained on the basis that the Jews named all of their inspired writings in exactly 22 or 24 listings in order to conform them to the same number as that of the letters in the Hebrew Alphabet, which, of course, was an altogether artificial arrangement. Furthermore, as Keil-Delitzsch stated it, "Although the Masoretes regarded and reckoned both Ezra and Nehemiah as a single work, that affords no grounds for supposing them actually to have been but a single book; for in that case, we should be obliged to consider all twleve of the Minor Prophets as a single book"![5]

In addition to all this, there is nothing either in the contents or the form of Ezra that is incompatible with the premise that it is a unified production of a single author.

B. *The Authorship of Ezra.* "Although the author of Ezra is not mentioned in the book, and in spite of the fact that both the first and second persons are used in the narrative, it is highly probable that Ezra himself wrote this book."[6]   Many radical scholars date Ezra as late as the times of Alexander the Great, but we

---

[4] CFK, Vol. 3c, p. 6.

[5] Ibid, p. 7.

[6] WYC, *Ezra*, p. 423.

appreciate Bowman's telling us exactly why they wish to late-date Ezra, "By thus assuming that the Chronicler (Ezra) wrote more than a century after the events he records, it is easy to understand why his statements can be challenged as unhistorical."[7] So there it is! The plain reference to the Law of Moses (Ezra 7:6) is a contradiction of that darling *P Document* hypothesis which is the cornerstone of radical criticism, and which this writer rejects out of hand as being itself, imaginative, fraudulent, and absolutely unhistorical. It is encourageing that Whitcomb flatly declared that this text (Ezra 7:6), "Cannot be used as an argument against Ezra's authorship."[8]

The long chronological gap between the two sections of Ezra has led most modern scholars to decide that Ezra compiled the first section from authentic records available to him, and that he wrote from his own experience and knowledge in the second section. We find no fault with this, believing it to be fully compatible with the Hebrew tradition of, "Ezra's authorship of the whole book."[9]

C. *The Name of the Book of Ezra.* There are two very good reasons for this name. (1) It is the name of the principle character in the book; and (2) it was written by Ezra. The book of Nehemiah was so named for the same reasons.

---

[7] IB, Vol. 3, p. 553.
[8] WYC, op. cit., p. 423.
[9] FCC, *Ezra*, p. 435.

D. *The Date of Ezra*. Without any doubt, Ezra
was written during the final one third of the fifth
century BC. Williamson, in his great award winning
commentary, noted that, "We do not accept a late date
for Ezra ... It cannot have been earlier than about 430
BC, nor later than the death of Artaxerxes in 424 BC."
Students should always remember that the business of
dating biblical books is, at best, a somewhat precarious
assignment. The fifth century BC date which we here
assign to Ezra is supported by the presence in the text of
vocabulary, style, proper names, etc. which "Are either
known to be or suspected of being Persian."[10]

In this connection, we reject the conclusion of
Short that, "Ezra, along with Nehemiah and Chronicles
was complied about 330 BC."[11] He followed the
leadership of the radical critics in this date, basing it
upon the mention of Jaddua the high priest in
Nehemiah 12:11,22, who according to Josephus was
high priest when Alexander the Great threatened
Jerusalem in 331 BC.[12]

The argument based upon Jaddua's being high
priest in the times of Alexander the Great, however, is
worthless for two reasons; (1) Jaddua might well have
been high priest in both periods, that of Nehemiah, and
that of Alexander the Great, which would have been
nothing very remarkable, especially if he had lived to be
ninety years of age or older, as did Jehoiada who died at

---

[10] FCC, *Ezra*, p. 436.
[11] NLBC, p. 324.
[12] JOSA, pp. 344, 345.

age 130 (2C 24:15). That such a thing actually
happened is supported by the fact that Josephus
reported the death of Jaddua the very next year after his
going out to meet Alexander[13], indicating that Jaddua at
that time might very well have been a person of
extremely advanced age.

(2) The other reason that the late-daters of
Ezra may not use the name of Jaddua as an excuse for
doing so was succinctly stated by Whitcomb, "Even if
Josephus is right that a Jaddua was high priest in
Alexander's time (and he is highly untrustworthy in his
chronology of this period) we are still left with the
distinct possibilities that (1) there were two high priests
named Jaddua, or (2) that Jaddua lived to be about 100
years old."[14] Either one of these possibilities removes
Josephus' mention of Jaddua as any kind of a legitimate
argument for a late date of Ezra.

E *The Two Divisions of Ezra.* The book of Ezra
has two main parts.

(1) Chapters 1-6 provide a record of Israel's
return from Captivity during the twenty-three year
period between 538-516 BC. "During this period
Zerubbabel was governor. Jeshua was high priest, and
Zechariah and Haggai were prophets."[15]

(2) Chapters 7-10 skip a period of "fifty-seven
years"[16] from what is related in the first six chapters

---

13 Ibid., p. 346.
14 WYC, op. cit., p. 443.
15 FCC, Ezra, p. 435.
16 Ibid.

without any mention whatever of events during that time. They relate the commission given by Artaxerxes to Ezra in the seventh year of his reign (458 BC), his journey to Jerusalem, and his doings there during the year between the Aprils of 458-457 BC.[17]

F. *The Purpose of Ezra.* Keil-Delitzsch stated that the purpose of Ezra was, "To show the manner in which the Lord God, after the lapse of seventy years of exile, fulfilled his promise, as conveyed by the prophets, by the deliverance of his people from Babylon, the rebuilding of the temple in Jerusalem, the restoration of the temple worship according to the law, and the preservation of the restored community from fresh lapses into heathenism and idolatry by the dissolution of their marriages with Gentile women."[18]

G. *Archaeological Support of the Book of Ezra.* Scholars earlier in this century rejected the fourth chapter of Ezra as "unhistorical"; but, "Once more a verdict against such radical critical views has now come to light in the famous Elephantine papyri. These letters are in Aramaic, the language of diplomacy and trade during the Persian period. They date between 500-400 BC. They were written by Jews in the military colony on the island of Elephantine; and, discovered in 1903, they constitute the most important archaeological source for the books of Ezra and Nehemiah."[19] They completely devastate the old critical dictum that the

---

[17] Ibid.
[18] CFK, op. cit., p. 5.
[19] WFA, p. 307.

language did not fit the times. It did fit, exactly!

Another important revelation from the Elephantine papyri is that the high priest called Jaddua by Josephus (see under 'D,' above) was actually named Jehohanan, who held that office in 408 BC.[20]

A great many other things might be included in an introduction to Ezra, but our principal concern lies in the study of what the text says. The disagreements and speculations of men regarding this or that question such as these addressed here have little or no importance. As the Lord said, "Till heaven and earth pass away, one jot or one tittle shall in no wise pass away from the law till all things be accomplished" (Matthew 5:18). All of the enemies of the Old Testament combined have been unable to remove a single sentence from it, despite their Gargantuan efforts to do so. If every verse of the Bible could be endowed with a human voice and the ability to speak, they might pass in review before the radical critics and say, as Paul said to the jailor at Philippi, "Sirs, do thyself no harm; we are all here"!

xxx

---

[20] BBC, Vol. 3, p. 422

CHAPTER 1
The Lord Moved to Fulfil His Promise of Ending the Exile

The seventy years of Israel's captivity had expired, exactly as Jeremiah had prophesied; and one of the most unbelievable events in human history promptly occurred, when, during the very first year of Cyrus' authority over the Chaldean kingdom (which at that time included Israel), the great ruler of Persia not only granted Israel permission to return to Palestine, but aided them very substantially in other ways also. There was no precedent whatever for such a thing. Where, in all the wretched history of the human race, was there ever anything that could be compared with a development like this? The very uniqueness of this return of Israel to their homeland is the only proof needed that it was accomplished by the direct intervention of God himself in the sordid affairs of sinful men.

Isaiah had prophesied the end of Israel's captivity, even foretelling the very name of the key instrument of God in the accomplishment of it, declaring emphatically that Cyrus would accomplish the rebuilding of Jerusalem and the temple (Isaiah 44:28-45:7). Only those who are blinded by the false axiom of radical critics who deny the possibility of predictive prophecy can accept their unfounded, passionate, and vehement denials of this passage in Isaiah. There it stands! And here in Ezra, as well as in the final verses of Second Chronicles, we have the record of God's fulfilment of his sacred word. See our discussion of Isaiah's prophecy on pp. 421-423 in our Commentary on Isaiah.

Cyrus's Decree Authorizing the Return of Israel to Palestine

Verses 1-4, Now in the first year of Cyrus king of Persia, that the word of Jehovah by the mouth of Jeremiah might be accomplished, Jehovah stirred up the spirit of Cyrus king of Persia, so that he made a proclamation throughout all his kingdom, and put it also in writing, saying, 2 Thus saith Cyrus king of Persia, All the kingdoms of the earth hath Jehovah, the God of heaven, given me; and he hath charged me to build him a house in Jerusalem, which is in Judah. 3 Whosoever there is among you of all his people, his God be with him, and let him go up to Jerusalem, which is in Judah, and build the house of Jehovah, the God of Israel (he is God), which is in Jerusalem. 4 And whosoever is left, in any place where he sojourneth, let the men of his place help him with silver, and with gold, and with goods, and with beasts, besides the freewill-offering for the house of God which is in Jerusalem.

In the first year of Cyrus king of Persia (v. 1). A number of scholars place this date at 538 BC;[1] but Darius was ruler of Persia (as Cyrus' deputy) for a couple of years; and Keil's placement of this date at 536

---

[1] FCC, *Ezra*, p. 437.

BC[2] is a more accurate discernment, as that was Cyrus' first year of sole sovereignty over Babylon.

That the word of Jehovah by the mouth of Jeremiah might be accomplished (v. 1). This is a reference to Jeremiah 15:12-14 which records that prophet's announcement of the seventy-year duration of the exile. See our extensive comments on that in the Commentary on Jeremiah, pp. 279-290.

Oesterley asserts that, "The seventy years is a dsignation for a long period of time, and is not to be taken in a literal sense";[3] however, this comment, in spite of its being echoed by a number of scholars, is simply not true. The captivity began in 606 BC and lasted till 536 BC, a period of exactly seventy years, as Keil has fully explained.[4] The point which many scholars overlook is that from the very first day of the accession of Jehoiakim, Israel was no longer an independent nation. That the seventy years was indeed a precise and exact prophecy, and not a mere idiom for "a long time," is proved by the fact that God designed it to give the land its sabbaths, which Israel had totally neglected during the 490 years from the accession of Saul to the Captivity. It required *exactly seventy years* to accomplish that. This fact is stressed by the sacred author in 2 Chronicles 36:21.

Cyrus ... made a proclamation throughout his

---

2 CFK, *Jeremiah*, p. 374.
3 ASP, p. 325
4 CFK, op. cit., p. 374.

kingdom, and put it also in writing (v. 1). This statement that the proclamation was made both orally and written, "Should not be surprising; it was quite usual in the ancient world for oral messages to be backed up by written documents, as in 2K 19:9-14."[5]

Many critics have challenged the authenticity of Cyrus' edict; but, "Archaeology has demonstrated that Cyrus' concession to Jewish exiles was not an isolated act, but the general policy of a remarkably humane leader of conciliating his new subjects by showing favor to their religions."[6] Some have pointed out that Cyrus' knowledge of the true God Jehovah was by no means perfect and that in a similar way he honored the pagan deity Marduk and the Moon god Sin. Still, the honors and guidance of his successes which Cyrus mentioned in the particular proclamations mentioned here as pertaining to Jehovah, the God of Israel, are certainly included in those inscriptions found upon the bricks in one of the gates of Babylon, namely, "The great gods have delivered all lands into my hands; the land I have caused to dwell in a peaceful habitation."[7]

The objection may then be raised that Cyrus's knowledge of Jehovah was far from perfect. So what? Did not Isaiah's prophecy indicate that very fact regarding Cyrus? "I have called thee by thy name; I have surnamed thee, though thou hast not known me"

---

[5] WBC, *Ezra*, p. 10.
[6] WFA, p. 303.
[7] Sir Frederic Kenyon, *The Bible and Archaeology* (New York, 1940), p. 141.

(Isaiah 45:4). It was altogether natural, therefore, that the author of Ezra should have stressed Jehovah alone, and not the pagan deities, in his report of the decree.

All the kingdoms of the earth hath Jehovah, the God of heaven, given me (v. 2). Williamson and others have repeated the inaccurate declaration found frequently in the writings of early 20th century critics that, "*The God of heaven* makes its first appearance here as a description of the God of the Bible."[8] There is only one thing wrong with such a comment; it is simply not true! In the eighth century BC, Jonah told the mariners on their storm-threatened ship that, "I am a Hebrew; and I fear the *God of heaven* who hath made the sea and the dry land" (Jonah 1:9). For any who may doubt the date of Jonah, we have thoroughly explored this in our introduction to that prophecy in Vol. 1 of our Minor Prophets Series. Furthermore, the very first book in the Bible, namely, Genesis, refers to *the God of heaven* twice (Genesis 24:3, 7)!

The absolute historicity and validity of this great decree of Cyrus is impossible of any intelligent denial. Furthermore, the biblical narrative of how it came about that Israel was delivered from Babylonian captivity must be accepted as the only logical explanation of it. Unbelievers may scoff at the pertinent prophecies God gave through Jeremiah and Isaiah; but what else could have led to that remarkable deliverance? If God himself did not indeed "stir up the spirit of Cyrus," as related in v. 1, then *who did?* The

---

[8] WBC, op. cit., p. 12.

entire operation that brought Israel back to Palestine, rebuilt Jerusalem, and the Second Temple, and reestablished a nation that had languished in slavery for seventy years ---that whole operation, first and last, was an act of Almighty God.

Let the men of his place help him with silver and gold (v. 4). It is disputed as to whether or not the helpers here were Israelites only, or if they also included their neighboring Babylonians. There is more than a hint of the Exodus here; for it will be remembered that the Egyptians enriched the children of Israel on the occasion of their leaving Egypt. Something of that same Divine Providence might have been effective upon this occasion also.

One might wish that all Israel had heeded the edict of Cyrus and made their way back to Palestine; but it was not to be. Isaiah's great prophecy of "The Remnant" would be literally fulfilled. Only a relative handful of the captives, considerably less than 50,000, ever made their way back to Judah and Jerusalem. The vast majority had accomodated themselves to the lifestyle, the riches, and the religion of the Babylonians.

Cyrus Returns to Israel the Sacred Vessels Looted from the Temple by Nebuchadnezzar

Verses 5-11, Then rose up the heads of the fathers' houses of Judah and Benjamin, and the priests, and the Levites, even all whose spirit God had stirred up to go up to build the house of God which is in Jerusalem. 6 And all they that were round about them strengthened their hand with vessels of silver, with gold, with goods, and with beasts, and with precious things, besides all that was willingly offered. 7 Also Cyrus the king brought for the vessels of the house of Jehovah, which Nebuchadnezzar had brought forth out of Jerusalem, and put in the house of his gods; 8 even these did Cyrus king of Persia bring forth by the hand of Mithredath the treasurer, and numbered them unto Sheshbazzar, the prince of Judah. 9 And this is the number of them: thirty platters of gold, a thousand platters of silver, nine and twenty knives, 10 thirty bowls of gold, silver bowls of a second sort four hundred and ten, and other vessels a thousand. 11 All the vessels of gold and of silver were five thousand and four hundred. All these did Sheshbazzar bring up, when they of the captivity were brought up from Babylon unto Jerusalem.

The heads of the fathers' houses of Judah and Benjamin (v. 5). Although Cyrus' decree was broad enough to have included any of the northern tribes who might have survived the Assyrian captivity (v. 3), this mention of those who responded makes it clear that there was no significant response from any of the tribes except that of Judah and Benjamin

And all that were about them strengthened their hand (v. 6). "This is usually held to include Babylonians";[9] and why not? The generous example set by the king himself would have prompted many others to follow his lead; and, as the text stands, it could hardly fail to include all the neighbors, even the Babylonians.

---

[9] BBC, Vol. 3, p. 434.

*Even these did Cyrus king of Persia bring forth ...
and numbered them unto Sheshbazzar, the prince of Judah
(v. 8).* "This is a reference to Nebuchadnezzar's looting
of the Temple of Solomon on both of those occasions
when he captured Jerusalem in 597 BC and in 587 BC.[10]
These sacred vessels he had laid up as trophies in the
house of his gods; and upon the night when Babylon
fell, the drunken king Belshazzar was having a great
feast for his lords and concubines, when he sent for the
sacred vessels of the Jewish Temple to drink from them.
That was the occasion (Daniel 5) when the fingers of a
man's hand wrote the doom of Babylon on the wall; and
the city fell that night.

*All these did Sheshbazzar bring up when they of the
captivity were brought up from Babylon to Jerusalem (v.
11).* Two things of importance should be noted here.
Sheshbazzar who here is seen to have led the first
emigration to Jerusalem disappears from the biblical
narrative after this brief mention; but as Williamson
noted, "This should not surprise us, because no first
hand account (of all that happened) has survived."[11]

Also, "The passive verb 'were brought up' is
deliberately chosen here to imply divine activity. The
narrative thus echoes the description of the Exodus
(Exodus 33:1), *Brought up from Babylon to Jerusalem*
thus becomes the counterpart of *brought up out of the
land of Egypt.*"[12]

---

[10] Ibid.
[11] WBC, op. cit., p. 19.
[12] Ibid.

CHAPTER 2
The Register of the Returned Exiles

Very little comment is needed on this chapter. The purpose of the sacred author was that of establishing the continuity of the nation of God's Chosen People; and, just as the return itself was presented by him as a "Second Exodus," so this list of names was designed to link the present company of returnees with the glorious names of their previous history, with the implied teaching that they were still the Chosen People and that God would continue to bless them.

"This same list of names appears in Nehemiah 7:6-73 and in Esdras 5:4-46. It is not easy to account for the discrepancies."[1] In fact, we have never seen any attempt by any scholar to harmonize the lists. They satisfied the people who returned from Babylon; and that is really all that matters.

"Seven distinct groups of people are mentioned."[2] These are (1) the leaders, (2) the men of Israel, (3) the priests, (4) the Levites, (5) the temple servants, (6) the sons of Solomon's servants, and (7) those of uncertain genealogy.

The return from exile was not an "all at once" experience. It went on somewhat gradually over a period of years; and this list might have been revised or corrected from time to time; and some scholars believe that it included some who had never been in captivity at

---

[1] NBCR, p. 399.
[2] Ibid.

all, "but who were in full sympathy with the returnees."[3]

It is amazing that Sheshbazzar to whom Cyrus' treasurer counted out the sacred vessels is not mentioned here; and it is not at all impossible, as suggested by Hamrick, that the author of Ezra here identified him and Zerubbabel as the same person.[4]

Regardless of our questions, many of which are impossible of any perfect solution, these names are of abiding interest in their own right. These are the names of those who kept alive the sacred hope, who did not give up, even when it seemed that all was lost, and whose children lived to turn their backs upon their shameful humiliation in Babylon, cross the burning sands of the desert, and return to that sacred elevation in Jerusalem where they built again the altar of Jehovah and faithfully resumed the worship of the God of their fathers.

"This chapter is certainly among the most uninviting portions of the Bible for the modern reader both because of its tedious nature and because of its overtones of racial exclusivism and pride."[5] However, the importance of the chapter lies in the evidence it presents concerning the development of that priestly heirarchy that came to be, in time, the total ruin of Israel.

---

[3] BBC, Vol. 3, p. 435.

[4] Ibid.

[5] WBC, *Ezra*, p. 38.

List of the Leaders

Verses 1-2, Now these are the children of the province, that went up out of the captivity of those that had been carried away, whom Nebuchadnezar the king of Babylon had carried away into Babylon, and that returned unto Jerusalem and Judah, every one into his city; 2 who came with Zerubbabel, Jeshua, Nehemiah, Seraiah, Reelaiah, Mordecai, Bilshan, Mispar, Bigvai, Rehum, Baanah.

The children of the province (v. 1). "This expression indicates that the Jewish exiles, although now released from captivity and allowed to return to their own land, were nevertheless still under the sovereignty of Cyrus, occupying a tributary province of the Persian empire."[6] This was a dramatic contrast with the glory days of David and Solomon.

Who came with Zerubbabel (v. 2). "Here Zerubbabel appears as the leader of the return to Jerusalem. The name means *seed of Babylon*, indicating that he was born there. He is usually described as the son of Shealtiel (3:2); but 1C 3:19 shows him to have been the son of Shealtiel's brother Pedaiah. Probably Shealtiel died childless, whereupon a Levirate marriage (Dt. 25:5ff) resulted in the birth of Zerubbabel, who was thus the actual son of Pedaiah but the legal son of Shealtiel."[7]

---

[6] JFB, p. 288.
[7] NLBC, p. 326.

A List of What May be Called the Laity

Verses 2c-35, The number of the men of the people of Israel: 3 the children of Parosh, two thousand a hundred seventy and two. 4 The children of Shephatiah, three hundred seventy and two. 5 The children of Arah, seven hundred seventy and five. 6 The children of Pahath-moab, of the children of Jeshua and Joab, two thousand eight hundred and twelve. 7 The children of Elam, a thousand two hundred fifty and four. 8 The children of Zattu, nine hundred and forty and five. 9 The children of Zaccai, seven hundred and threescore. 10 The children of Bani, six hundred forty and two. 11 The children of Babai, six hundred twenty and three. 12 The children of Azgab, a thousand two hundred twenty and two. 13 The children of Adonikam, six hundred sixty and six. 14 The children of Bigvai, two thousand fifty and six. 15 The children Adin, four hundred fifty and four. 16 The children of Ater, of Hezekiah, ninety and eight. 17 The children of Bezai, three hundred twenty and three. 18 The children of Jorah, one hundred twelve. 19 The children of Hashum, two hundred twenty and three. 20 The children of Gibbar, ninety and five. 21 The children of Bethlehem, a hundred twenty and three. 22 The men of Netophah, fifty and six. 23 The men of Anathoth, a hundred twenty and eight. 24 The children of Azmaveth, forty and two. 25 The children of Kiriath-arim, Chephirah, and Beeroth, seven hundred and forty three. 26 The children of Ramah and Geba, six hundred twenty and one. 27 The men of Michmas, a hundred twenty and two. 28 The men of Bethel and Ai, two hundred three. 29 The children of Nebo, fifty and two. 30 The children of Magbish, a hundred fifty and six. 31 The children of the other Elam, a thousand two hundred fifty and four. 32 The children of Arim, three hundred and twenty. 33 The children of Lod, Hadid, and Ono, seven hundred and twenty and five. 34 The children of Jericho, three hundred forty and five. 35 The children of Senaah, three thousand and six hundred and thirty.

The children of Bethlehem, a hundred twenty and three (v. 21). "Thus without any warning or transition, the list ceases to identify families by ancestors and begins to identify them by hometowns."[8] "Why this was done remains most uncertain."[9]

The List of the Priests Who Returned

Verses 36-39, The priests: the children of Jedaiah, of the house of Jeshua, nine hundred seventy and three. 37 The children of Immer, a thousand fifty and two. 38 The children of Pashhur, a thousand two hundred forty and seven. 39 The children of Harim, a thousand and seventeen.

It is very significant that the priests listed here numbered 4,287, a tenth of the entire number who returned. Why was this? "It reflects the fact that they

---

[8] BBC, Vol. 3, p. 436.
[9] WBC, Vol. 16, p. 34.

had most to gain from it."[10] Furthermore, "In the post-exilic period, there was a steady development of the priestly hierarchy,"[11] resulting finally in that godless concentration of evil men who controlled and exploited the temple and all who worshipped there, who engineered the crucifixion of the Son of God, rebelled against Rome, and brought total ruin upon Jerusalem and their entire system.

The Levites Who Returned

Verses 40-42, The Levites: The children of Jeshua and Kadmiel, of the children of Hodaviah, seventy and four. 41 The singers: the children of Asaph, a hundred twenty and eight. 42 The children of the porters: the children of Shallum, the children of Ater, the children of Talmon, the children of Akkub, the children of Hatita, the children of Shobai, in all a hundred thirty and nine.

Only 341 Levites returned to Palestine. Evidently something important had happened during the closing years of the monarchy and during the captivity that had resulted in the wholesale discouragement and disaffection of the Levites. Rawlinson explained this as due to the, "Jealousy of the priests, like that which animated Korah (Numbers 16:1-10), must have grown up during the captivity."[12] The

---

10 Ibid.
11 Ibid., p. 35.
12 PC, Vol. 7a, p. 18.

priestly conclave had also succeeded in reducing the importance and significance of the Levites and their office. By the times of Christ, the High Priest and his hierarchy had seized complete control over the whole nation, except that of the secular government; and shortly after the crucifixion of Christ they would rebel against Rome in their vain attempt to make their control total. Right here we can detect the tap root of that priestly conspiracy that led to the final ruin of Israel.

Why then did so few Levites return? "It was because of the decrease in their significance during this period and because of their lower status."[13]

The Nethinim Who Returned

Verses 43-54, The Nethinim: the children of Ziha, the children of Hasupha, the children of Tabbaoth,   44 the children of Kerios, the children of Siaha, the children of Padon,   45 the children of Lebanah, the children of Hagabah, the children of Akkub, 46 the children of Hagab, the children of Shamlai, the children Hanan,   47 the children of Gibbel, the children of Gahar, the children of Reaiah,   48 the children of Rezin, the children of Nekoda, the children of Gazzam,   49 the children of Uzza, the children of Paseah, the children of Besai, 50 the children of Asnah, the children of Meunim, the children of Nephisim,   51 the children of Bakbuk, the children of Hakupha, the children of Harhur,   52 the children of

---

13 WBC, Vol. 16, p. 35.

*Bazluth, the children of Mehida, the children of Harsha,
53 the children of Barkos, the children of Sisera, the
children of Temah,   54 the children of Nezeiah, the
children of Hatipha.*

The Nethinim (v. 43). "The name comes from a
Hebrew expression which means, 'given as helpers,' that
is, bondmen of the temple."[14] Cook also referred to
these as, "The sacred slaves given to assist the
Levites."[15] However, Williamson believed that, "The
name might mean no more than *devoted*."[16]   To this
writer, the more likely meaning is that given by Cook.
This is supported by the prominence of foreign names
in the list, names connected with the ancient
Canaanites, and also by their being classified with the
"children of Solomon's servants" (v. 55), who were most
certainly slaves. A plausible theory, supported by the
considerable number of foreign names, is that they were
prisoners of war allocated to the temple for the more
mundane tasks."[17]

The Rest of the Nethinim

*Verses 55-58, The children of Solomon's servants:
the children of Sotai, the children of Hassophereth, the
children of Peruda, 56 the children of Jaalah, the children*

---

14 PC, Vol. 6a, p. 112.
15 FCC, *Ezra*, p. 439.
16 WBC, op. cit., p. 36.
17 NBCR, p. 399.

of Darkon, the children of Giddel, 57 the children of Shephatiah, the children of Hattil, the children of Pochereth-hazebaim, the children of Ami. 58 All the Nethinim, and the children of Solomon's servants, were three hundred ninety and two.

Some Were Put Out of the Priesthood

Verses 59-63, And these were they that went up from Tel-melah, Tel-harsha, Cherub, Addan, and Immer; but they could not show their fathers' houses, and their seed, whether they were of Israel: 60 the children of Delaiah, the children of Tobiah, the children of Nekoda, six hundred fifty and two. 61 And the children of the priests: the children of Ha-baiah, the children of Kakoz, the children of Barzillai the Gileadite, and was called after their name. 62 These sought their register among those that were reckoned by genealogy, but they were not found: therefore were they deemed polluted and put from the priesthood. 63 And the governor said unto them, that they should not eat of the most holy things, till there stood up a priest with Urim and Thummin.

The children of Barzillia the Gileadite (v. 61). Barzillia, of course, was the famous friend of David who aided him during the rebellion of Absalom, a man of great wealth. Barzillia was not a priest; but his children, probably by his daughters who had married priests, and who therefore were indeed true sons of the priests; but they had retained the famous name of their distinguished ancestor. The priests, of course, intent on restricting everyone possible from joining their company, rejected their claims. The governor decided against them.

It is not exactly clear what the governor meant. There is no proof whatever that the Urim and Thummin survived the captivity, or for that matter, even the repeated sack of the temple; so what he might have meant was, that it would take a direct act of God to put the sons of Brazillia in the priesthood.

The heartless pride and arrogance of the Jewish priesthood are clearly visible here. "Concern for pedigree and purity can easily turn to pride and superiority; and this trend was tragically exemplified by many of the community's later descendants."[18]

The Sadducees and Pharisees of the times of Christ prided themselves upon the purity of their descent from Abraham, supposing that their kinship with the patriarch alone would assure them of eternal life. How wrong they were! John the Baptist had warned them that God was "Able of these stones to raise up children to Abraham" (Mt. 3:9); and Paul thundered the verdict in the ears of the nation that, "They are not all Israel who are of Israel" (Ro. 9:6); but, alas, pride and arrogance can blind the eyes and harden the hearts of all who thus delude themselves.

Summary of All Those Who Returned

Verses 64-67, The whole assembly together was

---

[18] WBC, op. cit., p. 39.

forty and two thousnd three hundred and threescore, 65
besides their men-servants and their maid-servants, of
whom there were seven thousand three hundred thirty and
seven: and they had two hundred singing men and singing
women. 66 Their horses were seven hundred thirty and six;
their mules two hundred forty and five; 67 their camels,
four hundred thirty and five; their asses, six thousand seven
hundred and twenty.

"The numbers given earlier in the chapter add up
to twelve thousand less than the total of 42,380 given in
this verse. Reckoning up the smaller numbers we have
29,818 as given here and 31,089 as given in the parallel
in Nehemiah. Ezra mentions 491 not mentioned by
Nehemiah; and Nehemiah mentions 1765 not given in
Ezra. If we add Ezra's 491 to Nehemiah's total and
Nehemiah's 1765 to Ezra's total, they both equal 31,583,
which is a deficiency of exactly 10,777."[19] They may
have been left out, either because they were not
members of Abraham's posterity, and from the Jewish
viewpoint therefore did not count. There is also the
possibility that these were women, the wives of the
returnees.[20]

Two hundred singing men and singing women (v.
65). "These were not singers appointed for use in the
worship but musicians retained by the wealthy for their
entertainment."[21] Significantly, they were not listed as

---

[19] JFB, p. 289.
[20] WBC, op. cit., p. 38.
[21] Ibid.

part of the assembly but along with other properties, the horses, mules and camels. Whitcomb thought that these singers were, "Hired by the Israelites for festivities and lamentations";[22] but Hamrick, and others, insist that, "They were slaves maintained for the entertainment of the rich."[23]

"This catalogue of the property that Israel brought back to Palestine indicates the general poverty and low estate of the returnees. They had but one slave and one ass for every six of their number, one horse to every sixty, one camel to every hundred, and one mule to every one hundred and seventy and five."[24]

Contributions Made Toward Rebuilding the Temple

Verses 68-70, And some of the heads of fathers' houses, when they came to the house of Jehovah which is in Jerusalem, offered willingly for the house of God to set it up in its place: 69 they gave after their ability into the treasury of the work threescore and one thousand darics of gold, and five thousand pounds of silver, and one hundred priests garments. 70 So the priests and the Levites and some of the people, and the singers, and the porters, and the Nethinim, dwelt in their cities, and all Israel in their cities.

Threescore and one thousand darics of gold (v. 69).

---

22 WYC, p. 425.
23 BBC, op. cit., p. 440.
24 PC, op. cit., p. 19.

During the years when this writer was in college, the radical critics were shouting to high heaven that, "The *daric* was a Greek coin that could not possibly have been current in Palestine till after the conquests of Alexander the Great. And upon the basis of their false allegations declared that Ezra, Nehemiah and the Chronicles could not possibly have been writen prior to 250 BC."[25]

"Archaeological evidence now shows that the Attic (Greek) drachma (the *daric* of this passage) was in use as a standard coin in Palestine from the middle of the fifth century BC and afterwards. Archaeologists have actually unearthed specimens of these coins near Jerusalem; and this *daric* became the official Jewish coinage, and specimens inscribed with the Aramaic name of Judah have been discovered."[26]

xxx

[25] AAOT, p. 305.
[26] Ibid.

CHAPTER 3
The Altar Erected; the Foundation of the Temple Laid, And the Peoples' Response

The Altar Erected at its Old Place

Verses 1-5, And when the seventh month was come, and the children of Israel were in the cities, the people gathered themselves together as one man in Jerusalem. 2 Then stood up Jeshua the son of Jozadak, and his brethren the priests, and Zerubbabel the son of Shealtiel, and his brethren, and builded the altar of the God of Israel, to offer burnt-offerings thereon, as it is written in the law of Moses the man of God. 3 And they set the altar upon its base; for fear was upon them because of the peoples of the countries: and they offered burnt-offerings thereon unto Jehovah, even burnt-offerings morning and evening. 4 And they kept the feast of tabernacles, as it is written, and offered the daily burnt-offerings by number, according to the ordinance, as the duty of every day required; 5 and afterward the continual burnt-offering, and the offerings of the new moons, and of all the set feasts of Jehovah that were consecrated, and of every one that offered a freewill-offering unto Jehovah.

And when the seventh month was come (v. 1). "This was the month Tishri, corresponding to our September-October."[1] "This was the first day of the month (v. 6), The Feast of Trumpets (Numbers 29:1-6), a foreshadowing of Israel's final regathering. Assuming

---

[1] H. Porter in ISBE, p. 532.

a two-year delay in the beginning of the journey from Babylon after Cyrus' decree, this would have been September 25, 536 BC. The laying of the temple foundation the following spring would thus have brought to an official close the seventy-year captivity prophesied by Jeremiah (25:1-12), i. e., from 605 to 535 BC.[2]

And builded the altar of God (v. 2). "This altar was hastily constructed in less than a day (v. 6) of field stones in accordance with the earliest prescriptions for altars in the law of Moses (Exodus 2):25)."[3]

Scholars are in disagreement over the date of the foundation's being laid; because, "Both Haggai and Zechariah date the beginning of the building activity of Zerubbabel in the second year of Darius I (520 BC)." The writings of Josephus, however, are ambiguous on this point, for he placed the laying of the foundation in the period prior to the hostility of the Samaritans, or at least, at the very beginning of it, but went on to mention it later as taking place in the reign of Darius I.[4] Since the "foundation" of any building may be (1) the excavated earth where it will be constructed, (2) the basic masonry, or (3) the support of the whole structure on top of the masonry, there can be no criticism of the two mentions of the foundation as being laid in the second year of Israel's return while Cyrus was still living, and again in the reign of Darius Hystaspes

---

2 WYC, p. 426.
3 IB, Vol. 3, p. 589.
4 JOSA, p. 323.

(Darius 1), who was the second ruler after Cyrus' death. Critics will have to come up with something harder to explain than this in order to establish what some of them call the "unhistorical" statements in Ezra.

The Persian Rulers from 559-358 BC.[5]

559-530	Cyrus
530-522	Cambyses
522-486	Darius I (Hystaspes)
486-465	Xerxes I (Ahashuerus)
465-424	Artaxerxes (Longimanus)
424-423	Xerxes II
423-404	Darius II (Nothus)
404-358	Artaxerxes (Mnemon)

And they kept the feast of tabernacles, as it is written (v. 4). This feast was kept on the fifteenth of Tishri (See Leviticus 23:34-42 and related passages of the law of Moses). "The Hebrew name of it was Sukkoth *(Booths),* a reference to the way in which the Israelites dwelt in booths during their journey through the wilderness."[6] The day of Atonement was also held on the tenth day of this month; but no mention of it is made here. The observance of that solemn occasion would have to wait upon the building of the second temple.

As it is written (v. 4). The inspired author is

---

5 NBCR, p. 395.

6 ASP, p. 326.

making it clear that Israel, upon their return to Palestine, were determined to do everything exactly according to the instructions in the law of Moses. *They kept ... all the set feasts of Jehovah (v. 5).* These were the Passover, the Pentecost (Feast of Weeks) and Tabernacles.

The True Worship Restored, They Planned to Rebuild the Temple

Verses 6-7, From the first day of the seventh month began they to offer burnt-offerings unto Jehovah: but the foundation of the temple of Jehovah was not yet laid. 7 They gave money also unto the masons and to the carpenters; and food, and drink, and oil unto them of Sidon, and unto them of Tyre, to bring cedar trees from Lebanon to the sea, unto Joppa, according to the grant that they had of Cyrus king of Persia.

There was never any doubt that the returnees would rebuild the temple, which they would do as soon as possible. They wasted no time in raising money for that purpose.

The grant they had of Cyrus (v. 7). "The full terms of this grant are found in 6:-3-5."[7] "The Lebanon range of mountains where those wonderful cedar trees grew belonged, at this point in history, to the kings of Persia."[8]

---

[7] WYC, p. 426.
[8] ASP, p. 327.

A number of dependable scholars have mentioned "corruptions" in the text of this chapter. Keil stated that, "This text cannot be regarded as authoritative";[9] and Oesterley stated, with regard to both verses 8 and 9 that, "The text here is corrupt."[10] In spite of this, the basic truth of what is here proclaimed is unimpeachable; and the alleged "corruptions" do not change that.   Furthermore, we believe that the allegations regarding a corrupt text are related to the false assumption of scholars that "laying the foundation" occurred only one time.   We reject that as unreasonable. How do men know that it was not done twice, once at the very beginning,   during the reign of Cyrus, and many years later under Darius 1?

The First Laying of the Foundation

Verses 8-10,   Now in the second year of their coming unto the house of God in Jerusalem, in the second month, began Zerubbabel the son of Shealtiel, and Jeshua the son of Jozadak, and the rest of their brethren the priests and the Levites, and all they that were come out of the captivity into Jerusalem, and appointed the Levites from twenty years old and upward, to have the oversight of the work of the house of Jehovah. 9 Then stood Jeshua with his sons and his brethren, Kadmiel and his sons, the sons of Judah, together, to have the oversight of the workmen in the house of God: the sons of Henadad, with their sons and

---

[9] CFK, Vol 3c, p. 54.
[10] ASP, p. 327.

their brethren the Levites. 10 And when the builders laid the foundation of the temple of Jehovah, they set the priests in their apparel with trumpets, and the Levites the sons of Asaph with cymbals, to praise Jehovah, after the order of David the king of Israel.

All of the ceremonies mentioned here would seem to have been something like what is known today as "Ground breaking." It is a major misassumption to suppose that the structural foundations of the Second Temple were at this time completed. Years would pass before that could occur, during which the opposition of the "peoples of the land" would be vented against Israel in their full hostility.

Bowman, of course, insisted that what took place here occurred during the reign of Darius 1, Sept. 21, 520 BC.[11] This writer, however, believes that there were two occasions when the foundation "was laid," and that the one in 520 BC was the second. This chapter plainly states that the first time was during the reign of Cyrus, or at least leaves that impression.

The Levites twenty years old and upward (v. 8). Various ages are given in scripture when the Levites were accounted able to do service in the temple. Those ages vary from the age of 20, as here, up to 25, 30, or 35. The reasons for the differences are not given; but one possible explanation is that suggested by Simmons' statement that, "There were 24,000 Levites to see after

---

[11] IB, Vol. 3, p. 592.

the work of Solomon's temple (1C 23:4); and only 341 Levites returned from Babylon."[12]   It hardly takes a genius to figure out why they lowered the required age: *they needed more men!*

Celebrating the Occasion

Verses 11-13,   And they sang one to another in praising and giving thanks unto Jehovah,saying, For he is good; for his lovingkindness endureth for ever toward Israel. And all the people shouted with a great shout, when they praised Jehovah, because the foundation of the house of Jehovah was laid.   12 But many of the priests and Levites and heads of fathers' houses, the old men that had seen the first house, when the foundaion of this house was laid before their eyes, wept with a loud voice; and many shouted aloud for joy: 13 so that the people could not discern the noise of the shout of joy from the noise of the weeping of the people; for the people shouted with a loud shout, and the noise was heard afar off.

They sang one to another (v. 11). This means that the musical renditions were done antiphonally, from one choir answering another, or from a priestly soloist answered by the singers, or by some other antiphonal arrangement.   "The Psalm they sang on that occasion was Psalm 136, which shows that they were thinking in terms of Jeremiah's great prophecy (33:11)."[13]   The

---

12 TBC, p. 253.
13 WYC, p. 426.

overwhelming joy of the occasion came from the fact that nearly three quarters of a century of hopes and fears, sorrows and frustrations, had reached a happy climax; God had forgiven and restored his Chosen People to their homeland.

However, there were those whose weeping rivalled the shouts of joy! Why? The relative insignificance and poverty of that projected New Temple was in no way comparable to that magnificent and glorious Wonder of the World that was the Temple of Solomon. There is no wonder that the old men who could remember the former Temple in its glory could find only tears as they saw the projection of the structure that would take its place. And yet, the glory of the Second Temple would far surpass that of Solomon, because the Christ himself would appear in the Second!

The people could not discern the noise of the shout of joy from the noise of the weeping (v. 13). This does not mean that the shout of joy was drowned out by the weeping; but that those who heard could not discern between them.[14] "Among Eastern people expressions of sorrow are by loud wailing, the howl of which is sometimes not easily distinguished from joyful acclamations."[15]

xxx

---

[14] CFK, p. 56,

[15] JFB, p. 290.

CHAPTER 4
Nearly a Century of Opposition to Israel

Twenty-Five Years from 535 to 520 BC

Verses 1-5, Now when the adversaries of Judah and Benjamin heard that the children of the captivity were building a temple unto Jehovah, the God of Israel; 2 then they drew near to Zerubbabel, and to the heads of the fathers' houses, and said unto them, Let us build with you; for we seek your God, as ye do; and we sacrifice unto him since the days of Esarhaddon king of Assyria who brought us hither. 3 But Zerubbabel and Jeshua, and the rest of the heads of the fathers' houses of Israel said unto them, Ye have nothing to do with us building a house unto our God; but we ourselves together will build unto Jehovah, the God of Israel, as king Cyrus the king of Persia hath commanded us. 4 Then the people of the land weakened the hands of the people of Judah, and troubled them in building, 5 and hired counsellors against them, to frustrate their purpose, all the days of Cyrus, even until the reign of Darius king of Persia.

This is an extremely abbreviated report, as a glance at the chronology of the rulers of Persia, given in the preceding chapter will show. A full twenty-five years of opposition is recorded in these five verses. These years included the remaining years of Cyrus' dominion, the twelve year reign of Cambyses, and into the second year of Darius I (Hystaspes).

Evidently, the great prophet Daniel was deceased early in this period, because it is evident that

no powerful voice was available to defend the interests
of Israel until the times of Darius I.

**Let us build with you, for we seek your God, as ye
do (v. 2).** The people who thus approached the Jews
were the remnants of the Northern Israel which
remained after the fall of Samaria in 722 BC; and when
wild animals became a threatening problem after many
of the people were carried away by Assyria, the
Assyrian kings repeopled the land with non-Israelites.
It is true that they worshipped Jehovah, after a fashion;
but their worship was corrupted by idolatry.
Zerubbabel and all Israel were very wise to reject this
offer of the Samaritans. The proof that they really had
no love at all for Israel appears in their continued
opposition.

Since the days of Esarhaddon (v. 2). "Isaiah had
prophesied in 734 BC that Northern Israel would cease
to be a distinct people within sixty-five years (Isa. 7:8);
and this was fulfilled by 669 BC, during the reign of
Esarhaddon (680-668 BC)."[1]

The following verses 6-23 are, in fact, an
unusually long parenthesis which describes the
continual opposition of the people of the land to the
development of Jerusalem until the times of Artaxerxes.

---

[1] WYC, p. 426.

Samaritan Opposition Continued Till 446 BC

Verses 6-23, And in the reign of Ahasuerus, in the beginning of his reign, wrote they an accusation against the inhabitants of Judah and Jerusalem. 7 And in the days of Artaxerxes wrote Bishlam, Mithredath, Tabel, and the rest of his companions, unto Artaxerxes king of Persia; and the writing of the letters was written in the Syrian character, and set forth in the Syrian tongue. 8 Rehum the chancellor and Shimshai the scribe wrote a letter against Jerusalem to Artaxerxes the king in this sort: 9 then wrote Rehum the chancellor, and Shimshai the scribe, and the rest of their companions, the Dinaites, the Apharsathchites, the Tarpelites, the Apharsites. the Archevites, the Babylonians, the Shushanchites, the Dehaites, the Elamites, 10 and the rest of the nations whom the great and noble Osnappar brought over, and set in the city of Samaria, and in the rest of the country beyond the River, and so forth.

11 This is the copy of the the letter they sent to Artaxerxes the king: Thy servants, the men beyond the River, and so forth. 12 Be it known unto the king, that the Jews that came up from thee are come to us unto Jerusalem; they are building the rebellious and the bad city, and have finished the walls, and repaired the foundations. 13 Be it known now unto the king, that, if this city be builded, and the walls finished, they will not pay tribute, custom, or toll, and in the end it will be hurtful unto the kings. 14 Now because we eat the salt of the palace, and it is not meet for us to see the king's dishonor, therefore have we sent and certified the king: 15 that search may be made in the book of the records of thy fathers: so shalt thou find in the book of the records, and know that this city is a rebellious city, and hurtful unto kings and provinces, and that they have moved sedition within the same of old time; for which cause was this city laid waste. 16 We certify the king that, if this city be builded, and the walls finished, thou shalt have no portion beyond the River.

17 Then sent the king an answer unto Rehum the chancellor, and to Shimshai the scribe, and to the rest of their companions that dwell in Samaria, and in the rest of the country beyond the River: Peace, and so forth. 18 The letter which ye sent unto us hath been plainly read before me. 19 And I decreed, and search hath been made, and it is found that this city of old time hath made insurrection against kings, and that rebellion and sedition have been made therein. 20 There have been mighty kings also over Jeruslaem, who have ruled over all the country beyond the River; and tribute, custom, and toll was paid unto them. 21 Make ye now a decree to cause these men to cease, and that the city be not builded, until a decree shall be made by me. 22 And take heed that ye be not slack herein: why should damage grow to the hurt of the kings?

23 Then when the copy of king Artaxerxes' letter was read before Rehum the chancellor, and Shimshai the scribe, and their companions, they went in haste to Jerusalem unto the Jews and made them to cease by force and power.

Here is the end of the long parenthesis. Note that this letter to Artaxerxes was followed promptly by his decree to shut down the building of Jerusalem (not the house of God; that had been finished long ago).

"We must date this decree in 446 BC; and it was the news of this disaster which so shocked Nehemiah and forced him into mourning and prayers (Nehemiah 1.3, 4)."[2] From this it is clear that the Samaritan opposition lasted from 535 BC to 446 BC, a period of at least 89 years.

Cause these men to cease ... until a decree shall be made by me (v. 21). This was a very important line in the letter, because, according to the foolish tradition of Persian kings, "Their laws of the Medes and the Persians could not be altered." Artaxerxes, here, very wisely left the door open either for himself or a successor to change his mind and let the building of Jerusalem continue.

Having disposed of this long parenthesis in which he spelled out the Samaritan opposition, the author of Ezra at once resumed the narrative regarding the building of the temple, which had been delayed because of the Samaritan opposition, and as we learn from the Minor Prophets, because of the indifference of God's people themselves. Thus between v. 23 and v. 24 there is a retrogression in time from 446 BC to 520 BC, which was the second year of Darius 1. Thus he leaps backwards in the narrative some 74 years!

Verse 24, Then ceased the work of the house of God which is at Jerusalem; and it ceased until the second year of Darius I the king of Persia.

---

[2] Ibid., p. 427.

Chronologically, this verse comes exactly after verse 5, above, where it was stated that, "The people of the land hired counsellors against them, to frustrate their purpose ... all the days of Cyrus king of Persia." In fact, this lobbying against the rebuilding of the temple went on throughout the remainder of the reign of Cyrus, through all the days of Cambyses, and until the second year of Darius I (520 BC).

A little later in Ezra (chapter 6) we shall have a detailed report of how the opposition of the Samaritans was successfully checkmated and how Darius 1 ordered the temple to be rebuilt.

One of the significant revelations of the chapter is the racial makeup of what we have loosely called the "Samaritans." A remnant of those people was descended from the ten northern tribes of Israel; but as the letter to Artaxerxes shows, there were not less than nine different nationalities besides Israelites who constituted the population of Samaria.

The great and noble Osnappar (v. 10). This is the only mention in the Bible of this name. Rawlinson supposed that he was an officer of Esarhaddon;[3] Oesterley identified him as, "Ashurbanipal (668-626 BC), the son and successor of Esarhaddon."[4]

xxx

---

[3] PC, Vol. 7a, p. 53.
[4] ASP, p. 328.

CHAPTER 5

After a 15-year Delay, Work On the Temple Resumed; The
Governor Reports to Darius I

The Historical Situation

The opposition of the people of the land had succeeded in weakening the purpose of Israel to rebuild the temple. As we learn from Haggai and others of the Minor Prophets, the lack of zeal and devotion on the part of God's people themselves had also contributed to this long delay (Haggai 1:2-11). Under the urgent admonitions of Haggai, both Zerubbabel and Jeshua rose up and vigorously began work on the temple. The foundation had been laid much earlier, but that foundation was probably little more than a groundbreaking that projected the size of the structure but did little else.

Also a new governor, operating from his headquarters in Damascus, under the authority of the Persian ruler who, at this time was Darius Hystaspes, was in charge of the satrapy that included Palestine. The governor was Tattenai, a far more noble person than the evil Rehum, a governor who came much later, and whose sympathies were totally in favor of the Samaritans and who was bitterly opposed to Israel.

We may be sure that when work was resumed on the temple that the Samaritans went immediately to Damascus to enlist the aid of the new governor in stopping it. Tattenai, however, refused to take any action against the temple work until he had consulted his overlord Darius I.

This chapter provides the sacred record of these developments.

Work on the Temple Resumed

Verses 1-2, Now the prophets, Haggai the prophet, and Zechariah the son of Iddo, prophesied unto the Jews that were in Judah and Jerusalem; in the name of the God of Israel, prophesied they unto them. 2 Then rose up Zerubbabel the son of Shealtiel, and Jeshua the son of Jozadak, and began to build the house of God which is at Jerusalem; and with them were the prophets of God helping them.

Now the prophets (v. 1). The record here does not mention what the prophets prophesied; but it is clear that they demanded that the Jews resume work on their temple. See Vol. 3 of our Commentaries on the Minor Prophets (Haggai), pp. 187-197, for a discussion of just how urgent the message of the prophets was. At any rate, Israel heeded it, and began to build the temple.

Haggai and Zechariah (v.). "The work on the temple was renewed only three weeks after Haggai began preaching, which was Sept. 20, 520 BC."[1] "Zerubbabel is highly honored in Haggai and in Zechariah 4; Jeshua is honored in Zechariah 3 and 6."[2]

---

[1] WYC, p. 428.
[2] Ibid.

And began to build the house of God (v. 2). This supports our view that the first laying of the foundation was a very elementary thing. Haggai complained that the house of God "lay in waste" (1:4); and that is the same terminology that was used after Nebuchadnezzar destroyed it. Furthermore, as Hamrick pointed out, "Haggai 1:12-15 does not mention any previous attempt to build the temple; and this probably means that Sheshbazzar's beginnings had been so meager that the project had to be started anew."[3]

Zerubbabel the son of Shealtiel (v. 2). See our note on p. 11, above.

The Governor Tattenai Investigates

Verses 3-5, At the same time came to them Tattenai, the governor beyond the River, and Shethar-bozenai, and their companions, and said unto them, Who gave you a decree to build this house, and to finish this wall? 4 Then we told them after this manner, what the names of the men were that were making this building. 5 But the eye of their God was upon the elders of the Jews, and they did not make them cease, till the matter should come to Darius, and then answer should be returned by letter concerning it.

At the same time ... came Tattenai (v. 3). "The Persian Empire at that time was divided into twenty satrapies, presided over by governors under the

---

[3] BBC, Vol. 3, p. 449.

authority of Darius. The territory ruled by Tattenai included Syria, Palestine, Phoenicia and Cyprus."[4] This satrapy was called Syria, and Tattenai's capital was Damascus. We do not have to wonder how he happened to appear at that particular time when the Jews had taken up work on the temple. That evil racial mix of ten strains of people under the title of Samaritans had run like the tattletales they were to inform the governor against Israel. They found a governor who was fair-minded and who refused to become their instrument of hatred against Israel. He allowed the work to proceed till he could consult Darius the king.

The governor beyond the River (v. 3). "Beyond the River" in Ezra is always a reference to the territory west of the Euphrates. The perspective is from that of Darius' capital in Babylon, or Shushan.

Shethar-bozenai (v. 3). This man was apprently the secretary of Tattenai, just as, at a later time, Shimshai was the secretary of Rehum.

The eye of their God was upon the elders of the Jews (v. 4). The providence of God most certainly entered into this new development; however, God's instrument of blessing Israel here was in His appointment of Tattenai, a governor who would not be controlled or manipulated by the evil Samaritans.

---

[4] JFB, p. 290.

Governor Tattenai's Letter to Darius I

Verses 6-17, The copy of the letter that Tattenai the governor beyond the River, and Shethar-bozenai, and his companions the Apharsachites, who were beyond the River, sent unto Darius the king; 7 they sent a letter unto him, wherein was written thus: Unto Darius the king, all peace. 8 Be it known unto the king, that we went into the province of Judah, to the house of the great God, which is builded with great stones, and timber is laid in the walls; and this work goeth on with diligence and prospereth in their hands. 9 Then asked we those elders, and said unto them thus, Who gave you a decree to build this house, and to finish this wall? 10 We asked them their names also, to certify thee, that we might write the names of the men that were at the head of them. 11 And thus they returned us answer, saying, We are the servants of the God of heaven and earth, and are building the house that was builded there many years ago, which a great king of Israel builded and finished. 12 But after that our fathers had provoked the God of heaven unto wrath, he gave them into the hand of Nebuchadnezzar king of Babylon, the Chaldean who destroyed this house, and carried the people away into Babylon. 13 But in the first year of Cyrus king of Babylon, Cyrus the king made a decree to build this house of God. 14 And the gold and silver vessels also of the house of God, which Nebuchadnezzar took out of the temple that was in Jerusalem, and brought into the temple of Babylon, those did Cyrus the king take out of the temple of Babylon, and they were delivered unto one whose name was Sheshbazzar, whom he had made governor; 15 and he said unto him,

*Take these vessels, go, put them in the temple that is in
Jerusalem, and let the house of God be builded in its place.
16 Then came the same Sheshbazzar, and laid the
foundations of the house of God which is in Jerusalem: and
since that time, even until now, hath it been in building, yet
it is not completed. 17 Now therefore, if it seem good to the
king, let there be search made in the king's treasure-house,
which is there at Babylon, whether it be so, that a decree
was made of Cyrus the king to build this house of God at
Jerusalem; and let the king send his pleasure to us
concerning this matter.*

One must admit that this letter is a fair and
honorable presentation of the truth as Tattenai laid it
out before Darius the king. What a contrast there is
here with that prejudiced and derogatory letter that the
evil governor Rehum would, at a later time, send to
Artaxerxes.

Builded with great stones (v. 8). "The Hebrew
here is *rolling stones*, that is, stones so large that they
would have to be moved by rolling them on rollers."[5]
Dummelow gave the dimensions of some of those
stones as "Sixty-seven feet long, seven and one half feet
high, and nine feet wide."[6]

Sheshbazzar (v. 14). This is the man to whom
was counted the sacred vessels that he restored to
Israel, even those that Nebuchadnezzar had looted from
the Temple of Solomon. He was evidently Cyrus' man in

---

5 NBCR, p. 401.
6 JRD, p. 701.

charge of that first expedition to Jerusalem; and scholars differ on just what connection he had with Zerubbabel. Hamrick thought that he might have been the same person as Zerubbabel,[7] in which case his Babylonian name might have been Sheshbazzar. However, the opinion of Cundall may be correct: "If Sheshbazzar was the Persian appointed leader, it would account for the fact that in this official communication he would be tactfully mentioned as the one who laid the foundations of the Temple, whereas Zerubbabel, the popular leader would be given the prominence in the domestic account."[8]

Let there be search made ... whether it be so ... that a decree was made of Cyrus the king to build the house of God at Jerusalem (v. 17). This was the key request of Darius by Tattenai. If indeed it was true that Cyrus had made such a decree, then according to the Medo-Persian tradition it was impossible to change it. Daniel twice referred to the "Law of the Medes and Persians which altereth not" (Daniel 6:8, 12). Daniel commented that, "It is a law of the Medes and Persians that no interdict nor statute which the king establisheth may be changed" (Daniel 6:15). If the projected search proposed by Tattenai revealed that Cyrus indeed had made such a decree as the Jews claimed, then it was settled; the law could not be changed.

xxx

---

[7] BBC, Vol. 3, p. 435.

[8] NBCR, p. 401.

CHAPTER 6
The Second Temple Completed and Dedicated

Verses 1-5, Then Darius the king made a decree, and search was made in the house of the archives, where the treasures were laid up in Babylon. 2 And there was found at Achmetha, in the palace that is in the province of Media, a roll, and therein was thus written for a record: 3 in the first year of Cyrus the king, Cyrus the king made a decree: Concerning the house of God at Jerusalem, let the house be builded, the place where they offer sacrifices, and let the foundations thereof be strongly laid; the height thereof threescore cubits, and the breadth thereof threescore cubits; 4 with three courses of great stones, a course of new timber: and let the expenses be given out of the king's house. 5 And also let the gold and silver vessels of the house of God, which Nebuchadnezzar took forth out of the temple which is at Jerusalem, and brought unto Babylon, be restored, and brought again unto the temple which is at Jerusalem, every one to its place; and thou shalt put them in the house of God.

In the house of the archives where the treasures were stored up (v. 1). This verse is another example of scholarly tampering with the sacred text in order to make it say what the scholars suppose it should have said. The RSV renders this line, "in the house of the archives where the documents were stored"; but Bowman rejects this as "unnecessary,"[1] because archaeological discoveries have proved that such

---

[1] IB, Vol. 3, p. 614.

decrees were kept in the same vaults where the treasures were also kept.

It is to Darius' great credit that when Cyrus' decree was not found in Babylon, he did not abandon the search, which he might well have done unless he had been motivated by a favorable inclination toward the Jews. Also, he might well have heard about that decree and thus had personal knowledge that it certainly existed.

And there (it) was found at Achmetha (Echbatana) (v. 2). "This was in Media, the summer residence of Persian kings."[2] "*Echbatana* is the Persian name for this place, as it came to light in the discovery of the Behistun Inscription."[3]

"The Behistun Inscription was discovered in 1835 by Sir Henry Rawlinson, a British army officer. On Behistun mountain, 200 miles N. E. of Babylon, there was a great isolated rock rising 1700' out of the plain; and on the face of that rock, on a perpendicular cliff , 400' above the road, Rawlinson noticed a large smoothed surface upon which there were carvings and inscriptions. These had been inscribed there by Darius I (Hystaspes) in the yearr 516 BC, the very year that the Second Temple was finished in Jerusalem. These inscriptions were written in the Persian, Elamite, and Babylonian languages; and Rawlinson, standing on a narrow 1' ledge at the base of these writings, made squeezes of them. The inscriptions were an account,

---

2 ASP, p. 328.
3 FCC, *Ezra*, p. 446.

the same account, of the conquests of Darius, written in three languages; and Sir Henry Rawlinson had found the key to the ancient Babylonian language, which unlocked for the world the vast treasures of the ancient Babylonian literature."[4]

Regarding this edict of Cyrus, "The old (critical) objections against the authenticity of this edict, on the supposition that Cyrus would not have concerned himself with the details and size of the temple, can no longer be sustained."[5]

"The variations between this decree of Cyrus and that report of it in Ezra 1 is due to the fact that this one was an official document relating to the expenditure of public money, and that one was an oral, public proclamation."[6]   There is no disharmony whatever between them.

The dimensions for the temple listed by Cyrus are a problem. There are different accounts of the size of Solomon's temple, in 2C 3 and in 1K 6; and, "It it is difficult to reconcile the dimensions given here with the statements made in Zechariah 4:10 and Haggai 2:3, implying that the second temple was smaller than the first. Perhaps the dimensions here are those which Cyrus required the Jews not to exceed."[7]   Keil solved the problem with the suggestion that Cyrus' dimensions

---

4 HHH, p. 47.
5 WBC, Vol. 16, p. 80.
6 WYC, p. 429.
7 FCC, op. cit., p. 446.

included the external structures,[8] and others have suggested that the smaller size of the second temple was due to the fact that it was the largest the returnees could afford, due to their impoverished condition.

Darius' Reply to Tattenai, Governor Beyond the River

Verses 6-7, Now therefore, Tettanai, governor beyond the River, Shethar-bozenai, and your companions the Apharsachites, who are beyond the River, be ye far from thence: 7 let the work of this house of God alone; let the governor of the Jews and the elders of the Jews build this house of God in its place.

"This order must have stunned Tettanai and his companions."[9]   Not only did Darius confirm the existence of the decree of Cyrus, he added his own authority and power to back it up, and even commanded the expenses of the project to be borne by the tax revenues which Tattenai controlled; and that probably meant that some of the expense would come out of Tattenai's own pockets.
Be ye far from thence (v. 6).   This should not be interpreted to mean that the governor was not to go near the temple for purposes of inspection; but, "It meant do not interfere with or impede the work on the building."[10]   Matthew Henry commented that, "The

---

8 CFK, *Ezra*, p. 83.
9 WYC, p. 419.
10 WBC, Vol. 16, p. 81.

manner of Darius' expression here indicates that he knew that Tattenai and his companions had a mind to hinder the work."[11]

Darius' Orders Expenses to Be Paid out of Tax Revenues

Verses 8-10, Moreover I make a decree what ye shall do to these elders of the Jews for the building of this house of God: that of the king's goods, even of the tribute beyond the River, expenses be given with all diligence to these men, that they be not hindered. 9 And that which they have need of, both young bullocks, and rams, and lambs, for burnt-offerings to the God of heaven; and also wheat, salt, wine, and oil, according to the word of the priests that are at Jerusalem, let it be given them day by day without fail; 10 that they may offer sacrifices of sweet savor unto the God of heaven, and pray for the life of the king, and of his sons.

And pray for the life of the king, and of his sons (v. 10). "Jeremiah's admonition for the Jews to *seek the peace* of Babylon during their residence there in the captivity (Jer. 29:7), was interpreted as a requirement that they should pray for their civil rulers, which the Jews do even until this day. In view of the kindness to them of the Persian kings, they would not have neglected to do this."[12] Furthermore this has come down even into Christianity as an apostolical order (1

---

[11] MH, Vol. 2, p. 1047.

[12] PC, Vol. 7a, p. 81.

Tim. 2:1-2).

Offerings to the God of heaven (vv. 9, 10). Many
able commentators have warned us that actions and
words as we find here should not be construed as
meaning that men like Darius were genuine believers in
the one true God. "Such acknowledgements as this we
find here by Persian kings they could make without any
renunciation of their polytheism. They could honor
Jahve as a mighty god, yea, even as the mightiest god,
without being unfaithful to the pagan gods of their
fathers."[13]

Crucifixion Set as Penalty for Violators

*Verses 11-12, Also I have made a decree, that
whosoever shall alter this word, let a beam be pulled out
from his house, and let him be lifted up and fastened
thereon; and let his house be made a dunghill for this: 12
and the God that hath caused his name to dwell there
overthrow all kings and peoples that shall put forth their
hand to alter the same, to destroy this house of God which
is at Jerusalem. I Darius have made a decree; let it be done
with all diligence.*

There are two parts of this penalty: (1) the
crufixion of the offender, and (2) an invocation that the
God of heaven would also execute divine justice upon
him.

"The extremely favorable impact of Darius'

---

13 CFK, op. cit., p. 87.

decree upon the temple project was no doubt due, in part, to the influence of Cyrus, two of whose daughters Darius had married; but it also came, no doubt, from the deep impressions made upon the idolatrous peoples of that age with regard to the being and providence of the God of Israel."[14]

Let him be hanged thereon (v. 11). This, of course, was crucifixion, a punishment widely used by the Persians. "Keil cites a word from Herodotus as saying that Darius impaled 3,000 Babylonians when he took their city. Therefore, this was no idle threat."[15] Cook added that, "Crucifixion was the most common form of punishment among the Persians."[16]

The Temple Finished Within About Four Years

Verses 13-15, Then Tattenai the governor beyond the River, Shethar-bozenai, and their companions, because that Darius the king had sent, did accordingly with all diligence. 14 And the elders of the Jews builded and prospered, through the prophesying of Haggai the prophet and Zechariah the son of Iddo. And they builded and finished it, according to the commandment of the God of Israel, and according to the decree of Cyrus, and Darius, and Artaxerxes king of Persia. 15 And this house was finished on the third day of the month Adar, which was in the sixth year of Darius the king.

---

[14] JFB, p. 291.
[15] WYC, p. 429.
[16] FCC, op. cit., p. 447.

And Artaxerxes king of Persia (v. 14). There was a lapse of 82 years between the end of Darius' reign (486 BC) and the beginning of that of Artaxerxes (404 BC) (See p. 25, above); and some have wondered just why his name should have been mentioned along with that of Cyrus and Darius. "He was probably included here because he, at a later date, contributed to the beautifying of the temple (7:21-28)."[17]

The third day of the month Adar (v. 15). "This was March 12, 515 BC, four and one half years after work had begun in earnest."[18] It will be remembered that it required over seven years in the building of Solomon's temple.

The Dedication of the Second Temple

Verses 16-18, And the children of Israel, the priests and the Levites, and the rest of the children of the captivity, kept the dedication of this house of God with joy. 17 And they offered at the dedication of this house a hundred bullocks, two hundred rams, four hundred lambs, and for a sin-offering for all Israel, twelve he-goats, according to the number of the tribes of Israel. 18 And they set the priests in their divisions, and the Levites in their courses, for the service of God, which is at Jerusalem; as it is written in the book of Moses.

---

[17] NBCR, p. 402.
[18] WYC, p. 429.

Critical scholars are very sensitive about any mention of *the book of Moses*; and their usual knee-jerk reaction is to challenge the passage as being from a different editor or some later hand. However, there is no reason whatever to believe such challenges. They are not scientific, they are founded upon scholarly imagination, and not upon any fact. The silly reason for such a challenge, according to Hamrick, was that the word *Jews* was the author's usual term for Israel; but here he referred to them as *the children of Israel.*[19] What a stupid assumption it must be that Ezra was not familiar with both expressions and that he would never have used both. At this glorious moment when God's people had been returned from captivity and their temple restored, the more formal term *children of Israel,* was not only appropriate, it was required.

As Hamrick noted, "This story indicates that there was a conscious attempt to imitate the ceremony associated with the dedication of Solomon's temple (1K 8, and 2C 5-7)."[20] However, the relative poverty of the people made it impossible to duplicate it. "Solomon offered over two hundred times as many oxen and sheep at the dedication of his temple as were offered on this occasion (1Kings 8:63)."[21]

---

[19] BBC, Vol. 3, p. p. 454.

[20] Ibid.

[21] WYC, p. 429.

The Children of Israel Keep the Passover

Verses 19-22, And the children of the captivity kept the passover upon the fourteenth day of the first month. 20 For the priests and the Levites had purified themselves together; all of them were pure: and they killed the passover for all the children of the captivity, and for their brethren the priests, and for themselves. 21 And the children of Israel that were come again out of the captivity, and all such as had separated themselves from the filthiness of the nations of the land, to seek Jehovah, the God of Israel, did eat, 22 and kept the feast of unleavened bread seven days with joy: for Jehovah had made them joyful, and had turned the heart of the king of Assyria unto them, to strengthen their hands in the work of the house of God, the God of Israel.

Verse 19. "With this verse, the writer resumes the Hebrew language, which he had discarded for the Chaldee, beginning at 4:8. With the exception of the letter of Artaxerxes (7:12-26), the remainder of the book is in Hebrew."[22]

All of them were pure (v. 20). It is not exactly clear, as the translation reads, but Cook assures us that a contrast is drawn between the universal purity of the Levites and the more general purity of the priests. "This made it fitting that the Levites should slaughter *all* the

---

[22] FCC, op., cit., p. 447.

consume."[23]

And all such as had separated themselves from the filthiness of the nations of the land (v. 21). Here, these are contrasted with the returnees from captivity. "These were those who were left in Palestine by Nebuchadnezzar and had become mixed with the heathen population."[24]

Jehovah ... turned the heart of the king of Assyria (v. 22). This is a reference, of course, to Darius I the king of Persia. However it is definitely not "a scribal error"[25] as charged by Cundall. Darius was king of Persia and also king of Babylon, but as the ruler of the former Assyrian Empire, he was also "King of Assur,"[26] as Keil stated it.

xxx

23 Ibid.
24 WYC, p. 429.
25 NBCR, p. 402.
26 CFK, op. cit., p. 93.

CHAPTER 7
Under Artaxerxes I, Ezra Returns from Babylon

Verse 1, After these things in the reign of Artaxerxes king of Persia, etc.

This verse establishes the chronology of this chapter which features Ezra's journey from Babylon to Jerusalem; but the problem centers in the question of just which one of the two kings of Persia named Artaxerxes is the one spoken of here.

Those kings were Artaxerxes I (Longimanus) who reigned 465-425 BC, and Artaxerxes II (Mnemon) who ruled in 405(4) to 358 BC. Depending upon which one of these monarchs was meant, there is a gap between chapters 6 and 7 here of either 58 years or 117 years. There is a sharp disagreement among scholars on this. C. F. Keil,[1] Merrill F. Unger,[2] Henry H. Halley,[3] John C. Whitcomb, Jr.,[4] F. C. Cook,[5] and Stephen S. Short[6] affirm that Artaxerxes I is the monarch mentioned; and Raymond A. Bowman[7] and Emmett Willard Hamrick[8] designate Artaxerxes II as the ruler spoken of here. H. G. M. Williamson in his

---

[1] CFK, Vol 2c, p. 94.
[2] AAOT, p. 309.
[3] HHH, p. 217.
[4] WYC, p. 429.
[5] FCC, *Ezra,* p. 448.
[6] NLBC, p. 530.
[7] IB, Vol. 3, p. 622.
[8] BBC, Vol. 3, p. 400.

award winning commentary (in 1985) made no choice
between them writing that, "Assuming that this king is
Artaxerxes I (465-425 BC), 'after these things' covers
some fifty-seven years (much more, of course, if
Artaxerxes II is intended)."[9] This writer's opinion is that
the evidence strongly favors Artaxerxes I.

In the interval indicated by the words "after
these things," Ahasuerus had ruled, during which the
events centering around the names of Mordecai and
Esther had occurred; and some scholars have supposed
that Esther's influence might have been a factor in the
favorable attitude of Artaxerxes I.

The Abbreviated Genealogy of Ezra

*Verses 1b-10, Ezra the son of Seraiah, the son of
Azariah, the son of Hilkiah, 2 the son of Shallum, the son
of Zadok, the son of Ahitub, 3 the son of Amariah, the son
of Azariah, the son of Meraioth, 4 the son of Zerahiah,
the son of Uzzi, the son of Bukki, 5 the son of Abishua, the
son of Phinehas, the son of Eleazar, the son of Aaron the
chief priest--- 6 this Ezra went up from Babylon. And he
was a ready scribe in the law of Moses, which Jehovah, the
God of Israel, had given; and the king granted him all his
request, according to the hand of Jehovah his God upon
him. 7 And there went up some of the children of Israel,
and of the priests, and the Levites, and the singers, and the
porters, and the Nethinim, unto Jerusalem, in the seventh
year of Artaxerxes the king. 8 And he came to Jerusalem in*

---

[9] WBC, Vol. 16, p. 91.

the fifth month, which was in the seventh year of the king.
9 For on the first day of the first month began he to go up
from Babylon; and on the first day of the fifth month came
he to Jerusalem, according to the good hand of his God
upon him. 10 For Ezra had set his heart to seek the law of
Jehovah, and to do it, and to teach in Israel statutes and
ordinances.

The events centered around the name of Ezra
must be accounted among the most wonderful things
that ever happened to God's people. The immense
dimensions of Ezra's request of Artaxerxes stagger the
imagination; and the authority given to Ezra by that
monarch, making him, in fact, ruler of the entire
province beyond the River, with the power of life and
death to enforce his reforms appears to have been
directly the result of Divine favor and intervention, as
positively indicated by Ezra's thanksgiving at the end of
the chapter. It seems quite unlikely that Ezra's 'request'
would have included all that the king gave, unless the
request came following the king's decision to turn the
government of the satrapy over to Ezra.

The purpose of this genealogy is to show the
importance of Ezra as a direct descendant of the great
High Priest Aaron. It is also significant that he had a
copy of the Law of Moses (v. 14); and this, we may
believe, was also true of many faithful descendants of
Aaron through the long centuries between the Exodus
and the return from Babylon, making it utterly
impossible for any forged document such as the so-
called *P Code* to have been fraudulently imposed upon

Israel. That Ezra was in full possession of the Torah indicates the preservation of it through the ages.

Priests, Levites, singers, porters, Nethinim, etc (v. 6). Oesterley wrote that, "That all these various classifications of Israelites should have been available to return with Ezra witnesses a considerable communal organization among the Jews during their captivity."[10]

On the first day of the first month began he to go up from Babylon, and on the first day of the fifth month came he to Jerusalem (v. 9). All of this journey occurred in the seventh year of Artaxerxes I; and Whitcomb gave the date of this journey as being, "From March 27 to July 24, 457 BC, a journey of exactly four months."

"The direct distance between Babylon and Jerusalem is about 520 miles; but the circuitous route usually followed by armies or other large groups was not direct, but went through Carchemish and the Orontes Valley, a distance of about 900 miles."[11] That Ezra and his company required 120 days to complete this journey, averaging only about eight miles a day was probably due to the dangers encountered and other difficulties associated with moving a large number of people.

---

[10] ASP, p. 329.
[11] FCC, op. cit., p. 448.

The Letter of Artaxerxes Commissioning Ezra
(Verses 11-16)

Verses 11-12, Now this is the copy of the letter that the king Artaxerxes gave unto Ezra the priest, the scribe, even the scribe of the words of the commandments of Jehovah, and of his statutes to Israel: 12 Artaxerxes, king of kings, unto Ezra the priest, the scribe of the law of the God of heaven, perfect, and so forth.

Beginning with verse 12, the letter of Artaxerxes is written in Aramaic, following which, in v. 27, Ezra again wrote in Hebrew.

Artaxerxes, king of kings (v. 12). As learned from the Behistun Inscription and other Babylonian inscriptions, the title 'King of Kings' was assumed by Babylonian kings, and frequently used by them.

Perfect, and so forth (v. 12). The Aramaic word from which *perfect* comes is unknown; and the RSV omitted it.[12]

Ezra Commanded to Go to Jerusalem

Verses 13-17, I make a decree, that all they of the people of Israel, and their priests and the Levites, in my realm, that are minded of their own free will to go to Jerusalem, go with thee. 14 Forasmuch as thou art sent of the king and his seven counsellors, to inquire concerning Judah and Jerusalem, according to the law of thy God

---

[12] RSV footnote on Ezra 7:12.

which is in thy hand, 15 and to carry the silver and gold, which the king and his counsellors have freely offered unto the God of Israel, whose habitation is in Jerusalem, 16 and all the silver and gold that thou shalt find in all the province of Babylon, with the freewill-offering of the people, and of the priests, offering willingly for the house of their God which is in Jerusalem; 17 therefore thou shalt with all diligence buy with this money bullocks, rams, lambs, with their meal-offerings and their drink-offerings, and shalt offer them upon the altar of the house of your God which is in Jerusalem.

Forasmuch as thou art sent of the king and his seven counsellors (v. 14). The first clause here may also be translated, "Forasmuch as thou art sent from before the king,"[13] indicating the possibility that Ezra was the holder of some high official position in the government of Artaxerxes. This is supported by the vast authority conveyed to Ezra by this commission, which was supported also by the seven counsellors of the king.
The law of thy God which is in thy hand (14). This was a copy of the Torah, the law of Moses.
Whose habitation is in Jerusalem (v. 15). Rawlinson construed this remark as merely a reference to the temple in Jerusalem, stating that, "Artaxerxes did not believe that the God of Israel was merely a local deity."[14] His reference to the God of Israel as the God of heaven in v. 21 indicates that this is true.

---

[13] Marginal reference in the Cross-Reference Bible.
[14] PC, Vol. 7c, p. 110.

And all the silver and gold that thou shalt find ... in all the province of Babylon (16). This refers to all of the freewill-offerings which Ezra might be able to receive in a widespread fund-raising campaign.

Instructions Regarding the Money

Verses 18-22, And whatsoever shall seem good to thee and to thy brethren to do with the rest of the silver and the gold, that do ye after the will of your God. 19 And the vessels that are given thee for the service of the house of thy God, deliver thee before the God of Jerusalem. 20 And whatsover more may be needed for the house of thy God, which thou shalt have occasion to bestow, bestow it out of the king's treasure-house. 21 And I, even I, Artaxerxes the king, do make a decree to all the treasurers that are beyond the River, that whatsoever Ezra the priest, the scribe of the law of the God of heaven, shall require of you, it be done with all diligence, 22 unto a hundred talents of silver, and to a hundred measures of wheat, and to a hundred baths of wine, and to a hundred baths of oil, and salt without prescribing how much.

Whatsoever shall seem good to thee and to thy brethren (v. 18). This commission to Ezra was about as near a blank check with unlimited authority as any king ever granted. It exhibits the utmost confidence and trust in Ezra by Artaxerxes. The only limit imposed here is that of the maximum withdrawals in v. 22. "The surplus was actually used in beautifying the temple, as indicated in v. 27."[15]

The king's treasure-house (v. 20). This is a reference to the sub-treasury of the satrapy of Syria, which included all of the territory beyond the River, the resources of which were made available to Ezra up to the limits indicated in v. 22.

A hundrd talents of silver (v. 22). Some critics have cited this as an exaggeration, based upon their claim that the whole revenue of the province beyond the River was only 350 talents of silver; and even Williamson stated that this amount, "seemed disproportionate."[16] However, the amount seems reasonable to this writer. "A talent of silver weighed 75 lbs.,"[17] and that is only seven pounds above the weight of one thousand silver dollars; and a hundred talents would therefore have amounted to only a little more than $100,000.00, which to this writer appears as a rather insignificant amount as it would have been considered in the treasury of a king.

A Tax Exemption for All Religious Employees

Verses 23-24, Whatsoever is commanded by the God of heaven, let it be done exactly for the house of the God of heaven; for why should there be wrath against the king and his sons? 24 Also we certify you, that touching any of the priests and Levites, the singers, porters,

---

[15] PC, op. cit., p. 111.

[16] WBC, op. cit., p. 103.

[17] Ibid.

*Nethinim, or servants of this house of God, it shall not be
lawful to impose tribute, custom, or toll, upon them.*

**Why should there be wrath against the king and his
sons (v. 23)?** This discloses the motive which prompted
Persian kings to honor the gods of all the nations they
conquered.

It shall not be lawful to impose tribute, etc. (v. 24).
Regarding this blanket tax exemption provided for the
entire religious community, according to Rawlinson,
"This was absolutely permanent and probably continued
in force till the close of the empire."[18]

Ezra's Authority Extended to Include
all Beyond the River

There was some quality of mind and character
among a number of ancient Jewish leaders that earned
for them the respect and honor of world rulers who
observed them. Joseph under Pharaoh, Daniel under
Nebuchadnezzar, and now Ezra under Artaxerxes I
were all granted a status under their respective
overlords that was little less than that of a deputy
monarch. Note the following:

**Verses 25-26, And thou, Ezra, after the wisdom of
thy God that is in thy hand, appoint magistrates and
judges, who shall judge all the people who are beyond the**

---

[18] PC, op. cit., p. 110.

River, all such as know the laws of thy God; and teach ye him that knowth them not. 26 And whosoever will not do the law of thy God, and the law of the king, let judgment be executed upon him with all diligence, whether it be unto death, or to banishment, or to confiscation of goods, or to imprisonment.

This concludes the letter of Artaxerxes I. It gave Ezra almost despotic power over the whole Persian province beyond the River. Also, of very great significance, it recognized the Law of Moses as the supreme law of the land, along with that of the king, which are here understood to be one and the same thing. From this we must recognize in Artaxerxes I an unusually brilliant mind, in that he recognized the utility of the Mosaic Law, including, of course, the Decalogue, as a fit charter of government for the whole kingdom. How strange it is that forty-seven of the forty-eight contiguous states of the U. S. A., in their various constitutions, have specifically listed the Ten Commandments as the basic law in every one of them. Clarence Manion, Dean of the College of Law at Notre Dame University, declared this to be a fact.

Let judgment be executed upon him with all diligence (v. 26). Here is another vital principle of just government that was commanded by Artaxerxes, namely, that punishment of violators of the law, should be executed immediately, promptly, *with all diligence.* Our own system of government in the U. S. A. today is tragically unjust and inefficient in their rejection of this vital principle. The average time between the conviction of some brutal and heartless murderer and his execution is measured in years, and sometimes reaches more than a decade. There is no wonder that criminals hold the law in utmost contempt. Half a millennium before Christ, a pagan Persian king, knew the futility and worthlessness of such a system as we in America have imposed upon ourselves.

An Analysis of Ezra's Commission

We are indebted to Rawlinson for this summary of Ezra's commission.[19]

A. The temporary provisions: (1) permission for all Israelites who desired to do so to go with Ezra to Jerusalem; (2) permission to carry the monetary gifts of the king and his counsellors to Jerusalem; (3) permission to draw upon the royal sub-treasury large grants up to the limits set in verse 22; (4) permission to convey to Jerusalem all of the money that Ezra might receive from an area-wide fund-raising effort; and (5) a royal mandate to "inquire" concerning Judah and Jerusalem.

B. Permanent provisions: (1) Ezra was endowed with the chief authority over all the great satrapy beyond the River, with power to appoint magistrates and judges, and to require their knowledge of the Mosaic Law. (2) He was empowered to enforce his decisions by penalties of fines, imprisonment,

---

[19] Ibid., p. 109.

banishment, or even death. (3) A permanent status of tax exemption was granted for the entire religious community concerned with services in the temple.

Having recorded, without translating it, the important document in Aramaic by which Artaxerxes conveyed to Ezra his commission, "Ezra then resumed the use of the more sacred Hebrew language and employed it uninterruptedly to the end of the narrative."[20]

God's Hand in This Acknowledged by Ezra

Verses 27-28, Blessed be Jehovah, the God of our fathers, who hath put such a thing as this in the king's heart, to beautify the house of Jehovah which is in Jerusalem; 28 and hath extended lovingkindness unto me before the king, and his counsellors, and before all the king's mighty princes. And I was strengthened according to the hand of Jehovah my God upon me, and I gathered together out of Israel chief men to go up with me.

To beautify the house of Jehovah ... in Jerusalem (v. 27). This reveals the use which Ezra made of the surplus money available to Ezra, over and beyond what was needed to carry out the specific instructions of the king.

Jehovah ... extended lovingkindness to me before the king (v. 28). This could be interpreted as a reference to

---

[20] Ibid., p. 112.

the favor God gave Ezra when he made request (v. 6) before the king for what he received; but the inclusion of the words, *before the king's counsellors, and before all his mighty princes,* makes it more likely that Ezra held some kind of office under Artaxerxes which had placed him under the observation of all such high officers of the king, and that God had given Ezra favor in the hearts of all of them. Besides that, Ezra here credited God himself with putting "such a thing" in the king's heart, with no reference at all to any request of Ezra.

xxx

CHAPTER 8
Further Details of Ezra's Journey to Jerusalem

List of Familes, Chief Men, With
Numbers of Returnees

Verses 1-14, Now these are the heads of their fathers' houses, and this is the genealogy of them that went up with me from Babylon, in the reign of Artaxerxes the king: 2 of the sons of of Phinehas, Gershom. Of the sons of Ithamar, Daniel, Of the sons of David, Hattush. 3 Of the sons of Shecaniah, of the sons of Parosh, Zechariah; and with him were reckoned by genealogy of the males a hundred and fifty. 4 Of the sons of Pahath-moab, Elie-hoenai the son of Zerahiah; and with him two hundred males. 5 Of the sons of Shecaniah, the son of Jahaziel; and with him three hundred males. 6 And of the sons of Adin, Ebed the son of Jonathan; and with him fifty males. 7 And of the sons of Elam, Jeshaiah the son of Athaliah; and with him seventy males. 8 And of the sons of Shephatiah, Zebadiah the son of Michael; and with him fourscore males. 9 Of the sons of Joab, Obadiah the son of Jehiel; and with him two hundred and eighteen males. 10 And of the sons of Shelomith, the son of Josiphiah; and with him a hundred and threescore males. 11 And of the sons of Bebai, Zechariah the son of Bebai; and with him twenty and eight males. 12 And of the sons of Azgad, Johanan the son of Hakkatan; and with him a hundred and ten males. 13 And of the sons of Adonikam, that were the last: and these are their names: Eliphelet, Jeuel, and Shemaiah; and with them threescore males. 14 And of the sons of Bigvai, Uthai and Zabbud; and with them seventy males.

This list is parallel with that of chapter 3:3-19; and there are many similarities. Generally, the same family names appear in both lists, although not in the same order. "The numbers here are much smaller, never reaching even a third of the totals in the other list, and sometimes falling below one twelfth."[1] Only in verses 5 (Shecaniah), 9 (Joab) and 10 (Shelomith) do we find new families mentioned; and two of these are disputed.

The authenticity of his list has been challenged; but Bowman mentioned that, "It has also been defended, and that it fits."[2] "The reliability of this list is also supported by its appearance with only slight variations in 1 Esdras 8:28-40."[3]

The whole number of those accompanying Ezra on this journey, including the Levites and Nethinim finally recruited by Ezra, was placed at 1,773 males. Rawlinson placed the total number, including women and children, at about 9,000, estimating five per family.[4] Wlliamson, however, estimated the total number as "some 5,000."[5]

The most remarkable name in the whole list is that of Hattush the son of Schechaniah. "Beyond any reasonable doubt, he was the descendant of David (1C

---

[1] PC, Vol. 8a, p. 122.

[2] IB, Vol. 3, p. 632.

[3] NBCR, p. 402.

[4] PC, op. cit., p. 122.

[5] WBC, Vol. 16, p. 110.

3:22), through Shemaiah; and he was Zerubbabel's great-great-grandson."[6]

A Second Beginning of the Journey at Ahava

Verses 15-20, And I gathered them together at the river that runneth to Ahava; and there we encamped three days; and I viewed the people, and the priests, and found there none of the sons of Levi. 16 Then sent I for Eliezer, for Ariel, for Shemaiah, and for Elnathan, and for Jarib, and for Elnathan, and for Nathan, and for Zechariah, and for Meshullam, chief men; also for Joiarib, and for Elnathan, who were teachers. 17 And I sent them forth unto Iddo the chief of the place Casiphia; and I told them what they should say unto Iddo, and his brethren the Nethinim, at the place Casiphia, that they should bring unto us ministers for the house of God. 18 And according to the good hand of our God upon us, they brought us a man of discretion, of the sons of Mahli the son of Levi the son of Israel; and Sherebiah with his sons and his brethren, eighteen; 19 and Hashabiah, and with him Jeshaiah of the sons of Merari, his brethren and their sons, twenty; 20 and of the Nethinim, whom David and the princes had given for the service of the Levites, two hundred and twenty Nethinim: all of them were mentioned by name.

I gathered them together to the river than runneth to Ahava (v. 15). Ezra's company had already left Babylon on the first day of the month; and they were

---

6 PC, op. cit., p. 122.

delayed here until the twelfth day when the journey was resumed. Some time had elapsed in their journey to this station, and there was more delay while Ezra recruited the Levites and the Nethinim.

The river that runneth to Ahava (v. 15) Several current scholars insist that this place is unknown; but Rawlinson wrote that, "It is now generally identified with the place IS in Herodotus (i. 179), a small stream flowing into the Euphrates from the east, some eight days' journey from Babylon. This place is mentioned under the slightly variant names of *Ava* and *Ivah* in 2K 17:24, 19:13, and in the LXX under the name *Aba* ... the modern name is *Hit*.[7] This information fully explains why the departure from Ahava was on the twelfth day of the month. Eight days had been required for their journey to that place, and the other four days were for recruiting the Levites.

Casiphia, also unknown, was evidently quite near this first way-station, otherwise, more time would have been required for enlisting the Levites. "Ezra knew of a settlement of Levites nearby at a place called Casiphia (the location of which is unknown to us)."[8]

I found there none of the sons of Levi (v. 15). The difficulty in recruiting Levites was probably due to the reduction of their status by the encroaching activities of the post-exilic priesthood, whose criminal activity was so dramatically exposed in the book of Malachi, so terrible, in fact, that God even cursed them (Malachi

---

[7] Ibid.

[8] NLBC, p. 531.

2:1-2).   The disaffection of the Levites is demonstrated by the fact that, "Only 341 returned with Zerubbabel, compared with 4,289 priests."[9]

Regarding Ezra's determination to include Levites in his migration, Williamson pointed out that, "Ezra regarded his company as 'an ideal Israel,"[10] which of course required the presence of Levites.   "And as presented in the book of Ezra, it was a 2nd Exodus."[11]

And of the Nethinim ... two hundred twenty (v. 20). The original Nethinim were the Gibeonites (Joshua 9:23).

Ezra Proclaims a Fast for Three Days

Verses 21-23, Then I proclaimed a fast there at the river Ahava, that we might humble ourselves before our God, to seek of him a straight way for us, and for our little ones, and for all our substance. 22 For I was ashamed to ask of the king a band of soldiers and horsemen to help us against the enemy in the way, because we had spoken unto the king saying, The hand of our God is upon all them that seek him for good; but his power and his wrath is against all them that forsake him. 23 So we fasted and besought our God for this: and he was entreated of us.

I proclaimed a fast there at the river Ahava (v. 21). Ezra had good reason behind this proclamation. Due to

---

[9] WYC, p. 430.

[10] WBC, op. cit., p. 111.

[11] Ibid.

his previous remarks to the king, he was ashamed to request a military escort to Jerusalem; and, since he was transporting a vast sum of money, and as the way was always a dangerous one, he felt a special need of God's protection.

Fasting, as a means of seeking God's favor, was a common practice in Israel; and even in the NT, Jesus prophesied that his followers would fast (Matthew 6:15, 8:14).

There was a long tradition in Israel that the civil rulers had the authority to proclaim a fast; and one was even called by Jezebel (1K 21:12).

And he was entreated of us (23). Ezra wrote this after his safe arrival in Jerusalem; but here he included this word that God had indeed answered their prayers. As a consequence of their prayers, "The journey was successfully accomplished, God's gracious protection delivering them from the bands of enemies and marauders."[12]

The Priests and Levites Entrusted With the Treasures

Verses 24-30, Then I set apart twelve of the chiefs of the priests, even Sherebiah, Hashabiah, and ten of their brethren with them, 25 and weighed unto them the silver, and the gold, and the vessels, even the offering for the house of our God, which the king, and his counsellors, and his princes, and all Israel there present, had offered: 26 I weighed into their hand six hundred and fifty talents of

---

[12] CFK, Vol. 3c, p. 112.

silver, and silver vessels a hundred talents; of gold a hundred talents;   27 and twenty bowls of gold, of a thousand darics; and two vessels of fine bright brass, precious as gold.   28 And I said unto them, Ye are holy unto Jehovah, and the vessels are holy; and the silver and the gold are a freewill-offering unto Jehovah, the God of your fathers.   29 Watch ye, and keep them, until ye weigh them before the chiefs of the priests and the Levites, and the princes of the fathers' houses of Israel, at Jerusalem, in the chambers of the house of Jehovah.   30 So the priests and the Levites received the weight of the silver and the gold, and the vessels, to bring them to Jerusalem unto the house of our God.

"The value of these gifts was well over a million pounds; but this is by no means inconceivable in view of the immense wealth of the Perisan kings."[13]

Responsibility for transporting this vast sum of money, "Was vested in twelve priests and twelve Levites especially chosen for the task. This was in accordance with the Pentateuchal care and movement of the tabernacle furnishings (Numbers, Chs. 3, 4)."[14]

Ye are holy ... the vessels are holy (v. 28). Ezra here heeded the prophecy of Isaiah who had prophesied the return of Israel from captivity, saying, "Cleanse yourselves, ye that bear the vessels of Jehovah." (Isa. 52:11). As Matthew Henry stated it, "We have here an

---

[13] NBCR, p. 403.
[14] WBC, op. cit., p. 119.

account of the particular care which Ezra took,"[15] in the handling of the treasures entrusted to him. It is always of the greatest importance that God's servants should take the greatest precautions in handling sacred contributions that their actions should exhibit to all men the utmost honesty and integrity.

The Journey Completed and the Treasures Weighed Before the Temple Custodians

Verses 31-34, Then we departed from the river Ahava on the twelfth day of the first month, to go to Jerusalem; and the hand of our God was upon us, and he delivered us from the hand of the enemy and the lier-in-wait by the way. 32 And we came to Jerusalem, and abode there three days. 33 And on the fourth day the silver and the gold and the vessels were weighed in the house of our God into the hand of Merimoth the son of Uriah the priest (and with him was Eleazar the son of Phinehas: and with them was Jozabad the son of Jeshua, and Noadiah the son of Bennuni, the Levites) ---34 the whole by number and by weight: and all the weight was written at that time.

"After four months of travelling (7:9), they came to Jerusalem; the fact of their having been unmolested on the way (v. 31) vindicated their faith in God's protection; and the treasures were weighed in with the proper temple authorities, indicating that none had

---

[15] MH, Vol, 2, p. 1057.

been misappropriated."[16]

We departed from the river Ahava on the twelfth day of the month (v. 31). Williamson seemed perplexed by the fact that, "Whereas in 7:9 the departure date was the first day of the month; here the actual date is given as the twelfth day of the month (so stated as to leave the impression that these dates are in some manner contradictory)."[17]   Once more we find that a careful reading of the Bible completely clears up what some critics view as a contradiction. Read the text:

On the first day of the first month began (Ezra) to go up from Babylon (7:9).

Then we departed from the river Ahava on the twelfth day of the first month (v. 31).

It does not take a genius to understand that on the first day of the month they left Babylon, and on the twelfth day of the month they left the river Ahava. Some of the scholars are mixed up on this because they have erroneously interpreted "the river Ahava" as being one of the canals in Babylon. See the comment of Herodotus on this as given in our comment on v. 15, above.

And we ... abode there three days (v. 32). This is a reference to the three-days' rest which they enjoyed after their arrival in Jerusalem. No doubt they needed it, because the journey had lasted four months and was attended by many dangers and anxieties. "Like Nehemiah (2:11), Ezra was content with a three days'

---

[16] NLBC, p. 531.

[17] WBC, op. cit., p. 120.

rest, before getting on with the business at hand."[18]

Sacrifices Offered for the Twelve Tribes of Israel

Verses 35-36, The children of the captivity, that were come out of exile, offered burnt-offerings unto the God of Israel, twelve bullocks for all Israel, ninety and six rams, seventy and seven lambs, twelve he-goats for a sin-offering: all this was a burnt-offering unto Jehovah. 36 And they delivered the king's commissions unto the king's satraps, and to the governors beyond the River: and they furthered the people and the house of God.

Twelve bullocks for all Israel, etc. (v.35). All except one of the sacrifices mentioned here were either twelve or multiples of that number, indicating that, "Ezra believed that the restored community represented all twelve of the tribes of Israel."[19]

Matthew Henry believed that these offerings "for all Israel" indicated that, "The union of the two Israels was then accomplished, as prophesied by Ezekiel 37:22."[20]

Keil pointed out that, "The sin-offering had served as an atonement for Israel; and that the burnt-offering typified the surrender of the entire nation of Israel to the service of the Lord, and was a declaration that those who had returned were henceforth resolved,

---

[18] PC, op. cit., p. 128.
[19] IB, op. cit., p. 643.
[20] MH, op. cit., p. 1058.

together with all Israel, to dedicate themselves to the service of the Lord their God."[21]

They delivered the king's commissions to the ... satraps (v. 36). These were the Persian lieutenants and governors under Artaxerxes the king who were in charge of all that vast territory west of the Euphrates River. "These satraps were the military chiefs in charge of the provinces, and they were also endowed with the civil authority as well."[22] As a result of this royal directive, "They furthered the people and the house of God as Artaxerxes had commanded."[23]

xxx

---

[21] CFK, op. cit., p. 113.

[22] Ibid.

[23] Ibid.

CHAPTER 9
Ezra's Prayerful Response to The Mixed Marriages
of Israel With Pagans

Actually, both of these final chapters of Ezra are devoted to the solution of the problem presented by Israel's intermarriage with foreigners. It is easy for us to see how this problem developed. In the first place there might have been a shortage of women in that company of returnees which came with Zerubbabel; and again, the great men of Israel's history had repeatedly taken foreign wives. Both Abraham and Joseph had married Egyptians; Judah also married a Gentile; Moses married a Cushite; one of David's wives was a foreigner (2S 3:3); and Solomon's harem was apparently dominated by pagan wives. Under the circumstances, therefore, it is easy to see how this problem developed.

Nevertheless, in spite of what some view as the violation of human rights, and the incredible grief, sufferings, and emotional distress that resulted from Ezra's drastic solution of this crisis, it needed to be corrected; and there can be no doubt whatever that God's will was accomplished in the epic severance of Israel from their idolatrous wives. "There is no doubt that if the practice of intermarriage had continued and extended, then the Jews would have lost their national identity; and it is of the greatest significance that the NT warns against marriages with unbelievers (2C 6:14)."[1]

In this connection, we must reject the liberal view that, "The Israelites did not originally condemn

---

[1] NBCR, p. 403.

intermarriage."[2] Deuteronomy 7:3 specifically forbade intermarriage with non-Israelites; and it is a gross mistake to identify that restriction with some alleged "Deuteronomist."   The prohibition against Israel's mingling with non-Israelites in marriage was an integral part of the entire Mosaic covenant, as taught in Exodus 23:32, where God forbade making "any covenant" with the pagan populations, a restriction which absolutely included the marriage covenant as well as all other covenants. Again, "Is it not that we are separated, I and thy people, from all the people that are upon the face of the earth" (Exodus 33:16)? The wholesale violation of God's law in this matter by many of Israel's famous leaders in no way invalidated God's specific orders.

Before proceeding to examine the text of this chapter, we notice another liberal viewpoint which we must reject. It seems to be a presumptive privilege falsely arrogated to themselves which prompts many critical scholars to proceed with rearranging the biblical text to conform to their imaginative theories and prejudices, apparently overlooking the fact that they are absolutely without any divine mandate to do any such rearranging of the biblical text.

We thank God that the custodianship of the sacred scriptures was not entrusted to the radical critical enemies of the Bible whose writings have proliferated during the current century. The inspired writings of the apostle Paul tell us exactly who received that commission of custodianship. Here it is:

---

[2] BBC, Vol. 3, p. 465.

WHAT ADVANTAGE THEN HATH THE JEW? ...
MUCH EVERY WAY; FIRST OF ALL BECAUSE THEY
WERE ENTRUSTED WITH THE ORACLES OF GOD
(ROMANS 3:1, 2).
Well, there we have it. The Jews were entrusted
with keeping the sacred scriptures of the OT; and
because of that, we cannot receive the proposition that,
"The story of the reading of the law and its aftermath
(Nehemiah 7:73b-9:37) originally stood between the
chapters 8 and 9 in the book of Ezra."[3] There are
excellent explanations of the gap of several months
between Ezra's arrival in Jerusalem and his getting
down to the problem of the mixed marriages; and we
shall note these below.

This is a remarkably interesting and important
chapter. There are ten divisions in these final two
chapters, three of which appear in this chapter. These
are: (1) "The complaint of the princes regarding the
mixed marriages (9:1-2); (2) Ezra's astonishment and
horror (9:3-4); and (3) Ezra's confession and prayer to
God (9:5-15)."[4]

Ezra Gets the Bad News About the Mixed Marriages

Verses 1-2, Now when these things were done, the
princes drew near unto me, saying, The people of Israel,
and the priests, and the Levites have not separated
themselves from the peoples of the lands, doing according

---

[3] Ibid., p. 465.
[4] PC, Vol. 7a, p. 138.

to their abominations, even of the Canaanites, the Hittites, the Perizzites, the Jebusites, the Ammonites, the Moabites, the Egyptians and the Amorites. 2 For they have taken of their daughters for themselves and for their sons, so that the holy seed have mingled themselves with the peoples of the lands: yea the hands of the princes and the rulers have been chief in this trespass.

Now when these things were done (v. 1). Hamrick wrote that, "These words seem to imply that the controversy over mixed marriages occurred immediately upon Ezra's arrival in Jerusalem."[5] A number of current scholars take the same view; and then, because Ezra's action to correct the situation did not take place till the twentieth day of the ninth month (10:9), the critical scholars at once account for this "gap," as they call it, by supposing that, "The story of the reading of the law and its aftermath (Neh. 7:73b-9:37) should be inserted into the book of Ezra, between chapters 8-9."[6]

As noted above, we believe in the integrity and authenticity of both Ezra and Nehemiah; and we do not accept the assumed authority of 20th century scholars to revise the Holy Bible and to do any kind of a scissors and paste job on it that pleases them.

Their error here is in the failure to see that "*after these things*" in the text says nothing about Ezra's actions being "immediately after his arrival in Jerusalem." It simply means that Ezra received the word about the

---

[5] BBC, op. cit., p. 464.
[6] Ibid.

mixed marriages after he had completed his assignment from the king. And how long was that?

Keil explained that several months elapsed before the word about the mixed marriages came to Ezra. "The delivery of the king's commands to the satraps and governors ... occupied weeks, or months; because the king's command was not merely to transmit the royal decree, but to come to such an understanding with them as would secure their goodwill and support in furthering the people and the house of God."[7] In view of the vast distances involved in Ezra's delivery of the king's decree to all the satraps and governors *beyond the River,* it is surprising that he confronted the mixed marriage situation as early as he did.

The Canaanites, the Hittites, Perizzites, ... etc. (v. 1). There were seven of the Canaanite nations (Exodus 3:8, 23:23, Deuteronomy 7:), five of whom are mentioned here. The Ammonites, Moabites and Egyptians are here mentioned in addition to five of the seven Canaanite races. "If any effectual check was to be put upon Israel's relapse into heathenism, the prohibition against marriages with all of these groups, under existing circumstances, was absolutely necessary."[8]

The problem was aggravated and intensified by the violations of many of the princes and rulers of the Israelites by such marriages.

---

7 CFK, Vol. . 3c, p. 115.

8 Ibid., p. 116.

The Astonishment and Horror of Ezra

Verses 3-4, And when I heard this thing, I rent my garment and my robe, and plucked off the hair of my head and of my beard, and sat down confounded. 4 Then were assembled unto me every one that trembled at the words of the God of Israel, because of the trespass of them of the captivity; and I sat confounded until the evening sacrifice.

Ezra's reaction to the bad news was extreme. There is hardly anything more painful than pulling out the hairs of one's beard. Similar actions were customary among Oriental peoples as an expression of grief, dismay, or consternation (Job 1:20, Ezekiel 7:18). "Notice that Ezra's appeal was moral and religious ... reformation can never be achieved by force."[9] As the chief civil authority, Ezra could have ordered the needed reforms and enforced them even with the death penalty; but he chose the better way.

Oesterley commented that, in Ezra's strict enforcement of the prohibition of mixed marriages, "His zeal in this matter resulted in his going beyond the requirements of the law (Deut. 23:7)."[10] That passage states that, "Thou shalt not abhor an Edomite ... or an Egyptian ... The children of the third generation of them that are born unto them shall enter into the assembly of Jehovah"; but there is nothing in that passage that justifies Oesterley's conclusion.

---

[9] NBCR, p. 403.
[10] ASP, p. 329.

Ezra's Prayer Re: Israel's Sin in the Mixed Marriages

Verses 5-15, And at the evening oblation I arose up from my humiliation, even with my garment and my robe rent; and I fell upon my knees, and spread out my hands unto Jehovah my God; 6 and I said, O my God, I am ashamed and blush to lift up my face to thee, my God; for our iniquities are increased over our head, and our guiltiness is grown up unto the heavens. 7 Since the days of our fathers we have been exceeding guilty unto this day ; and for our iniquities have we, our kings, and our priests, been delivered into the hand of the kings of the lands, to the sword, to captivity, to plunder, and to confusion of face, as it is this day. 8 And now for a little moment grace hath been showed from Jehovah our God, to leave us a remnant to escape, and to give us a nail in his holy place, that our God may lighten our eyes, and give us a little reviving in our bondage. 9 For we are bondmen; yet our God hath not forsaken us in our bondage, but hath extended lovingkindness unto us in the sight of the kings of Persia, to give us a reviving, to set up the house of our God, and to repair the ruins thereof, and to give us a wall in Judah and in Jerusalem. 10 And now, O our God, what shall we say after this? for we have forsaken thy commandments, 11 which thou hast commanded by thy servants the prophets, The land, unto which ye go to possess it, is an unclean land through the uncleanness of the peoples of the lands, through their abominations, which have filled it from one end to another with their filthiness: 12 now therefore give not your daughters unto their sons, neither take their daughters unto your sons, nor seek their peace or their prosperity for ever; that ye may be strong, and eat the good of the land, and leave it for an inheritance to your children for ever. 13 And after all that has come upon us for our evil deeds, and for our great guilt, seeing that our God hast punished us less than our iniquities deserve, and hast given us such a remnant,   14 shall we again break thy commandments, and join in affinity with the peoples that do these abominations? wouldest thou not be angry with us till thou hadst consumed us, so that there should be no remnant, nor any to escape?   15 O Jehovah, the God of Israel, thou art righteous; for we are left a remnant that is escaped, as it is this day: behold, we are before thee in our guiltiness; for none can stand before thee because of this.

    At the evening oblation I arose up from my humiliation (v. 5). "This is probably to be identified with the ninth hour (3:00 P. M.) (Acts 3:1)."[11]

    Our guiltiness is grown up unto the heavens (v. 6). This was also the conviction of Nehemiah (9:29-35), and likewise that of Daniel (9:5-8).   "The captivity had effectively done its work in convincing a previously proud and self-righteous nation of their gross wickedness and unfaithfulness to God."[12]

    Since the days of our fathers we have been exceeding guilty (v. 7). "The guilt which Ezra confessed was not merely that of his contemporary generation but that of their whole history.   The guilt of the corporate

---

[11] WBC, Vol. 16, p. 133.

[12] FCC, *Ezra*, p. 453.

community transcended that of a given generation."[13]

To give us a nail in his holy place (v. 8). "This metaphor is probably derived from a tent-pin, driven into the earth to secure the tent."[14]

We are bondmen ... God hath not forsaken us ... to give us a wall in Judah and Jerusalem (v. 9). Although the Persian kings had granted favors to the Jews regarding their return to Jerusalem and the building of their temple, they nevertheless still remained subjects of the Persian king, bound to obey him in everything. The mention of "a wall" here does not mean that the walls of Jerusalem had been rebuilt. "The word *wall* means *a fence,* and is used of a fence around a vineyard; and it is used here metaphorically for *protection.*"[15]

Which thou hast commanded by thy servants the prophets (v. 11). Ezra here, by the words, "The land unto which ye go to possess it," clearly had the Mosaic age in mind; and we have already cited three references in the Books of Moses that forbade foreign covenants including marriages; but the mention here of "prophets" has led some scholars to point out that there are no specific commandments in the prophets regarding this. However, as Moses was the Great Prophet unto whom even the Christ was compared; and since all of the prophets endorsed the Mosaic Law and commanded the people to observe it, "It was proper for Ezra to designate the Mosaic Law as the sayings of the prophets

---

[13] BBC, op. cit., p. 466.
[14] FCC, op. cit., p. 452.
[15] ASP, p. 329.

also."[16]

God hast punished us less than our iniquities deserve (v. 13). It is significant that Ezra includes himself along with the guilty people, identifying himself in every way with the sinful nation. Note also that he acknowledges the righteous judgment of God in the acceptance of his punishments as being "less than they deserved."

We appreciate Bowman's rejection of the criticism of some radical scholars who deny the authenticity of this prayer, on the basis of several, erroneous assumptions and 'guesses.' He wrote: "This prayer does not have an artificial or secondary nature, but is psychologically as well as historically appropriate. It is relevant to the occasion and necessary for the development of the situation."[17]

This magnificent prayer was used by the Lord to rally Israel around Ezra and to provide sufficient support for the drastic rejection of the mixed marriages.

xxx

---

[16] CFK, op. cit., p. 122.
[17] IB, Vol. 3, p. 647.

CHAPTER 10
Israel's Putting Away of Their Foreign Wives and Children

They Accept Shechaniah's Proposal

Verses 1-4, Now while Ezra prayed and made confession, weeping and bowing himself down before the house of God, there was gathered together unto him out of Israel a very great assembly of men and women and children, for the people wept very sore. 2 And Shechaniah the son of Jehiel, one of the sons of Elam, answered and said unto Ezra, We have trespassed against our God, and have married foreign women of the peoples of the land: yet now there is hope for Israel concerning this thing. 3 Now therefore let us make a covenant with our God to put away all the wives, and such as are born of them, according to the counsel of my lord, and of those that tremble at the commandment of our God; and let it be done according to the law. 4 Arise; for the matter belongeth unto thee, and we are with thee: be of good courage, and do it.

Two things in this paragraph are disputed. (1) Shechaniah is identified by Hamrick[1] as the son of the violator (Jehiel) mentioned in v. 26; but Williamson denied the certainty of that identification, writing that, "Jehiel is a common enough name to preclude certainty of identity, even with a single extended family."[2] Keil wrote that, "This Shechaniah is a different person from the descendant of Zattu (8:5); nor is Jehiel identical

---

[1] BBC, Vol. 3, p. 467.
[2] WBC, Vol. 16, p. 150.

with the individual of that name mentioned in v. 26."[3]

(2) *Let us make a covenant ... according to the counsel of my lord (v. 3).* The words *my lord* are given in the ASV margin as *my Lord.* Some scholars consider them as a reference to Ezra; others view them as a reference to God. Williamson's comment is that, "Shechaniah here refers to 'the advice of my lord,' i. e. Ezra";[4] and, based upon this, there is a postulation that Ezra had already discussed the matter previously with Shechaniah. However, there is absolutely nothing in the text which supports a proposition like that. We believe that the Douay Version properly translates this verse, "Let us make a covenant ... according to the will of the Lord, and of them that fear the commandment of the Lord our God." Keil also agreed that in this passage the Hebrew text has, "According to the counsel of the Lord," and that "there is no critical authority for changing it."[5] It appears that translators have been too much influenced by the LXX.

And let it be done according to the law (v. 3). This was part of Shechaniah's proposal to put away the foreign wives and their children. Deuteronomy 24:1 gave instructions for the divorcing of a wife; but, "According to the teaching of the Rabbis, divorce was allowed for every cause (Mt. 19:3)."[6] Thus there would have been no legal impediment to the adoption of

---

[3] CFK, Vol. 3c, p. 126.
[4] WBC, op. cit., p. 250.
[5] CFK, op. cit., p. 126
[6] PC, Vol. 7a, p. 152.

Shechaniah's proposal, a proposal which on that occasion was received by the vast majority of the people present. Some phases of the implementation of this drastic remedy are not mentioned in the text.

Ezra, however, very wisely moved at once to require all the people to swear that they would accept and execute this requirement to put away their foreign wives and their children.

The Oath of the People and Ezra's Fast

Verses 5-6, Then arose Ezra, and made the chiefs of the priests, the Levites, and all Israel, to swear that they would do according to this word. 6 Then Ezra rose up from before the house of God, and went into the chamber of Jehohanan the son of the son of Eliashib: and when he came thither, he did eat no bread, nor drink water; for he mourned because of the trespasses of them in the captivity.

"By making the people to swear to follow the suggested course of action while feelings were still running high, Ezra ensured that there could be no turning back at a later stage."[7]

In v. 6, "The reference to Johanan the son of Eliashib has featured prominently in discussions of the date of Ezra."[8] However, Williamson in his award winning commentary, after several pages of discussions regarding the bearing this passage is alleged to have

---

[7] WBC, op. cit., p. 151.

[8] Ibid.

regarding the date of Ezra, concluded that, "The issue is too uncertain to be admitted as evidence for the dating of Ezra."[9] In his conclusion Williamson affirmed his preference for the early date of Ezra.

Bowman identified the arguments from this passage that are alleged as excuses for dating Ezra after Nehemiah as, "One of the strongest arguments for doing so";[10] and in the weakness of this argument we are assured that the traditional date of Ezra prior to Nehemiah is correct. Also, the Jewish conviction on this is paramount. They were the divinely appointed custodians of the Scriptures, not the current crop of critics.

Ezra's fast, which was secretly observed in one of the rooms of the temple, assures us of his sincerity. Furthermore, his prayer was not a mere pretense ostentatiously exhibited, "To produce an effect on the audience rather than upon God, like many other public prayers,"[11] as some critics have alleged.

All Israel Summoned to Assembly in Jerusalem

Verses 7-9, And they made proclamation throughout Judah and Jerusalem unto all the children of the captivity, that they should gather themselves together unto Jerusalem; 8 and that whosoever came not within three days, according to the counsel of the princes and the

---

[9] WBC, op. cit., p. 154.
[10] As quoted by Williamson in WBC, p. 152.
[11] Batten in ICC, as quoted by Cundall in NBCR, p. 403.

elders, all his substance should be forfeited, and himself separated from the assembly of the captivity. 9 Then all the men of Judah and Benjamin gathered themselves together unto Jerusalem within the three days (it was the ninth month, on the twentieth day of the month); and all the people sat in the broad place before the house of God, trembling because of this matter, and for the great rain.

All his substance should be forfeited (v. 7). This was indeed a great penalty, and, besides that, those refusing to appear within the three days would also lose their status among God's people. "The forfeiture of substance here was not its destruction, as described in Deuteronomy 13:13-17 (for a city fallen into idolatry), but the appropriation of the offender's substance to the benefit of the temple, as described in Leviticus 27:28)."[12]

All the men of Judah and Benjamin gathered themsleves together unto Jerusalem (v. 9). This apparently means all Israelites living in those areas and does not exclude members of other tribes who might have been among them. Yet, the number of the Ten Tribes who returned might have been so insignificant that the whole nation of returnees might well have been known merely as the "men of Judah and Benjamin."

(It was the ninth month, the twentieth day of the month) (v. 9). "This was the month Kislew, corresponding to our months of November-

---

[12] CFK, op. cit., p. 128.

December."[13] Whitcomb identified this date as Dec. 8, 457 BC.[14] It was the rainy season in Jerusalem, and the weather at that time could be very cold.

All the people sat in the broad place before the house of God (v. 9). "This was a stone-walled enclosure, about 500 feet long and 150 feet wide, which might have afforded sitting room for 20,000 men. Deducting the aged, the infirm, the sick, and those under twelve years of age, and all the women, the whole total of men returning from captivity would scarcely have reached that number."[15] "This broad place was an open area in front of the watergate at the southeastern corner of the temple court."[16] The first order of business was an address by Ezra, which happily, due to the severe conditions, was rather brief.

Trembling because of this matter, and for the great rain (v. 9). The addition of this detail assures us that this is an account by an eye-witness. The urgency in which Ezra and the princes and elders viewed the matter of Israel's intermarriage with foreigners is emphasized by their calling such a general meeting at that unfavorable time of the year.

---

13 H. Porter in ISBE, p. 542.

14 WYC, p. 431.

15 PC, op. cit.. p. 153,

16 WYC, p. 431.

Ezra's Address Before the People

Verses 10-14, And Ezra the priest stood up and said unto them, Ye have trespassed, and married foreign women, to increase the guilt of Israel. 11 Now therefore make confession unto Jehovah, the God of your fathers, and do his pleasure; and separate yourselves from the peoples of the land, and from the foreign women. 12 Then all the assembly answwered and said with a loud voice, As thou hast said concerning us, so must we do. 13 But the people are many, and it is a time of much rain, and we are not able to stand without: neither is this a work of one day or two; for we have greatly transgressed in this matter. 14 Let now our princes be appointed for all the assembly, and let all them that are in our cities that have married foreign women, come at appointed times, and with them the elders of every city, and the judges thereof, until the fierce wrath of our God be turned from us, until this matter be despatched.

"The crowd readily agreed to Ezra's decision; but the implementation of it was far too complex and complicated a thing to be accomplished immediately while they were standing there shivering in the cold from the wintry rain."[17]

A commission was appointed, as the people suggested; and the people were called before it in small groups, accompanied by their fellow-citizens, thus giving time and opportunity to work out the problems one by one.

---

[17] BBC, op. cit., p. 468.

Opposition to Ezra's Solution of the Problem

Verse 15, Only Jonathan the son of Asahel and Jahzeiah the son of Tikvah stood up against this matter: and Meshullam and Shabbethai the Levite helped them.

This verse indicates that there was some oppostion, of course, to such a drastic course of action; and the fact of there being some opposed to it is not nearly so remarkable as the insignificant number of the opponents ---only four people out of some 20,000 men, or more!

And the Children of the Captivity Did So

Verses 16-17, And the children of the captivity did so. And Ezra the priest, with certain heads of fathers' houses, after their fathers' houses, and all of them by their names, were set apart; and they sat down in the first day of the tenth month to examine the matter. 17 And they made an end with all the men that had married foreign women by the first day of the first month.

The opposition did not delay the repudiation of the foreign wives. Only about a week elapsed between the decision to do so and the first session of the commission appointed to execute it. "The case of each city (or village) was taken separately. The male inhabitants of full age attended, and the 'elders and judges' heard each case separately. The neighbors of each person investigated were available for questioning; and when a mixed marriage was proved, the wife was repudiated. In 112 cases, the commission decided that the foreign wives and the children born to them were to be sent away."[18] An emendation in the RSV results in the number being reduced to 111.

In any case, the number is surprisingly small. Out of at least 20,000 men, only a few more than a hundred were guilty of having violated God's law in this matter. However, the importance of it was greatly intensified and augmented by the high social position and importance of the violators. If these had remained unpunished, or if their unlawful marriages had been allowed to stand, there is no way that Israel could have continued to maintain their distinction as a separate nation. Ezra's listing the violators as to their distinction as priests, Levites, etc., doubtless had this very fact in focus. The whole project was completed in three months' time, which allowed the better part of a whole day for the investigation of each one convicted.

These Are The Names of Those With Foreign Wives

Verses 18-44, And among the sons of the priests there were found that had married foreign women: namely, of the sons of Jeshua, the son of Jozadak, and his brethren, Maaseiah, and Eliezer, and Jarib, and Gedaliah. 19 And they gave their hand that they would put away their wives; and being guilty, they offered a ram of the flock for their

---

[18] PC, op. cit., p. 155.

guilt. 20 And of the sons of Immer: Hanani and Zebadiah. 21 And of the sons of Harim: Maaseiah, and Elijah, and Shemaiah, and Jehiel, and Uzziah. 22 And of the sons of Pashhur: Elioenai, Maaseiah, Ishmael, Nathanel, Jozabad, and Elasah.

23 And of the Levites: Jozabad, and Shimei, and Kelaiah (the same is Kelita), Pethahiah, Judah, and Eliezer. 24 And of the singers: Eliashib. And of the porters, Shallum, and Telem, and Uri.

25 And of Israel: of the sons of Parosh: Ramiah, and Izziah, and Malchijah, and Benaiah. 16 And of the sons of Elam: Mattaniah, Zechariah, and Jehiel, and Abdi, and Jerimoth, and Elijah. 27 And of the sons of Zattu: Elioenai, Eliashib, Mattaniah, and Jerimoth, and Zabad, and Aziza. 28 And of the sons of Bebai: Jehohanan, Hananiah, Zabbai, and Athlai. 29 And of the sons of Bani: Meshullam, Malluch, and Adaiah, Jashub, and Sheal, Jeremoth. 30 And of the sons of Pahath-moab: Adna, and Cheial, Benaiah, Maaseiah, Mattaniah, Bezalel, and Bennui, and Manasseh. 31 And of the sons of Harim: Eliezer, Isshijah, Malchijah, Shemiah, Shimeon, 32 Benjamin, Malluch, Shemariah. 33 Of the sons of Hashum: Mattenai, Mattattah, Zabad, Eliphelet, Jeremai, Manasseh, Shimei. 34 Of the sons of Bani: Maadai, Amram, and Uel. 35 Benaiah, and Bedaiah, Cheluhi, 36 Vaniah, Meremoth, Eliashib, 37 Mattaniah, Mattenai, and Jaasu, 38 and Bani, and Binnui, Shimei, 39 and Shelemiah, and Nathan, and Adaiah, 40 Machnadebai, Shashai, Sharai, 41 Azarel, and Shelemiah, Shemariah, 42 Shallum, Amariah, Joseph. 43 Of the sons of Nebo: Jeiel, Matithiah, Zabad, Zebina, Iddo, and Joel, Benaiah.

*44 All these had taken foreign wives; and some of them had
wives by whom they had children.*

Whitcomb's count of all these violators found,
"Seventeen priests, ten Levites, and eighty-six others;
and each of these put away his foreign wife and offered
a ram as a guilt-offering."[19]   Some of the versions
support this count of 113 in all.

Drastic as this solution of the problem assuredly
was, "A comparison of Nehemiah 10:30 (12 years later)
and of Nehemiah 13:23 (30 years later) shows that the
evil was not permanently eliminated. Long association
with heathen neighbors made such a separation
difficult."[20]

One thing that modern readers will wonder
about is what provision, if any, was made for those
wives and children which were expelled from the Jewish
community. Jamieson has this: "Doubtless an adequate
provision was made for the repudiated wives and
children, according to the means and circumstances of
the husbands."[21]   Abraham had also made provision for
Hagar when he put her and Ishmael away.

We conclude this study of Ezra with the
following relevant comment of Williamson:

Israel's mission could make headway only if
she maintained the servant identity that
separated her from the nations to which she was

---

[19] WYC, p. 432.

[20] Ibid.

[21] JFB, p. 294.

commissioned to reveal God's will. In exactly
the same way, Christians individually, and as the
Church, are called to be 'light' and 'salt,'
elements that function effectively precisely
because of their difference from the setting in
which they are placed. 'But if the salt has lost its
savor ... ?' (Mt. 5:13-16)."[22]

xxx

---

[22] WBC, op. cit., p. 162.

Commentary On Nehemiah

INTRODUCTION

The inclusion of Ezra and Nehemiah as a single book in the Hebrew Bible was due to their forcing the number of inspired books to correspond to the number of letters in their alphabet. In the same manner they included all twelve of the Minor Prophets as a single book! Ezra and Nehemiah are separate books by separate authors.

Another common misunderstanding about this book is that of the radical critics who imagine that First and Second Chronicles, Ezra, and Nehemiah were all written by some anonymous person referred to as "The Chronicler."[1] However, the radical critics have stated that the author of Second Chronicles is a liar in every type of terminology known for such a purpose; and it is therefore a gratuitous insult to attribute Nehemiah (as well as Ezra) to that imaginary "chronicler."

The Name. "*Nehemiah* means 'The Lord has comforted,' and it is sometimes abbreviated as 'Nahum' (Nahum 1:1), 'Naham' (1C 4:19), or 'Nahamani' (7:7)."[2]

Authorship. Wilson wrote that, "We cannot be certain who was the composer of Nehemiah."[3]   Halley

---

[1] BBC, Vol. 3, p. 470.
[2] IB, Vol. 3, p. 882.
[3] R. Dick Wilson in ISBE, p. 1083.

wrote that, "There is a persistent Jewish tradition that Ezra wrote First and Second Chronicles, Ezra and Nehemiah";[4] but, although correct as regards all four of those books except Nehemiah, this writer holds that Nehemiah himself is the author of the work that bears his name. Why? The first sentence in the book reads: *"The words of Nehemiah the son of Hacaliah."* Thus the Bible itself tells us who wrote it. Is there any known fact that contradicts this? No!

Keil wrote that, "The contents of the book itself do not furnish the slightest opposition to the view that the whole composition was the work of Nehemiah."[5] Also Whitcomb pointed out that, "The fact that Nehemiah is written in the first person is evidence that Nehemiah is the author; and the places where he is mentioned in the third person can be explained in harmony with his authorship."[6]

Date. All efforts to date Nehemiah any later than the fifth century BC have been thoroughly repudiated by current scholars. "The date of Nehemiah is about 431-430 BC."[7] "There is not the slightest proof that any of Ezra and Nehemiah is unhistorical, or that they were not written in the fifth century BC."[8] Efforts to date Nehemiah in the times of the Greek period are based upon Nehemiah's mention of Jaddua in 12:11, 22;

---

[4] HHH, p. 220.

[5] CFK, Vol. 3c, p. 150.

[6] WYC, p. 435

[7] PC, Vo, 7b, p. ii.

[8] ISBE, p. 1084.

but for a thorough discussion of that and its consequent rejection as having any bearing whatever on the date of Nehemiah, see the recent work of Williamson.[9] He accepted the Persian period in the latter part of the fifth century BC as the date of Nehemiah.

Ezra, Nehemiah and Esther. There is a sense in which these three books have a single purpose. "They have the story of the Jews' return from Babylon, the rebuilding of the Temple, the wall of Jerusalem and the re-establishment of the Jews' national life in their homeland."[10] Ezra's focus was upon the rebuilding of the Temple, and Nehemiah's was upon the rebuilding of the walls. This one fact should establish the relative dates of the two books. Cyrus authorized the rebuilding of the Temple; Darius II authorized the rebuilding of the walls; therefore, Ezra is the earlier.

The general purpose. The grand purpose of all three of these books is to reveal God's restoration of Israel to Palestine according to the prophecies and to demonstrate God's continued blessing and protection of the Chosen People. In Nehemiah, "The principle purpose of the writer was to describe the circumstances that attended the rebuilding of the wall in 444 BC."[11]

The Three Returns. "(1) In 536 BC, Zerubbabel returned with 42,360 Jews, 7,337 servants, 200 singers, 736 horses, 245 mules, 435 camels, 6,720 asses, and 5,400 gold and silver vessels. (2) In 457 BC, Ezra

---

[9] H. G. M. Williamson in WBC, Vol. 16., pp. 149-154.
[10] HHH, p. 216.
[11] PC, op. cit., p. i.

returned with 1,754 males, 100 talents of gold, and 750 talents of silver. This journey required four months. (3) In 444 BC, Nehemiah returned as governor, with an army escort; and he quickly rebuilt the walls of Jerusalem and fortified the city at government expense."[12] Thus the return from captivity was in stages exactly after the manner of their deportation.

Regarding the Prophets of This Period. During approximately one century (536-432 BC) during which the events of the three books (Ezra, Nehemiah and Esther) occurred, the final prophets of the Old Covenant performed their ministries. Zechariah and Haggai prophesied during the first half of this period, and Malachi appeared in the times of Nehemiah. There was nothing accidental about this. In the ministries of those prophets and in the affairs of these three books, we have the concluding program by which God gave the Chosen Race one more (and the final) opportunity to become faithful to the God of their fathers. True to the prophecy of Isaiah, however, they continued to stop their ears, close their eyes, harden their hearts and refuse utterly to obey the commandments of God (Isaiah 6:9:10, Matthew 13:14-15, Acts 28:25-28). The principal agents of Satan in this disaster were the Jewish priesthood; and their evil determination becomes quite visible in Nehemiah.

The Opposition of the Priests. "Nehemiah's efforts to effect his reforms were thwarted and resisted by an important party of the priests and the nobles, a party

---

[12] HHH, p. 216.

which leaned toward secularism, approved of intermarriage with the heathen, and disregarded the sanctity of the Temple. This party, strong and powerful, was supported by the nobles and even the current high priest Eliashib." Right here, then, in the times of Nehemiah, we have a glimpse of those "Three False Shepherds" (Zechariah 11:8) who would eventually achieve the judicial hardening of racial Israel (Romans 11:25). Those false shepherds were the Pharisees, the Sadducees, and the Herodian, made up entirely of the priests and the nobles, exactly as in the times of Nehemiah.

The Historical Situation When Nehemiah Arrived. Nehemiah arrived in Jerusalem in 444 BC; Ezra had been there 13 years, but his work was limited to teaching religion. The Jews had been in Jerusalem about a hundred years; and, except for the rebuilding of the temple, they had made little or no progress. When they attempted to rebuild the wall, the peoples of the land interfered and would stop the work, either by threats, or through intrigue with the Persian ruler. It was a melancholy situation indeed that greeted Nehemiah.

Nehemiah's Arrival. He arrived as civil governor of Judaea, protected by a military escort, and armed with a commission from the king of Persia to rebuild the walls and fortify Jerusalem. And did he do it? He accomplished that task in less than ninety days.

The Masoretic Text. After a thorough examination of the Latin, Syrian, Septuagint (LXX) and Arabian versions of the OT, Wilson concluded that,

"The Hebrew text (MT) is of more value than that of the Versions."[13] The same writer also declared our text to be accurate in the very smallest particulars.

Characteristics of the Book of Nehemiah. "It is a plain, simple, straight-forward history of a short period of Jewish history; there are no miracles; nothing very extraordinary or exciting is included. The Jewish nation is in a state of depression; and that seems to be reflected in the matter-of-fact record of Nehemiah. Nevertheless, the ultimate failure of the Chosen People to discharge their principal commission to receive and advocate the Kingdom of Messiah begins in this final one of the Historical Books to appear as an absolute certainty for racial Israel as a whole. Only the "righteous remnant" would actually seize that opportuniity; the great majority would continue their headlong rush into rebellion and ruin. "There is no other portion of the Scriptures in which the individuality of the author is so vividly impressed as in Nehemiah."[14]

Outline of Nehemiah. After looking over a dozen different outlines, this writer has chosen the following by Stephen S. Short:[15]

    I.   Nehemiah's sad news re: Judaea (1:1-10).
    II. He is sent to Jerusalem (2:1-20).
    III. The walls are rebuilt (3:1-6:19).
    IV. List of returnees with Zerubbabel (Ch. 7).
    V.   Reading of the Law (7:73b-8:18).

---

[13] R. Dick Wilson in ISBE, p. 1084.
[14] PC, op. cit., p. iii.
[15] NLBC, p. 534.

Nehemiah, Israel's last chance. The events of Esther came chronologically between Zerubbabel and Nehemiah, therefore God's intervention in the secular affairs of Israel came to a conclusion with the efforts of Nehemiah. Never again would God take control of the government of Israel and attempt to bring the Chosen People back to their duty. Oh yes, there would be other providential help for the Chosen People; but never again would they have complete control of their government. Nehemiah is the last of the Historical books.

The evil priesthood grew steadily worse; God cursed them in the days of Malachi; although they remained vassals of pagan governments, the priesthood gradually came to exercise complete and total control over the religious affairs of God's people; but their insatiable ambition could never be satisfied till they ruled the secular government also. They tried to achieve that in their rebellion against Rome, which ended in the disaster of A. D. 70.

Concluding Word Regarding Nehemiah. "It must be said in conclusion, that no portion of the OT provides us with a greater incentive to dedicated, discerning zeal for the work of God than does Nehemiah. The example of his passion for the truth of God's word, whatever the cost or consequences, is an example sorely needed in the present hour. May the prayerful study of this book lead more of God's people today to, 'Earnestly contend for the faith once for all delivered unto the saints.' (Jude 3)."[16]

xxx

---

[16] WYC, p. 435.

CHAPTER 1
Nehemiah Gets the Bad News About Jerusalem

Josephus has a tale regarding the manner in which Nehemiah received this bad news. One day as he was walking around the palace in Susa, he heard some Jews speaking in the Hebrew language and inquired of them regarding conditions in Jerusalem. They told him of the constant enmity of the neighboring people, and of how they were subjected to harrassment day and night, and even that many dead people could be found along the roads.[1] The Scriptural account does not exactly correspond with this, unless we should set aside the usual opinion of commentators that Hanani was an actual brother of Nehemiah; but the narratives have one thing in common. Hanani was only one of several people who brought the bad news.

"It cannot be definitely ascertained whether or not Hanani was actually a blood brother of Nehemiah. However, in 7:2, Nehemiah again referred to him as his brother, leading to the speculation that he was really a brother in the ordinary sense."[2] Williamson wrote that, "It is likely that the word (brother) should be taken literally."[3]

Verses 1-2, The words of Nehemiah the son of Hacaliah.

Now it came to pass in the month Chislev, in the

---

[1] JOSA, p. 332.
[2] TBC, p. 258.
[3] WBC, Vol. 16, p. 171.

twentieth year, as I was in Shushan the palace, 2 that
Hanani, one of my brethren, came, he and certain men out
of Judah; and I asked them concerning the Jews that had
escaped, that were left of the captivity, and concerning
Jerusalem.

    The words of Nehemiah (v. 1). This stands as the
title of the whole book; and the critical canard that,
"These words were probably added by a later scribe,"[4]
should be rejected. "No other historical book begins in
this manner,"[5] and therefore no 'later scribe' could
possibly have been so foolish as to make such an
unheard of addition. However, all of the prophetical
books begin thus; and in all these cases they constitute
the title of the book, as they most certainly do here.
"Verse 1a here contains the title of the whole book."[6]
"This book is one of the outstanding autobiographical
masterpieces of the ancient world."[7]

    Nehemiah the son of Hacaliah (v. 1). The tribe
to which Nehemiah belonged is not revealed; but,
"Eusebius and Jerome assert that he was of the tribe of
Judah."[8] Jamieson supposed that this is true and added
further that, "He was of the royal family of David."[9]
Matthew Henry, however, stated that, "If 2 Maccabees
1:18 is the truth in their statement that Nehemiah

---

[4] ASP, p. 330.

[5] FCC, *Nehemiah*, p. 459.

[6] CFK, 3c, p. 155.

[7] NBCR, p. 404.

[8] CFK, op. cit., p. 155.

[9] JFB, p. 294.

offered sacrifices, then we must conclude that he was a priest and therefore of the tribe of Levi."[10] These references are an excellent example of scholarly comment on something which the sacred Scriptures do not reveal.

The month Chislev in the twentieth year (v. 2). The month Chislev corresponded to our November-December; and the twentieth year here is a reference to, "The twentieth year of the reign of Artaxerxes I (Longimanus), i. e. in the year 445 BC."[11]

In Shushan the palace (v. 2). "This is the same place as Susa, where Daniel saw the vision of the ram with two horns (Daniel 8:2),"[12] and, "Where, in the year 478 BC, Esther became Xerxes' queen in this palace."[13] "This place was the winter residence of Persian kings";[14] "It was located east of the river Tigris and near the head of the Persian gulf."[15]

Summary of the Bad News

Verse 3, And they said unto me, The remnant that are left of the captivity there in the province are in great affliction and reproach: the wall of Jerusalem also is broken down, and the gates thereof are burned with fire.

---

10 MH, Vol, 2, p. 1068,
11 NLBC, p. 534.
12 PC, Vol. 7b, p. 2.
13 WYC, p. 436.
14 ASP, p. 330.
15 NLBC, p. 534.

The wall of Jerusalem also is broken down (v. 3).
This should not be read as meaning that the breaking
down of the wall had happened only recently. At this
point in history, the wall had never been rebuilt since
Nebuchadnezzar had destroyed it. There had indeed
been an effort by the Jews to rebuild the wall, somewhat
earlier in the reign of this same Artaxerxes I; but that
had been totally frustrated by the hatred of Rehum and
Shimshai the deputy rulers beyond the River; and in
Ezra 4:17-22, we have the record of how the enemies of
Israel had forcefully stopped all such efforts to rebuild
the city. See our discussion of this in Ezra chapter 4,
above.

Nehemiah's Response to the Bad News

*Verse 4, And it came to pass, when I heard these
words, that I sat down and wept, and mourned certain
days; and I fasted and prayed before the God of Heaven.
And I said:*

As cupbearer of the king, Nehemiah was a
prominent and trusted member of the king's court,
living in honor, security and luxury; "But he could not
forget that he was an Israelite, and this was similar to
the emotions that governed the life of Moses."[16]
I prayed before the God of heaven (v. 4). "This title
of the Almighty is Persian rather than Jewish; but it was

---

[16] GDH, Vol. 2, p. 486.

a favorite of Nehemiah who had been brought up in Persia."[17] We keep encountering remarks of this kind in the writings of several commentators; but there is no way that they can be considered true. Jonah mentioned "The God of heaven" in the eighth century BC (1:9); and we find it also in the works of Moses about one millennium before Nehemiah's time (Genesis 24:3,7).

Nehemiah's Prayer

Verses 5-11, I beseech thee, O Jehovah, the God of heaven, the great and terrible God that keepeth covenant and lovingkindness with them that love him and keep his commandments: 6 let thine ear now be attentive, and thine eyes open, that thou mayest hearken unto the prayer of thy servant, which I pray before thee at this time, day and night, for the children of Israel, thy servants, while I confess the sins of the children of Israel, which we have sinned against thee. Yea, I and my father's house have sinned: 7 we have dealt very corruptly against thee, and have not kept the commandments, nor the ordinances, which thou commandedst thy servant Moses. 8 Remember, I beseech thee, the word that thou commandedst thy servant Moses, saying, If ye trespass, I will scatter you abroad among the peoples: 9 but if ye return unto me, and keep my commandments and do them, though your outcasts were in the uttermost part of the heavens, yet will I gather them from thence, and will bring them to the place that I have chosen, to cause my name to

---

[17] FCC, op. cit., p. 459.

dwell there. 10 Now these are thy servants and thy people, whom thou hast redeemed by thy great power, and by thy strong hand. 11 O Lord, I beseech thee, let now thine ear be attentive to the prayer of thy servant, and to the prayer of thy servants, who delight to fear thy name; and prosper, I pray thee, thy servant this day, and grant him mercy in the sight of this man.

If ye trespass, I will scatter you abroad among the peoples (v. 8). Here Nehemiah was remembering the words of Moses in Deuteronomy 30:1-8.

This is a fervent beautiful prayer, and there's not a word in it that suggests any other person than Nehemiah as the author of it. Yet the critics who profess to know everything, and who are unable to find any dependable record whatever in the Holy Bible, declare this prayer to be fraudulently ascribed to Nehemiah. Hamrick stated that, "This prayer is probably not a *ver batim* quotation from Nehemiah."[18] And Oesterley even professed to know who wrote it! "The Chronicler took this prayer from the Temple liturgy and put it into the mouth of Nehemiah"![19] It is difficult to imagine a more arrogant conceit than that which produces such comments. Where is there any prayer in the Temple liturgy that duplicates this? It simply does not exist.

"There was a grave personal risk to Nehemiah in his decision to champion the cause of the distressed

---

[18] BBC, Vol. 3, p. 471.
[19] ASP, p. 330.

citizens in Jerusalem, because his master Artaxerxes I had already accepted the charge of the Samaritans that Jerusalem was a bad and rebellious city (See Ezra 4:17-22); and any request of Nehemiah of Artaxerxes would involve asking him to rescind a decree that he himself had made only a few years previously."[20]

And grant him mercy in the sight of this man (v. 11). Speaking of himself in the third person here, Nehemiah prays that God will grant him mercy before the king. "What man he means is explained by the following supplementary remark, 'And I was cupbearer to the king,' without whose favor and permission Nehemiah could not have carried out his intention."[21]

"Mercy is what Nehemiah prays for, especially mercy from God, as he makes his petition before Artaxerxes."[22] It is significant that Nehemiah in this prayer did not speak of Artaxerxes as 'the king,' but as 'this man.' "Such expressions as 'a man,' or 'this man,'" according to Oesterley, "Come from a Hebrew word that carries 'a note of contempt.'"[23] Perhaps Nehemiah was thinking that, "After all the great king is only a man, subject in every way to the will of God."

xxx

---

[20] NBCR, p. 404.

[21] CFK, op. cit., p. 162.

[22] MH, op. cit., p. 1070.

[23] ASP, p. 330.

CHAPTER 2

*Nehemiah Arrives in Jerusalem With Authority to Rebuild
the Walls of the City*

Artaxerxes Granted Nehemiah's Request

*Verses 1:11b-2:8, Now I was cupbearer to the king.
1 And it came to pass in the month Nisan, in the twentieth
year of Artaxerxes the king, when wine was beside him, that
I took up the wine and gave it unto the king. Now I had
not been beforetime sad in his presence. 2 And the king
said unto me, Why is thy countenance sad, seeing thou art
not sick? this is nothing but sorrow of heart. Then I was
very sore afraid. 3 And I said unto the king, Let the king
live for ever: why should not my countenance be sad, when
the city, the place of my fathers' sepulchres, lieth waste, and
the gates thereof are consumed with fire? 4 Then the king
said unto me, For what dost thou make request? So I
prayed to the God of heaven. 5 And I said unto the king, If
it please the king, and if thy servant have found favor in thy
sight, that thou wouldest send me unto Judah, unto the city
of my fathers' sepulchres, that I may build it. 6 And the
king said unto me (the queen sitting beside him), For how
long shall thy journey be? and when wilt thou return? So it
pleased the king to send me; and I set him a time. 7
Moreover I said unto the king, If it please the king, let
letters be given me to the governors beyond the River, that
they let me pass through till I come unto Judah; 8 and a
letter unto Asaph the keeper of the king's forest, that he may
give me timber to make beams for the gates of the castle
that pertaineth to the house, and for the wall of the city,
and for the house that I shall enter into. And the king*

granted me, according to the good hand of my God upon me.

In all of the wonderful things that God did for the children of Israel, there are few things any more astounding than this. That a Persian king should have reversed a former decision stopping the work of the Jews on the walls of their city, and then have sent a trusted emissary, accompanied by a military escort, and endowed with full authority to reconstruct the walls and fortify the city of Jerusalem ---only God could have caused a thing like that to happen.

In the month Nisan (v. 1). This was four months after the time mentioned in 1:1, during which time Nehemiah had fasted and prayed "night and day" that something could be done to aid Jerusalem. During this period, Nehemiah had diligently tried to maintain his customary happy appearance; but his great grief finally became evident in his appearance.

I took up the wine, and gave it unto the king (v. 1). Jamieson has a description of how a cupbearer performed his service. "He washed the cup in the king's presence, filled it with wine, then poured from the cup into his own left hand a sufficient amount. Then he drank that in the king's presence and handed the cup of wine to the king."[1]

Then I was sore afraid (v. 2). "It was contrary to court behavior for a servant to appear sad."[2] "Being sad

---

[1] JFB, p. 295.
[2] ASP, p. 330.

in the king's presence was a serious offense in Persia (Esther 4:2); and, besides that, Nehemiah was well aware that the request which he would ultimately make of the king might indeed anger him."[3]

The place of my fathers' sepulchres lieth waste (v. 3). This reply kept Nehemiah's concern in the personal, rather than the political, sector.

For what dost thou make request (v. 4)? This was the moment of truth for Nehemiah. If the king was displeased, Nehemiah would lose his head; and therefore his first reaction was that, "I prayed to the God of heaven." There can be no doubt that God answered his prayer; because, "That prayer brought about one of the most astonishing reversals of royal policy in all history."[4] Furthermore, it happened in Persia, of all places, where their favorite proverb was, "The law of the Medes and Persians which altereth not."

"Send me unto Judah ... that I may build it (v. 5). A more daring request was never made. It had been only a few years since, "Artaxerxes had commissioned Rehum and Shimshai to bring a stop to the rebuilding and fortifying of Jerusalem (Ezra 4:8-23)."[5] The amazing thing is that Artaxerxes granted Nehemiah's request, lock, stock and barrel ---all of it.

Perhaps it is permissible for us to speculate a little on why Artaxerxes did so. Of course, the great reason is that God willed it; but, as is always the case,

---

[3] WYC, p. 436.
[4] Ibid.
[5] BBC, Vol. 3, p. 473

God uses ordinary men and events to achieve his purpose. Some of the satraps beyond the River had grown too powerful. "There is evidence that Megabyzos, one of the satraps beyond the River, had recently revolted; and the creation of a strengthened and fortified Jerusalem under a friendly governor might have appeared to Artaxerxes at that particular time as a wise strategy."[6] Also, by separating Judah from the powerful coalition of the peoples known collectively as "Samaritans," and by fortifying it, the aggressiveness of the Samaritan coalition would be dramatically checkmated. And of course, Artaxerxes' commission to Nehemiah definitely "Involved the separation of Judea from Samaria."[7] This substantially weakened the power of Sanballat.

The castle which appertaineth to the house (v. 8). This is a reference to the combination palace and fortress, "That protected the Temple and overlooked the northwest corner of the courts ... Herod later rebuilt it in NT times, and it was known as the Tower of Antonio. Nehemiah contemplated using it as his residence."[8]

Some critics have questioned how it came about that Nehemiah was in possession of such detailed knowledge of specific buildings in Jerusalem; but a man in Nehemiah's high official position was in possession of all kinds of options for procuring any kind of

---

[6] NBCR, p. 405.
[7] Ibid.
[8] WYC, p. 437.

information that he might have desired.

The queen also sitting beside him (v. 6). Polygamy was popular among Persian kings, nevetheless they also had one principal wife whom they designated as "the Queen." "The legitimate queen of Artaxerxes was Damaspia."[9] Williamson noted that the word is used here in the plural, and that upon occasions the word was applied to some favorite woman in the harem, or even to the queen-mother of the king, as in the book of Daniel. Some have concluded that the presence of the queen here indicated that this was a private banquet. Rawlinson's comment was that, "It appears that Artaxerxes Longimanus had only one legitimate wife, a certain Damaspia."[10] He backed this up with a reference to a statement by Ctesias in Persian history.

And I set him a time (v. 6). Nehemiah's first term as governor lasted twelve years; but it seems unlikely that he would have set such a time for his journey. Nehemiah evidently promised to return within a much shorter period, after which his leave of absence was extended. The speed with which he tackled the problem of building the wall suggests this. The journey itself would require three or four months each direction, and allowing enough time for the fortifications, suggests that his request must surely have been for, "a year or two."[11]

---

9 WBC, Vol. 16, p. 180.

10 PC, Vol. 7c, p. 10.

11 Ibid.

*Nehemiah Shows His Credentials to the Satraps,
Arrives in Jerusalem, and Surveys
the Broken Walls by Night*

Verses 9-16, Then I came to the governors beyond the River, and gave them the king's letters. Now the king had sent with me captains of the army and horsemen. 10 And when Sanballat the Horonite, and Tobiah the servant, the Ammonite, heard of it, it grieved them exceedingly, for that there was come a man to seek the welfare of the children of Israel. 11 So I came to Jerusalem, and was there three days. 12 And I arose in the night, and some few men with me; neither told I any man what my God put in my heart to do for Jerusalem; neither was there any beast with me, save the beast that I rode upon. 13 And I went out by night by the valley gate, even toward the jackal's well, and to the dung gate, and viewed the walls of Jerusalem, which were broken down, and the gates thereof were consumed with fire. 14 Then I went on to the fountain gate, and to the king's pool: but there was no place for the beast that was under me to pass. 15 Then I went up in the night by the brook, and viewed the wall; and I turned back, and entered by the valley gate, and so returned. 16 And the rulers knew not whither I went, or what I did; neither had I as yet told it to the Jews, nor to the priests, nor to the nobles, nor to the rest that did the work.

And I came to the governors beyond the River, and gave them the king's letters (v. 9). This must indeed have been a shock to Sanballat and Tobiah. The mention of "captains of the army, and horsemen," (v. 9) indicates a very considerable military escort; and they were strengthened by the full authority, permission and credentials of the king of Persia. This was particularly bad news to Sanballat, who, "According to the Elephantine Papyrus, was governor of Samaria, which at that time included Judea. He was possibly an Ephraimite."[12]

Sanballat would have been a fool not to have read this sudden arrival of Nehemiah in command of a division of the Persian army as the end of his domination of Judah.

"It grieved them exceedingly (v. 10). Of course, their normal reaction to the situation was to hinder Nehemiah in every possible manner.

I went out by night by the valley gate (v. 13). One must admire the skill, wisdom and ability of Nehemiah, who secretly developed his whole program of action, concealing it from every person who might have been in a position to discourage or hinder it.

The valley gate (v. 13). This was one of the nine gates of the city, located at the southwest corner of Jerusalem;[13] and Nehemiah's exploration of the walls extended along the southern elevation of the city, past the southeast corner and some distance up the Kidron valley as far as the king's pool. He did not go around the whole city, but turned back and reentered by the valley gate.

There was no place for the beast that was under me

---

[12] NBCR, p. 405

[13] AAOT, p. 313.

to pass (v. 14). Recent archaeological discoveries explain why Nehemiah was compelled to dismount and continue a part of his exploration on foot. "Excavations by Kathleen Kenyon[14] have revealed dramatically why Nehemiah's mount could not pass along the eastern wall. The steep slopes had been built up with gigantic stone terraces. When Nebuchadnezzar destroyed the city, those terraces with the buildings constructed on them collapsed into the valley below; and when Nehemiah came the entire area (around that southeastern section) was an incredible mass of fallen stones. Nehemiah abandoned the pre-exilic line of the east wall altogether and constructed a new wall along the crest of the hill."[15]

And the rulers knew not ... (v. 16). The 'rulers' were the local officials; and the fact that Nehemiah laid his plans secretly, excluding both the priests and the nobles from his confidence, at first, indicates that he was in possession of prior information regarding the opposition to be expected from them. Those people whom he had interviewed in Shushan had probably apprised him of the evil attitude of the priests and nobles.

And They Said, Let Us Rise Up and Build

Verses 17-20, Then said I unto them, Ye see the evil

---

[14] Kathleen Kenyon, *Jerusalem: Excavating 3,000 Years of History* (New York: McGraw-Hill, 1967), pp. 107-111.

[15] BBC, Vol. 3, p. 474.

*case that we are in, how Jerusalem lieth waste, and the
gates thereof are burned with fire: come, and let us build up
the wall of Jerusalem, that we be no more a reproach. 18
And I told them of the hand of my God which was good
upon me, as also the king's words that he had spoken unto
me. And they said, Let us rise up and build. So they
strengthened their hands for the good work. 19 But when
Sanballat the Horonite, and Tobiah the servant, the
Ammonite, and Gershem the Arabian, heard it, they
laughed us to scorn, and despised us, and said, What is this
thing which ye do? will ye rebel against the king? 20 Then
answered I them, and said unto them, The God of heaven,
he will prosper us; therefore we his servants will arise and
build: but ye have no portion, nor right, nor memorial in
Jeruslaem.*

Ye see the evil case we are in (v. 17). Not merely
the physical state of ruin of the city, but the shameful
subservience they suffered under the Samaritan
governor, the constant reproach and hatred of their
neighbors, and their current low estate compared to
their former glory ---all of these things oppressed and
discouraged the people. What a surge of new hope and
joy must have energized and excited the people with the
sudden apearance of Nehemiah, and his challenge to
Rise Up and Build!

And I told them ... (v. 18). Having carefully laid
his plans, and being then ready to act, Nehemiah
explained to the people his full power and permission of
the king to rebuild the wall and fortify the city. The
response of the people was spontaneous and jubilant,

"Let us rise up and build," they said.

Sanballat and Tobiah responded to the situation with scornful laughter, taunting and spiteful remarks, and accusations of rebellion against the king. Nehemiah had not told them of his full authority and power to rebuild and fortify Jerusalem. However Nehemiah did not tell them, even then, that he was acting with the king's full support and permission, saying rather that, "The God of heaven, he will prosper us." We may well suppose that Sanballat and Tobiah at once dispatched messengers to Artaxerxes; and we may only imagine their consternation and disgust when they got the bad news from the king himself.

xxx

CHAPTER 3
Details of How They All Worked on the Wall

The skill and ability of Nehemiah appear dramatically in this chapter. Even the high priest, of all people, was enlisted in the work. Nobody was exempt; the entire population of Judah, some twenty five or thirty thousand men, all went to work at one time on the city wall. No wonder it was finished in record time.

Eliashib the high priest, like many of the nobles and a large number of priests, would oppose some of Nehemiah's reforms; but this building of the city wall was a project that received the unanimous support of the whole population, a fact that clearly surfaces in this chapter.

Those Who Built the Wall at the Sheep Gate

Verses 1-2, Then Eliashib the high priest rose up with his brethren the priests, and they builded the sheep gate; they sanctified it, and set up the doors of it; even unto the tower of Hammeah they sanctified it, even unto the tower of Hananel. 2 And next unto him builded the men of Jericho. And next to them builded Zaccur the son of Imri.

It was quite appropriate that the high priest and his associate workers should have been assigned to build that section of the wall that included the sheep gate, because that was located at the northeastern corner of the city adjacent to the Temple area. We do not subscribe to the critical dictum that this chapter, in any manner, is some kind of an addition to Nehemiah's

account. Nehemiah was the one who planned and
engineered every portion of this remarkable building
project. Only Nehemiah had the ability to have done
such a thing.

"There were approximately forty sections of the
wall, in variable lengths and proportions; and, as they
are listed here, they appear in a succession to the left,
that is, counterclockwise, beginning here at the sheep
gate and finally ending at this same sheep gate."[1]

Those who Worked on the Wall Having the Fish Gate

*Verses 3-5, And the fish gate did the sons of
Hassenaah build; they laid the beams thereof, and set up
the doors thereof, the bolts thereof, and the bars thereof. 4
And next unto them repaired Meremoth the son of Uriah,
the son of Hakkoz, and next unto them repaired
Meshullum the son of Berechiah, the son of Meshezabel,
and next unto them repaired Zadok the son of Baana. 5
And next unto them the Tekoites repaired; but the nobles
put not their neck to the work of their lord.*

The fish gate was the northern gate of the city,
See map on page 138 by Merrill F. Unger.[2]

"The Tekoites lived south of the city and were
probably in sympathy with Sanballat, or afraid of
reprisals if they openly identified themselves with

---

[1] BBC, Vol. 3, 476.
[2] AAOT, p. 313.

Nehemiah."[3]   This would account for the fact that "Their nobles put not their neck to the work."

List of the Foremen Who Repaired the Old Gate

Verses 6-12, And the old gate repaired Joiada the son of Paseah and Meshullum the son of Besodeiah; they laid the beams thereof, and set up the doors thereof, and the bolts thereof, and the bars thereof. 7 And next unto them repaired Melatiah the Gibeonite and Jadon the Meronothite, the men of Gibeon, and of Mizpah, that appertained to the throne of the governor beyond the River. 8 Next unto him repaired Uzziel the son of Harhaiah, goldsmiths. And next unto them repaired Hananiah one of the perfumers, and they fortified Jerusalem even unto the broad wall. 9 And next unto them repaired Rephaih the son of Hur, the ruler of half the district of Jerusalem. 10 And next unto them repaired Jedaiah the son of Harumaph, over against his house. And next unto him repaired Hattush the son of Hashabneiah. 11 Malchijah the son of Harim, and Hasshub the son of Pahath-moab, repaired another portion, and the tower of the furnaces. 12 And next unto him repaired Shallum the son of Hallohesh, the ruler of half the district of Jerusalem, he and his daughters.

Critics attempting to make this chapter some kind of an interpolation claim that, "It is intent upon underscoring the role of the clergy in the rebuilding of

---

3 NBCR, p. 406.

the wall."[4] However, no such intention is evident in this chapter. On the other hand, the focus is not upon the clergy at all, but upon the fact that *everybody* engaged in the work. "All classes participated in the project, including priests (v. 1), goldsmiths and perfumers (v. 8), rulers of the city and even women (v. 12), also Levites (v. 17) and merchants (v. 32)."[5] Where is there any emphasis on the clergy in all that?

Not merely the population of Jerusalem engaged in this project, but their fellow-countrymen who lived throughout the area. "These included the men of Jericho (v. 2), the Tekoites (v. 5), the men of Gibeon and Mizpah (v. 7), the inhabitants of Zanoah (v. 13), those who lived in the district of Bethzur (v. 16), those in Keilah (v. 17), and the men of the Plain, i. e., the Jordan valley (v. 22)."[6] Again, we must ask, "Where is there any special emphasis upon the clergy in this chapter"?

Another factor that ties this chapter irrevocably to the person of Nehemiah is the frequent mention of the great beams used for the doors of the various gates. Only Nehemiah had the king's permission to bring these, presumably from the forest of Lebanon; and it was therefore the men directly obedient to the orders of Nehemiah who delivered these great timbers to the various locations. The fact of Nehemiah's name not being mentioned in these verses is of no importance

---

[4] BBC, Vol. 3, 476.

[5] NBCR, p. 405.

[6] NLBC, p. 536.

whatever.

The Wall That Included the Valley Gate
and the Dung Gate repaired

Verses 13-14, The valley gate repaired Hanun, and the inhabitants of Zanoah; they built it, and set up the doors thereof, the bolts thereof, and the bars thereof, and a thousand cubits of the wall unto the dung gate.

14 And the dung gate repaired Malchijah the son of Rechab, the ruler of the district of Beth-haccherem; he built it, and set up the doors thereof, the bolts thereof, and the bars thereof.

Thousands of the Israelites worked on the walls, but only the leaders of the companies working on the various sections were named. Note that one group of workers build a thousand cubits of the wall (v. 13). That is fifteen hundred feet! The Rechabites also appear to have made their contribution, as may be indicated by the name of the ruler mentioned in v. 14.

The next section of the wall mentioned is that including the fountain gate, on the southeastern section of the city, where the walls were the most completely demolished. That accounts for the fact that the majority of the workers were employed there.

Regarding The Wall Including the Fountain Gate

Verses 15-27, And the fountain gate repaired Shellun the son of Colhozeh, the ruler of the district of

*Mizpah; he built it, and covered it, and set up the doors
thereof, the bolts thereof, and the bars thereof, and the wall
by the pool of Shelah by the king's garden even unto the
stairs that go down from the city of David. 16 After him
repaired Nehemiah the son of Azbuk, the ruler of half the
district of Beth-zur, unto the place over against the
sepulchres of David, and unto the pool that was made, and
unto the house of the mighty men. 17 After him repaired
the Levites, Rehum the son of Bani. Next unto him
repaired Hashabiah, the ruler of the district of Keilah, for
his district. 18 After him repaired their brethren, Bavvai
the son of Henadad, the ruler of half the district of Keilah.
19 And next to him repaired Ezer the son of Jeshua, the
ruler of Mizpah, another portion, over against the ascent to
the armory at the turning of the wall. 20 After him Baruch
the son of Zabbai earnestly repaired another portion, from
the turning of the wall to the door of the house of Eliashib
the high priest. 21 After him repaired Meremoth the son of
Uriah the son of Hakkoz another portion, from the door of
house of Eliashib even to the end of the house of Eliashib.
22 And after him repaired the priests, the men of the Plain.
23 And after them repaired Benjamin and Hasshub over
against their house. After them repaired Azariah the son
of Maaseiah the son of Ananiah beside his own house. 24
After him repaired Binnui the son of Henadad another
portion, from the house of Azariah unto the turning of the
wall, and unto the corner. 25 Palal the son of Uzai
repaired over against the turning of the wall, and the tower
that standeth out from the upper house of the king, which
is by the court of the guard. After him Pedaiah the son of
Parosh repaired. 26 (Now the Nethinim dwelt in Ophel,*

unto the place over against the water gate toward the east,
and the tower that standeth out.)   27 After him, the
Tekoites repaired another portion, over against the great
tower that standeth out, and unto the wall of Ophel.

It is significant that many of the prominent
citizens of Jerusaelm, whose houses were near the wall,
elected to repair that section of the wall that was beside
their houses. This is easily understood, because their
own personal safety and security were thus procured
and protected.

The exact locations and extent of each one of
these various "repairs," although unknown to us, and
vigorously disputed as to details by special scholars in
the topography of ancient Jerusalem, are nevertheless
of little interest to present day Christians. The big point
in all of this is simply that the total population of Judah
and Jerusalem enthusiastically joined hands and hearts
and refortified the ancient city. No doubt, those walls
were finished, during the period when Sanballat and
Tobiah were either sending someone, or going
themselves to see Artaxerxes I in the hope of stopping
it. Such a journey, round trip, would have taken at least
six or eight months; and long prior to that, the walls
were completed, the great gates rebuilt, the bolts and
the bars put in place, and the city secured by the
military. What a magnificent achievement!

The Wall of Jerusalem Completely Rebuilt

Verses 28-32,   Above the horse gate repaired the

priests, every one over against his house. **29** *After them repaired Zadok the son of Immer over against his own house. And after him repaired Shemaiah the son of Shecanaiah, the keeper of the east gate.* **30** *After him repaired Hananiah the son of Shelemiah, and Hanun the sixth son of Zalaph, another portion. After him Meshullam the son of Berechiah over against his chamber.* **31** *After him repaired Malchijah one of the goldsmiths unto the house of the Nethinim, and of the merchants, over against the gate of Hammiphkad, and to the ascent of the corner.* **32** *And between the ascent of the corner and the sheep gate repaired the goldsmiths and the merchants.*

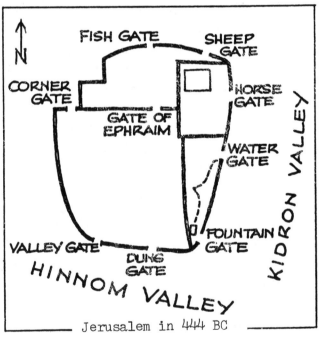

Jerusalem in 444 BC

CHAPTER 4
Bitter Enemies of Israel Oppose Rebuilding the Wall

Two false interpretations of Nehemiah thus far must be rejected. One we have already noted, namely, the allegation that chapter 3 was not written by Nehemiah and that it was "injected" into Nehemiah's narrative. The other is the inaccurate allegation that Verses 3-6 in chapter 3 "suggest the completion of the wall."[1] No such suggestion is found in chapter 3. Oh yes, it says various workers "repaired" this or that section of the wall; but that only designates the different assignments to the forty different companies of workers; and there's not a word in the whole chapter that even hints that the walls were completed. If Nehemiah had intended this third chapter to indicate the completion of the wall, the dedication of it would have followed at once.

This chapter records the hostility and bitterness of Israel's neighbors when they became aware of Nehemiah's rebuilding the city's fortifications. "Sanballat in Samaria on the north, Tobiah and the Ammonites on the east, Geshem and his Arabs to the south, and the Ashdodites and all the Philistines who had hated Israel from the times of Saul and David,"[2] --- all of these surrounding neighbors were outraged and disgusted with the prospect of Jerusalem's restoration; and they opposed it in every way possible.

---

[1] IB, Vol. 3, p. 696.
[2] NBCR, p. 406

The Enemies Begin Their Attack with Ridicule and Mockery

Verses 1-6, But it came to pass that, when Sanballat heard that we were building the wall, he was wroth, and took great indignation, and mocked the Jews. 2 And he spake before his brethren and the army of Samaria, and said, What are these feeble Jews doing? will they fortify themselves? will they sacrifice? will they make an end in a day? will they revive the stones out of the heaps of rubbish, seeing they are burned? 3 Now Tobiah the Ammonite was by him, and he said, Even that which they are building, if a fox go up, he shall break down their stone wall. 4 Hear, O our God; for we are despised: and turn back their reproach upon their own head, and give them up for a spoil in a land of captivity; 5 and cover not their iniquity, and let not their sin be blotted out from before thee; for they have provoked thee to anger before the builders. 6 So we built the wall; and all the wall was joined together unto half the height thereof: for the people had a mind to work.

This was only the first phase of Sanballat's efforts to stop the fortification of Jerusalem. When this failed, he would try other measures. However, except for the remarkable ability and skill of Nehemiah, this initial opposition of laughter, ridicule and insults might have proved successful. "Nothing makes the enemies of the Lord's work any more indignant than the success of God's people."[3]

---

[3] GDH, Vol. 2, p. 491.

The nature of the insults heaped upon the Jews
here was calculated to discourage them. They were
called, "feeble Jews"; "will they fortify themselves"? was
asked in a tone of unbelief. "The very idea that these
people would contemplate such a thing." "Will they
sacrifice"? was a way of asking, "Do they expect their
God to do this for them'? "Will they revive the stones ...
seeing they are burned"? "The effect of fire is to crack
and weaken stone";[4] and this insult was merely a charge
that the Jews did not have the material to rebuild the
walls. Insults hurt, even if they are untrue. This one
was only true in a very limited frame of reference. The
stones from the vast majority of the ruined walls were in
exellent condition. Only those ruined by the burned
wooden gates would have been affected.

*If a fox go up, he shall break down their stone wall
(v. 3).* "Foxes were mentioned, perhaps, from their
having been known in large numbers to infest the
ruined walls of Jerusalem, as recorded in Lamentations
5:18)."[5] This insult was that of Tobiah.

Hear, O our God, for we are despised ... (vv. 4, 5).
This writer agrees with Jamieson that, "This prayer is
not marked by hatred, vengeance, nor any other sinful
passion, and that it exhibits a pious and patriotic zeal
for the glory of God and the success of his cause."[6] As
we noted in our discussion of the so-called imprecatory
Psalms, many of the things that current scholars are

---

[4] NBCR, p. 406.
[5] JFB, p. 296.
[6] Ibid.

saying about such prayers evidences a claim of superior righteousness that we believe is unjustified.

Rawlinson wrote that, "Before men were taught to love their enemies and to bless them that cursed them (Mt. 5:44), they gave vent to their natural feelings of anger and indignation by the utterance of maledictions in their prayers."[7]   "The violence of Nehemiah's imprecations here (v. 4) grates harshly on modern ears; but it should be remembered that such vehemence against enemies appears repeatedly in the Pslams (79:4-12, 123:3-4, and 137:7-9)."[8]   We have discussed this fully under those references in our Commentary on The Psalms.

Christians should remember that when they pray for God's will to be done, for righteouness and truth to prevail, and for the righteous to be protected and blessed, that there is *most certainly a corollary to such a prayer;* and that is that falsehood shall be repudiated, the wicked defeated, frustrated, and checkmated, and that the wicked shall indeed be cast into hell.   There was nothing in Nehemiah's prayer that is not contained embryonicly in every prayer of a Christian today.

"Nehemiah's short prayer here is parenthetical; and such prayers form one of the most striking characteristics of Nehemiah's history. This is the first one, and others are in 5:19; 6:9, 14; and 13:14, 22, 29, and 31."[9]

---

7 PC, Vol. 7b, p. 37.

8 Charles W. Gilkey, in IB, op. cit., p. 698.

9 FCC, *Nehemiah*, p. 464.

So we built the wall ... unto half the height thereof (v. 6). "This means that the entire continuous wall had been constructed up to one half the contemplated height."[10] The taunting ridicule and mockery of the neighboring enemies had not succeeded in stopping construction.

Sanballat Threatens Violence Against the Builders

Verses 7-14, And it came to pass that, when Sanballat and Tobiah, and the Arabians and the Ammonites, and the Ashdodites, heard that the repairing of the walls of Jerusalem went forward, and that the breaches began to be stopped, then they were very wroth; 8 and they conspired, all of them together, to come and fight against Jerusalem, and to cause confusion therein. 9 But we made our prayer unto God, and set a watch against them day and night, because of them. 10 And Judah said, the strength of the bearers of burdens is decayed, and there is much rubbish; so that we are not able to build the wall. 11 And our adversaries said, They shall not know, neither see, till we come into the midst of them, and slay them, and cause the work to cease. 12 And it came to pass that, when the Jews that dwelt by them came, they said unto us ten times from all places, ye must return unto us. 13 Therefore set I in the lowest parts of the space behind the walls, in the open places, I set there the people after their families with their swords, their spears, and their bows. 14 And I looked, and rose up, and said unto the nobles, and to the rulers, and to

---

[10] PC, op. cit., p. 38.

the rest of the people, Be not afraid of them: remember the Lord who is great and terrible, and fight for your brethren, your sons, and your daughters, your wives, and your houses.

The Arabians (v. 7). The identity of these is questionable. "Some believe they were the descendants of one of the racial groups that Sargon planted in Samaria. This is possible, but they might also have been one of the desert tribes of Arabians induced to come forward in the hope of plunder, being influenced by the Ammonites, their neighbors."[11]

Oesterley has a summary of the crisis presented in these verses:

"This was a very critical time. The Jews were getting weary of the ceaseless work; their enemies had planted fear in the workers living beyond the walls by telling them of their plans suddenly to appear and kill the workers; the Jews from the surrounding area appealed to their neighbors at work on the wall to return home, abandoning the work. Nehemiah's presence of mind and firmness alone saved the situation." [12]

Note the manner in which Nehemiah moved to meet this crisis. (1) He prayed to God (v. 9). (2) He set a watch day and night (v. 9). (3) He set armed men at "the lowest parts," i. e., places were the walls might be most easily attacked (v. 13). (4) He brought in the Jews

---

11 PC, op. cit., p. 41.

12 ASP, p. 332.

with their families from the outlying areas, armed them and kept them overnight in the city. (5) He stationed armed men throughout the city near the construction workers. (6) He kept a close eye himself upon the situation. (7) He kept a trumpeter by his side, so that in case of an attack, he could promptly order all hands to repel it (v. 18). (8) He called the whole assembly together, saying, "Be not afraid of them ... Remember the Lord who is great and terrible" (v. 14). (9) He commanded the people to be ready to fight (v. 14). (10) And he ordered the work to go on full speed ahead! What a leader he proved to be!

"Nehemiah with faith in God, skilfully arming and arranging his men, drove straight ahead with the work; and in spite of all obstacles, the Wall was finished in 52 days; and Jerusalem was again a fortified city, 142 years after its destruction by Nebuchadnezzar in 586 BC."[13]

We prayed ... and set a watch (v. 9). Prayer to God does not eliminate the need for Christians to be alert and prepared to face emergencies. The old song from World War II, was, *Praise the Lord, and Pass the Ammunition.*

They shall not know, or see, till we come and slay them (v. 11). Sanballat by these threats was speaking as if he had an army at his disposal; but, "This was probably nothing more than the customary armed guard by which the satraps protected themselves; and Sanballat probably gambled that the king of Persia

---

might overlook a skirmish between such a band and the Jews."[14] As it turned out, his threatening words were only a bluff.

This chapter has some of the text that is corrupted, and "The chronology of the things mentioned here is not fully clear."[15]

They said unto us ten times ... Ye must return unto us (v. 12). "*Ten Times* is the equivalent here of *over and over,* or *repeatedly.*"[16] The Jews from the surrounding area were being intimidated and frightened by Sanballat. Nehemiah countered this by bringing the people into Jerusalem.

In Spite of Threatening Enemies the Work Went On

Verses 15-20, And it came to pass when our enemies heard that it was known to us, and God brought their counsel to naught, that we returned all of us to the wall every one unto his work. 16 And it came to pass from that time forth, that half of my servants wrought in the work, and half of them held the spears, and the shields, and the bows, and the coats of mail; and the rulers were behind all the house of Judah. 17 They that builded the wall and they that bare burdens laded themselves; every one with one of his hands wrought in the work, and with his other held his weapon; 18 and the builders every one had his sword girded by his side, and so builded. And he that sounded the

---

14 FCC, op. cit., p. 465.
15 WBC, Vol. 16, p. 226.
16 FCC, op. cit., p. 465.

trumpet was by me. 19 And I said unto the nobles, and to the rulers, and to the rest of the people, The work is great and large, and we are separated upon the wall, one from another: 20 in what place soever ye hear the sound of the trumpet, resort ye thither unto us; our God will fight for us.

God brought their counsel to naught (v. 15). This simply means that Sanballat, hearing and observing Nehemiah's preparations and determination to fight, backed down from his ugly threats. In his mind, no doubt, was the knowledge that the king of Persia was also behind Nehemiah's fortifying Jerusalem. "That no conflict came about shows that when the enemy approached, and saw from a distance, the whole people awaiting them in perfect order with all equipment and weapons at the ready, they simply lost heart and turned back."[17]

Half of my servants wrought in the work (v. 16). These are generally understood to have been "official servants that pertained to Nehemiah";[18] but there remains the possibility that the military escort provided by the king of Persia was yet with Nehemiah, there having been no report of its return to Persia. Therefore there is the possibility that these were meant.

Every one with one of his hands wrought in the work, and with the other held his weapon (v. 17). This expression is obviously somewhat figurative, as explained by the next clause, "Everyone had his sword

---

[17] PC, op. cit., p. 42.
[18] WYC, p. 438.

girded by his side, and so builded." The great London preacher Charles Haddon Spurgeon published a paper called *Sword and Trowel*, named after what is written here.

The coats of mail (v. 16). "Coats of mail were common in Assyria from the 9th century BC, and even earlier in Egypt; they were made of thin leaves of bronze or iron sewed upon leather or linen and overlapping one another."[19]

The sound of the trumpet (v. 20). "When an attack was made, the trumpet sounded at that point; all the workers rallied, and the enemy was either frightened or driven away. Even those who lived beyond the city came into Jerusalem at night to sleep."[20]

Worked Day and Night; Even Slept in Their Clothes

Verses 21-23, So we wrought in the work: and half of them held the spears from the rising of the morning till the stars appeared. 22 Likewise at the same time I said unto the people, Let everyone with his servant lodge within Jerusalem, that at night they may be a guard to us, and may labor in the day. 23 So neither I nor my brethren, nor my servants, nor my men of the guard that followed me, none of us put off our clothes, everyone went with his weapon to the water.

Half of them held the spears ... till the stars

---

[19] FCC, op. cit., p. 465.
[20] GDH, op. cit., p. 292.

appeared (v. 21). "These three verses are a summary of what was said above. Half of the servants and the guard worked in the daytime, and the other half stood guard at night."[21] Note also that the work continued without intermission throughout all the daylight hours.

Let everyone ... lodge within Jerusalem (v. 22). "This means let none return to his own village or city at night, but let all take their rest in Jerusalem."[22]

Everyone went with his weapon to the water (v. 23). All scholars speak of the damaged text in this verse. "As it stands, it is quite meaningless."[23] The footnote in our version (the ASV) reads, "The text is obscure." "Keil translated it, 'Each laid his weapon at the right,' that is, when he slept, his weapon was ready at hand."[24]

Various translations are:

None of us put off our clothes, saving that everyone put them off for washing (AV).

(We) did not put off our clothes; only every man stripped himself when he was to be washed (DOUAY).

Each kept his weapon in his hand (MOFFATT).

We all kept our weapons at hand (GNB).

Each kept his weapon in his hand (RSV).

Each kept his weapon in his right hand (New RSV).

xxx

---

[21] PC, op. cit., p. 42.

[22] FCC, op. cit., p. 466.

[23] ASP, p. 332.

[24] WYC, p. 439.

CHAPTER 5
Nehemiah's Handling of a Severe Social Crisis

There are conflicting views of reputable scholars regarding the nature of this chapter. Whitcomb labeled it "parenthetical";[1] but Williamson divided the chapter into two sections, making verses 1-13 a description of a crisis that came during the building of the wall, but admitting the rest of the chapter as a later parenthetical addition. Of the first section he wrote that, "The wives ... were more conscious of the approaching calamity, because they were having to manage at home while their husbands were engrossed in the wall-building."[2]

There are a number of reasons why this writer accepts the viewpoint that the whole chapter is parenthetical and that it was included at this point in Nehemiah's memoirs for reasons which we believe will appear later in the narrative.

"This parenthetical chapter describes how Nehemiah succeeded in stopping the practice of usury, which resulted in extreme poverty and even bondage for many Jews. There is also a record here of Nehemiah's example of unselfishness and generosity during his twelve years as governor."[3]

It seems to this writer that Nehemiah might well have included this chapter just here as an advance glimpse of the evil nobles who, along with the priests, would eventually vigorously oppose Nehemiah's

---

[1] WYC, p. 439.

[2] WBC, Vol. 16, p. 237.

[3] WYC, p. 439.

reforms.

A Major Social Crisis Confronts Nehemiah

Verses 1-5,   Then there arose a great cry of the people and of their wives against their brethren the Jews. 2 For there were that said, We, our sons and our daughters, are many: let us get grain that we may eat and live. 3 Some also there were that said, We are mortgaging our fields and our vineyards, and our houses: let us get grain, because of the dearth. 4 There were also those that said, We have borrowed money for the king's tribute upon our fields and our vineyards. 5 Yet now our flesh is as the flesh of our brethren, our children as their children: and lo, we bring into bondage our sons and our daughters to be servants, and some of our daughters are brought into bondage already: neither is it in our power to help it; for other men have our fields and our vineyards.

There are three classes of protesters here: "These were (1) the landless who were desperately short of food (v. 2), (2) the landowners who, because of famine had been compelled to mortgage their properties (v. 3), and (3) those who had been forced to borrow money at exhorbitant rates to meet the Persian king's property taxes (v. 4)."[4]

Man's inhumanity to man is tragically visible in the sad circumstances that precipitated this uprising of the people.

---

[4] NBCR, p. 406.

There are also three causes of the situation, as enumerated by Rawlinson. "These were over-population (v. 2), recent famine (v. 3), and heavy taxation (v. 4)."[5]

Because of the dearth (v. 3). "Dearth is the usual word for famine, as in Genesis 12:10, and in many other places."[6]

One reason for accepting this chapter as a record of events unrelated to the wall-building, is this mention here of a widespread shortage of food, due to famine. There was no hint of such a shortage during the building of the wall; besides that, "The wall-building did not take long enough (less than two months) to cause widespread suffering."[7]

For other men have our fields and our vineyards (v. 5). Keil explained the tragic significance of these words: "Since our fields and vineyards belong to others, what they produce does not come to us, and we are not in a position to be able to put an end to the sad necessity of selling our sons and our daughters for servants."[8]

---

5 PC, Vol. 7b, p. 48.

6 ASP, p. 332.

7 Ibid.

8 CFK, 3c, p. 210.

Nehemiah Moved Quickly to Solve the Problem

Verses 6-13, And I was very angry when I heard their cry and these words. 7 Then I consulted with myself and contended with the rulers and the nobles, and said unto them, Ye exact usury, every one of his brother. And I held a great assembly against them. 8 And I said unto them, We after our ability have redeemed our brethren the Jews, that were sold unto the nations; and would ye even sell your brethren, and should they be sold unto us? Then held they their peace, and said never a word. 9 Also I said, The thing that ye do is not good: ought ye not to walk in the fear of our God, because of the reproach of the nations our enemies? 10 And likewise, my brethren and my servants, do lend them money and grain. I pray you, let us leave off this usury. 11 Restore, I pray you, to them, even this day, their fields, their vineyards, their oliveyards, and their houses, also the hundredth part of the money, and of the grain, the new wine, and the oil, that ye exact of them. 12 Then said they, We will restore them, and will require nothing of them; so will we do, even as thou sayest. Then I called the priests and took an oath of them, that they would do according to this promise. 13 Also, I shook out my lap, and said, So God shake out every man from his house, and from his labor, that performeth not this promise; even thus be he shaken out and emptied. And all the assembly said, Amen, and praised Jehovah. And the people did according to this promise.

I was very angry when I heard these words (v. 6). Nehemiah restrained his anger, very wisely, and by his skilful handling ot the situation, "He avoided personally alienating the rulers and nobles, who after all were the leaders of the community, and the men upon whom he relied for the support of his administration."[9]

Then I consulted with myself (v.). This means that Nehemiah disciplined himself in the control of his anger. He carefully laid the plans by which he would put an end to their abuses.

Ye exact usury, every man of his brother (v. 7). This was a heartless violation of God's law (Exodus 22:25), which forbade God's people to charge interest on any loan to a brother Israelite. "He reminded the rulers and nobles that his own conduct had been the opposite of theirs; and that when he had seen Jewish slaves offered for sale in Gentile markets, he would pay the ransom price and give them their liberty. But those nobles and rulers were selling their poverty-stricken fellow Jews to heathen masters, knowing that Nehemiah would buy them back."[10]   That procedure, obviously, amounted to their selling their brethren to Nehemiah, as indicated by the terse words in v. 8, *And should they be sold unto us?*

Would ye even sell your brethren (v. 8)? It was against the Law of God for an Israelite to sell even a servant as a bondman, much less a brother (Leviticus 25:42). It is apparent that Nehemiah's inclusion of this episode parenthetically at this point in his book was due to his purpose of exposing the character of the rulers

---

[9] WBC, op. cit., p. 239.
[10] NLBC, p. 539.

and nobles as an advance explanation of trouble he
would have with them later.

*They held their peace, and found never a word (v.
8).* Nehemiah had completely checkmated any public
opposition by the rulers and nobles by his confronting
them before a general assembly of the whole
population. They had no excuse whatever for their
wholesale violations of the Mosaic Law. Their own
consciences condemned them.

*And I likewise, my brethren and my servants do
lend them money and grain (v. 10).* Nehemiah said
nothing at all here about charging interest on such
loans; and this writer does not believe that he was guilty
of violating the Moasic instructions against such
charges. If Nehemiah had been charging his brethren
usury, why would he have been so angry with the nobles
and rulers for doing so? The scholars who make the
word *likewise* in this verse prove that Nehemiah was a
usurer are in error.

Let us leave off this usury (v. 10). Ah! But does
not this clause prove that Nehemiah was doing the same
thing? Williamson so understood it, "Nehemiah here
candidly admits having been involved in these same
practices."[11]   No! This was merely a tactful
indentification of himself with the violators, in order to
promote good will and to avoid antagonism; and this is
by no means the only example of a biblical writer's using
that very same device for the sake of avoiding
unnecessary bitterness. "Ezra identified himself with

---

[11] WBC, op. cit., p. 240.

the marriage offenders (Ezra 9:6) although he had not contracted an illicit marriage."[12] Did not the apostle Paul write:[13]

LET _US_ PRESS ON ... NOT LAYING AGAIN A FOUNDATION OF REPENTANCE, ... AND THIS WILL _WE_ DO, IF GOD PERMIT (HEBREWS 6:1, 3)?

In this passage, Paul used the first person plural twice (underlined words in passage); but he was not confessing that he himself was guilty of the same errors he was attempting to correct in the recipients of his letter. In the same manner, here, Nehemiah's use of the first person plural was not a confession that he was the same kind of heartless usurer as the rulers and nobles.

Restore unto them their fields ... the hundredth part of the money ... and of the grain, etc. (v. 11). This was a public request, backed up by the support of the general assembly that all the abuses be ended at once. Several types of oppressing the poor are in evidence in this blanket request. (1) There was the interest charge (a hundredth part of the money. "This was a monthly charge, amounting to 12% a year."[14] (2) Then there were the fields confiscated through foreclosures, and (3) the extravagant rental charges "in kind," the grain, wine, oil, etc.

Then said they, We will restore them, and will

---

[12] BBC, Vol. 3, p. 482.

[13] See our defense of the Pauline Authorship of Hebrews in our introduction to that commentary.

[14] WYC, p. 439.

require nothing of them (v. 12). Wonderful! So far, so good. But Nehemiah knew the character of the evil men with whom he was dealing; and he moved at once to "swear them in" to do what they promised to do.

Then I called the priests and took an oath of them (v. 12). With honest men, this would have been unnecessary; but Nehemiah moved to thwart any violations of this agreement by swearing them in before the whole assembly.

I shook out my lap, and said, God so shake out every man ... that performeth not this promise (v. 13). The 'lap' that Nehemiah shook out was an improvised one, made by gathering up his robe in a fold, and then shaking it out as if he were emptying out things contained in it. This was a symbolical action, as were the deeds of many of the prophets, designed to emphasize their words. It was an appeal that God would drastically and completely punish and remove all violators of the promises they had sworn to honor.

And the people did according to this promise (v. 13). Nehemiah's precautions assured a full compliance with the public promises; and the people were relieved.

Nehemiah's Summary of His Conduct as Governor

Verses 14-19, Moreover from the time that I was appointed to be their governor in the land of Judah, from the twentieth year even to the two and thirtieth year of Artaxerxes the king, that is, twelve years, I and my brethren have not eaten the bread of the governor. 15 But the former governors that were before me were chargeable unto the people, and took of them bread and wine, besides forty shekels of silver; yea, even their servants bare rule over the people: but so did not I, because of the fear of God. 16 Yea, also I continued in the work of this wall, neither bought we any land: and all my servants were gathered thither unto the work. 17 Moreover there were at my table, of the Jews and the rulers,[15] a hundred and fifty men, besides those that came unto us from the nations that were round about us. 18 Now that which was prepared for one day was one ox and six choice sheep; also fowls were prepared for me, and once in ten days stores of all sorts of wine; yet for all this, I demanded not the bread of the governor, because the bondage was heavy upon this people. 19 Remember unto me, O God, for good, all that I have done for this people.

That is, twelve years (v. 14). "These years were 444 to 432 BC."[16] This verse is clearly retrospective, and from this the usual understanding is that this chapter was written some twelve years after the building of the wall. Shortly before this first term of Nehemiah as governor ended, "He returned to Babylon for a visit."[17] Many scholars have marvelled that the "time" set by Nehemiah for his return to Babylon (2:6) could have included the entire twelve-year term as governor. Evidently, there had been some other arrangement with the king in Babylon that would have extended the time. As Oesterley said, "If more fragments of Nehemiah's

---

[15] *Deputies, according* to the footnote in the ASV.

[16] WYC, p. 439.

[17] ASP, p. 332.

memoirs had been preserved, this would have been
explained."[18] This is a wise observation, and it would be
encouraging if more scholars took into account the fact
that all the difficulties which we find in the Bible would
doubtless disappear altogether if we had *all the facts.*

*I and my brethren have not eaten the bread of the
governor (v. 14).* This simply means that Nehemiah and
his staff did not accept the usual allotments of food and
money that the state provided for governors. He was a
truly patriotic soul, much as was George Washington,
who during the Revolutionary war built and outfitted
three naval ships, at his own expense; and he did not
seek a reimbursement after he became president. What
a pity that the birthday of a president like that should
not be accorded a separate celebration, apart from all
others.

*The former governors ... were chargeable unto the
people (v. 15).* We agree with Whitcomb that, "These
were probably the Persians who did not fear God, and
we are sure that the one's meant by Nehemiah did not
include Zerubbabel."[19]

*Those at my table were a hundred and fifty men (v.
17).* "This included his entire staff, and additionally
there were Jews from the surrounding area, who as yet
had no homes, who ate at his table, and all of this at his
own expense. Compare that with the entertainment by
Jezebel of 400 prophets of the Asherah 'at her table',
besides all of the provisions for their upkeep and

---

[18] Ibid.
[19] WYC, p. 439.

livelihood (1K 18:19)."[20] Also Jezebel did that at the expense of the people; and that says nothing of the far greater extravagant expenses of Ahab.

Besides those that came unto us from the nations that were round about us (v. 17). This not only meant those who voluntarily elected to return, but it also included those Jews whom the rulers and nobles had sold to the heathen neighbors as slaves, and whom Nehemiah, a wealthy man in his own right, had purchased back and restored to their liberty.

One ox and six choice sheep (v. 18). We learned in 1K 4:22, 23, that Solomon at his table served thirty oxen and one hundred sheep every day!

Remember, O my God, for good, all that I have done for this people (v. 19). Naturally, Nehemiah desired that the people would remember what he had done for them; but, "He wanted God to remember too."[21] It is certainly not sinful for a Christian to pray that God will remember the good that he might have done.

xxx

---

[20] Ibid.
[21] NLBC, p. 539.

CHAPTER 6
One Final Effort Made By Nehemiah's Enemies

Five Successive Attempts To Get Nehemiah
in Their Power

Verses 1-9, Now it came to pass when it was reported to Sanballat and Tobiah, and to Geshem the Arabian, and unto the rest of our enemies, that I had builded the wall, and that there was no breach left therein (Though even unto that time I had not set up the doors in the gates), 2 that Sanballat and Geshem sent unto me, saying, Come, let us meet together in one of the villages in the plain of Ono. But they thought to do me mishcief. 3 And I sent messengers unto them, saying, I am doing a great work, so that I cannot come down: why should the work cease whilst I leave it, and come down to you? 4 And they sent unto me four times after this sort, and; I answered them after the same manner. 5 Then sent Sanballat his servant unto me in like manner the fifth time with an open letter in his hand, 6 wherein was written, It is reported among the nations, and Gashmu saith it, that thou and the Jews think to rebel; for which cause thou art building the wall: and thou wouldest be their king according to these words. 7 And thou hast appointed prophets to preach of thee at Jerusalem, saying, there is a king in Judah: and now shall it be reported unto the king according to these words. Come now therefore, and let us take counsel together. 8 Then I sent unto him saying, There are no such things done as thou sayest, but thou feignest them out of thine own heart. 9 For they all would make us afraid, saying, Their hands shall be weakened from the work, that it be not done. But thou, O God, strengthen thou my hands.

"The narrative which was broken by the parenthetical chapter 5 is here taken up again."[1] "The enemies of Judah had found ridicule (4:1-6) ineffective, and their threatened military attack had not taken place (4:7-23); and their plan here was to kill Nehemiah, or at least kidnap him."[2]   The spiritual significance of Sanballat's proposal is that Satan is always attempting to induce God's servants to come down unto the plains of Ono, and to *take counsel* with evil men.   Satan's purposes are never otherwise than totally evil.   "The plain of Ono was near Lydda, twelve miles north of Jerusalem."[3]   Cundall located it 19 miles north of Jerusalem.[4]

With an open letter in his hand (v. 5). This open letter was not sealed, in order that the escort who carried it might read it and scatter the evil report as widely as possible. The very fact of sending such an open letter to the head of a government was an insult.

Gashmu (v. 6). This is the name as it appears in the MT; but it is believed to be the same as Geshem, as the word is translated in the RSV. He was an important official whose word might carry weight in Persia; and there was also the element of plausibility that such a

---

1 ASP, p. 332.
2 NLBC, p. 539.
3 Ibid.
4 NBCR, p. 407.

report might carry with it in Persia."[5] The whole report, however, was totally false.

Thou hast appointed prophets to preach of thee (v. 7). Sanballat here exhibits some knowledge of Hebrew history in which prophets did play a large part in the anointing of Israel's kings, as in the cases of Saul and David. This supports an earlier comment that Sanballat might have been an Ephraimite. However, Sanballat's omission of any reference to Nehemiah as being a descendant of the royal family of David, supports Williamson's argument that, "Nehemiah was not of Davidic descent."[6]

Thou feignest them out of thine own heart (v. 8). Nehemiah's response to this well-planned scheme to allure him into a meeting with Sanballat was merely to send him word that all of his charges were merely a pack of lies which he himself had invented.

But now, O God, strengthen thou my hands (v. 9). Here is another of Nehemiah's impromptu prayers, indicating his complete reliance upon the blessing of God in order to accomplish his objectives.

Sanballat and Tobiah had corrupted a priest named Shemaiah, who attempted to get Nehemiah killed, having been hired by Tobiah. That is our next episode.

---

[5] Ibid.

[6] WBC, Vol. 16, p. 257.

A Traitor Within Jerusalem Attempts to Bring
About Nehemiah's Death

Verses 10-14,   And I went into the house of
Shemaiah the son of Delaiah the son of Mehetabel, who
was shut up, and he said, Let us meet together in the house
of God, within the temple, and let us shut the door of the
temple: for they will come to slay thee; yea, in the night will
they come to slay thee. 11 And I said, should such a man
as I flee? and who is there, that, being such as I, would go
into the temple to save his life? 12 And I discerned, and,
lo, God had not sent him; but he announced this prophecy
against me: and Tobiah and Sanballat had hired him. 13
For this cause was he hired, that I should be afraid, and do
so, and sin, and that they might have matter for an evil
report, that they might reproach me. 14 Remember, O My
God, Tobiah and Sanballat according to these their works,
and also the prophetess Noadiah, and the rest of the
prophets who would have put me to fear.

There are many details of this plot which are not
fully explained in the Bible, but enough is revealed to
expose the traitors among the priests and prophets of
Jerusalem. "Shemaiah, a hired traitor, pretended to be
Nehemiah's friend. invited him into his home, told him
of a plot to kill him that very night (a lie), and suggested
that he hide within the temple. That suggestion about
entering the temple exposed Shemaiah to Nehemiah,
revealing that Shemaiah was a liar, for Nehemiah knew
that God would not have led him to break the Mosaic

injunction against entering the temple (Numbers 1:51)."[7]

The text does not say so; but given the treachery of Shemaiah and the hatred of the priesthood against Nehemiah, they would in all probability have murdered him for such a violation if they could have induced him to fall for their strategy. We do not know what part Noadiah and others of the prophets (and priests) had in this conspiracy; but evidently, the whole temple enclave were enemies of Nehemiah. That development, and the motivation for it, are revealed in the next paragraph.

All Enemies Frustrated, The Wall Finished

Verses 15-19, So the wall was finished in the twentieth and fifth day of Elul, in fifty-two days. 16 And it came to pass, when all our enemies heard thereof, that all the nations that were about us feared, and were much cast down in their own eyes; for they perceived that this work was wrought of our God. 17 Moreover in the days the nobles of Judah sent many letters unto Tobiah, and the letters of Tobiah came unto them. 18 For there were many in Judah sworn unto him, because he was the son-in-law of Shechaniah the son of Arah; and his son Jehohanan had taken the daughter of Meshullam the son of Berechiah to wife. 19 Also, they spake of his good deeds before me, and reported my words to him. And Tobiah sent letters to put me in fear.

---

[7] WYC, p. 440.

Here we have the explanation of the priesthood's hatred of Nehemiah. Tobiah had married one of their daughters and was the son-in-law of Shechaniah. Many of them were sworn allies of Tobiah and cooperated with Israel's enemies throughout the period of rebuilding the wall. Indeed, its completion was certainly *wrought of God* (v. 16).

xxx

CHAPTER 7

Nehemiah Prepares to Return to Babylon; Tackles the Problem of Repopulating Jerusalem

The Security of the City

Verse 1, Now it came to pass when the wall was built, and I had set up the doors, and the porters, and the singers, and the Levites were appointed.

The singers and the Levites are here named along with the keepers of the city gates; and, because that was something of an unusual assignment for Levites and singers, the critics promptly claim that their mention here is, "A mistaken addition by the Chronicler."[1] Of course, Nehemiah is the author here, not the mythical 'chronicler' of the radical critics, who, in their view was not merely incompetent, but an unqualified liar as well. This view regarding this verse was long ago disputed and disproved; but true to the critical 'style,' succeeding generations continue to parrot their old shibboleths. Hamrick, for example, wrote that, the addition of singers and Levites to the gatekeepers was due to, "Confusion,"[2] on the part of the author. There was no possibility whatever that Nehemiah was confused about whom he appointed as gatekeepers of Jerusalem.

And why were singers and Levites needed and appointed to this work? They were loyal to God and to

---

[1] ASP, p. 332.
[2] BBC, Vol. 3, p. 486.

Nehemiah; and the single largest group who populated the city at that time were the priests; and *they were not loyal.* Nehemiah was preparing to return to Persia, and he was taking the utmost precautions to leave Jerusalem's security intact.

Williamson refuted the usual critical claim that these words regarding the singers and Levites 'are a gloss,' adding that, "These were emergency arrangements only."[3]   F. C. Cook also agreed that the singers and Levites were assigned to this work, "Because their experience (as guardians of the Temple) pointed them out as the fittest persons for this task."[4]

Verse 2,   I gave my brother Hanani, and Hananiah the governor of the castle, charge over Jerusalem, for he was a faithful man, and feared God above many.

Hanani here is the same person who brought Nehemiah the sad news about the state of Jerusalem while Nehemiah was still cupbearer to king Artaxerxes. Scholars are in disagreement on whether there is one man mentioned in this verse or two. As the translators have it, there are clearly two persons, i.e., Nehemiah's brother, and another person who was in charge of the castle.   The RSV and most of the scholars we have consulted consider that two men are named. However, Bowman, in IB, wrote that, "*Hanani* and *Hananiah* are identical names, the former an abbreviation of the

---

[3] WBC, Vol. 16, p. 270.
[4] FCC, p. 469.

latter; and, obviously, the **and** joining the two names is explicative."[5] Nehemiah's use of the singular pronoun *he* in the final clause of the verse supports Bowman's view.

Despite this, we are unwilling to set aside the plain statements in the ASV and the RSV denoting two persons, not merely one. "He put his brother Hanani, and Hananiah the governor of the castle (on the north side of the temple, in charge of the city)."[6] "The high religious principle, as well as the patriotic spirit of these two men recommended them as being preeminently qualified for being invested with an official trust of such vast importance."[7] Supporting the apparent conviction of the translators of ASV and RSV, is the fact that Jerusalem was officially divided into two districts (Nehemiah 3:12), and that the custom of dual directorships of cities and districts was common (See also Nehemiah 3:18).

"It is believed that Nehemiah was preparing to return to Persia, and wanted to leave a dependable person in charge."[8]

Verse 3, And I said unto them, Let not the gates of Jerusalem be opened until the sun is hot; and while they stand on guard, let the doors be shut, and bar ye them: and appoint watches of the inhabitants of Jerusalem, every one

---

[5] IB, Vol. 3, p. 724.

[6] WYC, p. 440.

[7] JFB, p. 297.

[8] GDH, Vol . 2, p. 495.

his watch, and every one to be over against his house.

Let not the gates ... be opened till the sun is hot.
"The gates of Oriental cities were usually opened at sunrise,"[9] but Nehemiah ordered them to be opened somewhat later. Furthermore, "The gates were to be closed in the evenings prior to the departure of the guards."[10] After the closing of the gates, watchmen were to be placed along the wall, "every man over against his own house." As Cundall noted, "This is another example of Nehemiah's wise understanding of human nature."[11]

Verse 4, Now the city was wide and large; but the people were few therein, and the houses were not builded.

This verse is actually the key to the inclusion at once of that long list of genealogies. Jerusalem was in desperate need of more inhabitants, for it was far too large a city for the few who lived there; and "Nehemiah, at once, laid plans for populating the city with PURE JEWS; and the register of those who had returned with Zerubbabel becomes his basis for determining the purity of genealogy."[12]
And the houses were not builded. "This must be understood in a relative sense, because some houses are

---

[9] PC, 3b, p. 72.
[10] CFK, 3c, p.375
[11] NBCR, p. 407.
[12] WYC, p. 441.

referred to in v. 3."[13]

Verse 5, And my God put it into my heart to gather together the nobles, and the rulers, and the people, that they might be reckoned by genealogy. And I found the book of the genealogy of them that came up at the first, and I found written therein:

God put it into my heart. Nehemiah always gave God credit for whatever he did, giving all the glory to God.

The genealogy of them that came up at first. This can be understood only as a reference to them that came up with Zerubbabel, a number approaching 50,000. Older and more recent scholars alike affirm the identity of the following list with that in the book of Ezra. "This list is approximately the same as that of the exiles who returned under Zerubbabel; and it must have been found by Nehemiah in the archives in Jerusalem."[14] "Except for verses 70-72, this register is identical with that in Ezra 2:1-70."[15]

Nothing is of less interest to current readers than these genealogical registers in the OT; but the importance of them is great indeed. The great promise of God looking to the redemption of fallen humanity, and the bringing into our world of the Dayspring from On High, specifically tied that promise to the "Seed

---

[13] NLBC, p. 540.

[14] ASP, p. 333.

[15] WYC, p. 441.

(singular) of Abraham" (Genesis 12:3); and when Mary cradled the Son of God in the Bethelehem manger, it was absolutely necessary that all men should have been certain that Jesus of Nazareth was indeed that Seed. It was the concern and diligence of men like Nehemiah who preserved and honored the genealogies of the people that were absolutely the prerequisites of Christian confidence in the identifty of Jesus Christ.

We shall have little or no comment on this register of names.

Verses 6-73a, These are the children of the province, that went up out of the captivity of them that had been carried away, whom Nebuchadnezzar the king of Babylon had carried away, and that returned unto Jerusalem and to Judah, every one into his city; 7 who came with Zerubbabel, Jeshua, Nehemiah, Azariah, Raamaiah, Nahamani,, Mordecai, Bilshan, Mispereth, Bigvai, Nehum, Baanah.

The number of the men of the people of Israel: 8 the children of Parosh, two thousand a hundred and seventy two. 9 The children of Shephatiah, three hundred seventy and two. 10 The children of Arah, six hundred fifty and two. 11 The children of Pahath-moab, of the children of Jeshua and Joab, two thousand and eight hundred and eighteen. 12 The children of Elam, a thousand two hundred fifty and four. 13 The children of Zattu, eight hundred forty and five. 14 The children of Zaccai, seven hundred and threescore. 15 The children of Binnui, six hundred forty and eight. 16 The children of Bebai, six hundred twenty and eight. 17 The children of Azgad, two thousand three hundred twenty and two. 18 The children of Adonikam, six hundred threescore and seven. 19 The children of Bigvai, two thousand threescore and seven. 20 The children of Adin, six hundred fifty and five. 21 The children of Ater, of Hezekiah, ninety and eight. 22 The children of Hashum, three hundred twenty and eight. 23 The children of Bezai, three hundred twenty and four. 24 The children of Hariph, a hundred and twelve. 25 The children of Gibeon, ninety and five. 26 The men of Bethlehem and Netophah, a hundred fourscore and eight. 27 The men of Anathoth, a hundred twenty and eight. 28 The men of Beth-azmaveth, forty and two. 29 The men of Kiriath-jearim, Chephirah, and Beeroth, seven hundred forty and three. 30 The men of Ramah and Geba, six hundred twenty and one. 31 The men of Michmas, a hundred and twenty and two. 32 The men of Bethel and Ai, a hundred and twenty and three. 33 The men of the other Nebo, a hundred fifty and two. 34 The children of the other Elam, a thousand two hundred and fifty and four. 35 The children of Harim, three hundred and twenty. 36 The children of Jericho, three hundred forty and five. 37 The children of Lod, Hadid, and Ono, seven hundred twenty and one. 38 The children of Senaah, three thousand nine hundred and thirty.

39 The priests: The children of Jedaiah, of the house of Jeshua, nine hundred seventy and three. 40 The children of Immer, a thousand fifty and two. 41 The children of Pashur, a thousand two hundred forty and seven. 42 The children of Harim, a thousand and seventeen.

43 The Levites: the children of Jeshua, of Kadmiel,

*of the children of Hodevah, seventy and four. 44 The
singers: the children of Asaph, a hundred forty and eight.
45 The porters: the children of Shallum, the children of
Ater, the children of Talmon, the children of Akkub, the
children of Hatita, the children of Shobai, a hundred forty
and eight.*

*46 The Nethinim: the children of Ziha, the children
of Hasupha, the children of Tabbaoth,   47 the children of
Keros, the children of Sia, the children of Padon,   48 the
children of Lebana, the children of Hagaba, the children of
Salmai,   49 the children of Hanan, the children of Giddel,
the children of Gahar,   50 the children of Reaiah, the
children of Rezin, the children of Nekoda,   51 the children
of Gazzam, the children of Uzza, the children of Paseah,
52 the children of Besai, the children of Meunim, the
children of Nephushesim,   53 the children of Bakbuk, the
children of Hakupha, the children of Harhur,   54 the
children of Bazlith, the children of Mehida, the children of
Harsha,   55 the children of Barkos, the children of Sisera,
the children of Temah,   56 the children of Neziah, the
children of Hatipha.*

*57 The children of Solomon's servants: the children
of Sotai, the children of Sophereth, the children of Perida,
58 the children of Jaala, the children of Darkon, the
children of Giddel,   59 the children of Shephatiah, the
children of Hattil, the children of Pochereth-hazzebaim, the
children of Amon. 60 All the Nethinim, and the children of
Solomon's servants, were three hundred ninety and two.*

*61 And these were they that went up from Tel-
melah, Tel-harsha, Cherub, Addon, and Immer; but they
could not show their fathers' houses nor their seed, whether*

they were of Israel: 62 The children of Delaiah, the children of Tobiah, the children of Nekoda, six hundred forty and two.   63 And of the priests: the children of Hobaiah, the children of Hakkoz, the children of Barzillai the Gileadite, and was called after their name.   64 These sought their register among those who were reckoned by genealogy, but it was not found: therefore were they deemed polluted and put from the priesthood.   65 And the governor said unto them, that they should not eat of the most holy things, till there stood up a priest with Urim and Thummin.

66 The whole assembly together was forty and two thousand three hundred and threscore,   67 besides their man-servants and their maid-servants, of whom there were seven thousand three hundred thirty and seven: and they had two hundred forty and five singing men and singing women.   68 Their horses were seven hundred thirty and six; their mules two hundred forty and five;   69 their camels, four hundred thirty and five; their asses, six thousand seven hundred and twenty.

70 And some from among the heads of fathers' houses gave unto the work.   The governor gave to the treasury a thousand darics of gold, fifty basins, five hundred and thirty priests' garments.   71 And some of the heads of fathers' houses gave into the treasury of the work twenty thousand darics of gold, and two thousand and two hundred pounds of silver.   72 And that which the rest of the people gave was twenty thousand darics of gold, and two thousand pounds of silver and threescore and seven priests' garments.

73a So the priests, and the Levites, and the porters,

*and the singers, and some of the people, and the Nethinim,
and all Israel dwelt in their cities.   72b (And when the
seventh month was come, the children of Israel were in
their cities).*

The final parenthesis here is included as a part
of chapter 8 in our version.

For our comments on a number of things
regarding this list, please see the parallel account in
Ezra.   There is nothing further which we wish to add
here.

xxx

CHAPTER 8
Reading of the Law of Moses; the Feast of Tabernacles

Verse 73b (From chapter 7), And when the seventh month was come, the children of Israel were in their cities.

Our version (ASV) includes this line with chapter 8, because it identifies the time of the great reading of the Law discussed herein. The seventh month was Tishri, corresponding to our September-October.[1]

The chapters 8, 9 & 10 are a unit, incorporated, we believe, by the author Nehemiah as an explanation of the great celebration that followed the completion of the wall.

Keil wrote that the mention of the seventh month (Tishri) here should be understood as a reference to the very next month after the completion of the wall in the sixth month (Elul), "There is nothing against the inference that the seventh month of the same year is intended."[2] Short also agreed that the events of this chapter, "Came only a few days after the completion of the wall, which occurred on the 25th day of the month Elul (6:15), the sixth month."[3]

Throughout this whole century, from the times of James Moffatt till the present day, critical scholars have been advocating all kinds of rearrangements of the sacred text, some of them even attempting to place these chapters in the book of Ezra.

---

[1] H. Porter in ISBE, p. 542.
[2] CFK, Vol 3c, p. 227.
[3] NLBC, p. 540.

All such speculations, rearrangements, and allegations of all kinds of confusion, interpolations and mistakes on the part of their mythical 'chronicler' are, in the view of this writer, without any value. The book of Nehemiah still stands in the sacred text, as it has stood for ages, a unit, composed of "The Words of Nehemiah," and of course, including things that Nehemiah himself incorporated into his narrative. Williamson gives us the name of a current great scholar, "Y. Kaufmann, whose work, *History of the Religion of Israel, Volume IV*, carries a defense of the unity of these three chapters, and also maintains at the same time that they are in their correct historical setting."[4] It only remains to be said that there is absolutely no agreement whatever among the critics on any other viable alternative.

Gathering of a General Assembly to Hear the Law Read

Verses 1-8, And all the people gathered themselves together as one man into the broad place that was before the water gate; and they spake unto Ezra the scribe to bring the book of the law of Moses, which Jehovah had commanded to Israel. 2 And Ezra the priest brought the book of the law before the assembly, both men and women, and all that could hear with understanding, upon the first day of the seventh month. 3 And he read therein before the broad place that was before the water gate from early morning until midday, in the presence of the men and the

---

4 WBC, Vol. 16, p. 275.

women, and of those that could understand; and the ears of all the people were attentive to the book of the law. 4 And Ezra the scribe stood upon a pulpit of wood, which they had made for the purpose; and beside him stood Mattithiah, and Shema, and Anaiah, and Uriah, and Hilkiah, and Maaseiah, on his right hand; and on his left hand Pedaiah, and Mishael, and Malchiah, and Hashum, and Hashbaddanah, Zechariah, and Meshullum. 5 And Ezra opened the book in the sight of all the people (For he was above all the people); and when he opened it, all the people stood up. 6 And Ezra blessed Jehovah, the great God; and all the people answered, Amen, Amen, with the lifting up of their hands: and they bowed their heads, and worshipped Jehovah with their faces to the ground. 7 Also Jeshua, and Bani, and Sherebiah, Jamin, Akkub, Shabbethaih, Hodiah, Maaseiah, Kelita, Azariah, Jozebad, Hanan, Pelaiah, and the Levites caused the people to understand the law: and the people stood in their place. 8 And they read in the book, in the law of God, distinctly; and they gave the sense, so that they understood the reading.

They spake unto Ezra the scribe (v. 1). Where was Ezra during the rebuilding of the wall? We do not know. He might have been recalled to Persia years earlier, or he might have been temporarily absent from Jerusalem. "The most probable explanation is that he had been recalled to Persia in 456 BC, and that now, eleven years later in 444 BC, he was allowed to return to

Jerusalem."[5] It is not unreasonable at all to suppose that Nehemiah had sent for him to come and celebrate the dedication of the completed wall.

Some scholars have expressed amazement that the people requested Ezra to read to them from the Law of Moses; but Ezra was a popular leader, and the will of the people in that matter became manifest. "It was quite natural for the people to request Ezra to resume his work of exposition of the law of Moses, to which he had accustomed them on his former visit."[6]

We appreciate Bowman's admission that the author of Nehemiah, "Regarded it as the whole Pentateuch,"[7] which it most certainly was. We regard Nehemiah as the author; and his clear statement here that the law of Moses is that which was read is conclusive.

The dedication of the wall is not related till chapter 12; and, as Keil stated it, "All of the facts related in chapters 8-11 might easily have occurred in the interval between the completion of the wall and its dedication."[8] This understanding overwhelmingly supports the unity of the book of Nehemiah, the focus of which, first and last, is centered in the rebuilding of the wall of Jerusalem.

From early morning until midday (v. 3). "Early morning, i. e., daylight. He began as soon as it was

---

5 PC, Vol. 7b, p. 80.
6 FCC, *Nehemiah*, p. 471.
7 IB, Vol. 3, p. 733.
8 CFK, op. cit., p. 227.

daylight, and continued on, he and his assistants (v. 8), till noon."⁹ Many details of this great gathering are not revealed. The general assembly ---was it of people from the surrounding area, or merely all the people in the city? If the surrounding people were included, did they travel in darkness before daylight; and did they open the gates before the sun was hot? The absence of any detailed answers to such questions suggests caution in the acceptance of such quotations as that we just cited.

And Ezra stood upon a pulpit of wood (v. 4). Here we find the word *pulpit* used in the sense of a podium, or platform; because thirteen men are named as the persons standing side by side with Ezra. It is amazing to this writer that scholars have trouble accepting the number of those men as *thirteen.* *'It must have been fourteen, seven on each side, because the Jews thought the number seven was a perfect number'! 'Maybe, it was twelve men, six on each side, the twelve being symbolical of the twelve tribes of Israel'! In that case, perhaps one of the names was dropped out by mistake!* Such comments are ludicrous. What a shame that God did not employ some of those critics to revise the Bible! As a matter of fact, there were six of them on Ezra's right hand, and seven on his left. Cook identified them as, "The chief priests of the course at that time performing the Temple service."¹⁰

Ezra opened the book ... and when he opened it, all the people stood up (v. 5). Frequently, even today,

---

⁹ PC, op. cit., p. 80.
¹⁰ FCC, *Nehemiah,* p. 472.

Christians stand when the word of God is read.
However, there is no record that such a custom was
observed from the times of Moses and afterwards.
Furthermore, these words may not be tortured to mean
that all of the people stood during the entire morning.
"The people listened to Ezra and his fellow priests as
they read from various scrolls of the Pentateuch, no
doubt including Leviticus 23:23-25 regarding the Feast
of Trumpets, and the portions describing the Feast of
Tabernacles; but much moral instruction from various
parts of the Pentateuch must also have been read."[11]

*The Levites caused the people to understand the
law, and the people __stood__ in their place (v. 7).* It is not
known exactly what is meant by the Levites causing the
people to understand the law. Hamrick thought that
they did so, "By translating the words out of the Hebrew
into the Aramaic vernacular of the people."[12] Cook
believed that they might also have merely explained,
"Obscure words or passages."[13]

Of particular interest is the word *stood,* which
we have underlined in v. 5, above. It is italicized in the
ASV, indicating that the word is not in the Hebrew text
but has been added by the translators. The RSV reads,
'the people remaining in their place.'

Regarding this chapter, Oesterley has a very
excellent comment. While admitting that the text fails
to give us any complete account of all the details of

---

[11] NLBC, p. 541.

[12] BBC, Vol. 3, p. 489.

[13] FC C, op. cit., p. 472,

what happened, he wrote, "The really important point is clear enough, viz., that by Ezra's inspiration and under his guidance the Law (of Moses) was now for the first time put before the Jews in such a way as to convince them that it was the most important thing in the world that their lives should be conducted wholly in accordance with its precepts."[14] That being indeed true for ancient Israel, how much more is it important for Christians so to honor, trust and obey the word of inspiration in the New Testament!

The Weeping of the People Turned Into Joy

Verses 9-12, And Nehemiah who was the governor, and Ezra the priest the scribe, and the Levites that taught the people, said unto all the people, This day is holy unto Jehovah your God; mourn not nor weep. For all the people wept when they heard the words of the law. 10 Then he said unto them, Go your way, eat the fat, and drink the sweet, and send portions unto him for whom nothing is prepared; for this day is holy unto our Lord: neither be ye grieved; for the joy of Jehovah is your strength. 11 So the Levites stilled all the people, saying, Hold your peace, for the day is holy; neither be ye grieved. 12 And all the people went their way, to eat, and to drink, and to send portions, and to make great mirth, because they had understood the words that were declared unto them.

Nehemiah, who was the governor, and Ezra the

---

[14] ASP, p. 233.

priest the scribe (v. 9). In the light of this verse, we find it impossible to accept the declaration that, "Nehemiah's name in v. 9 is most certainly intrusive; and, apart from the strong evidence that Nehemiah and Ezra were not contemporaries, there are reasons to believe his name is not original in this context."[15] How could it be that Ezra and Nehemiah were not contemporary, since both of them were officials in the reign of Artaxerxes? That alone means that they *were contemporaries,* unless one of them died; and where is there any statement about that?

For all the people wept when they heard the words of the Law (v. 9). Who is he who, upon careful meditation upon all that the Law of God requires, can restrain emotions of grief and mournful feelings of sinful shortcomings and failures? Only those who close their eyes and stop their ears against what God says can refrain from similar grief. God's Law does not, however, leave the human heart depressed in sorrow. Ezra (and his helpers the Levites) quickly moved to turn the people's weeping into joy.

Send portions unto him for whom nothing is prepared (v. 10). Cook pointed out that this custom of sending portions on festive occasions grew out of the words in Deuteronomy 16:11, 14.[16] The poor, the sojourner, the servant, the neglected, and the dispossessed are not to be forgotten by God-fearing people.

---

[15] BBC, op. cit.,p. 489.
[16] FCC, op. cit., p. 472.

And all the people went their way ... to make great mirth (v. 12). The reason for this great joy is stated in the words, "Because they had understood the words that were declared unto them." What a glimpse of the New Covenant there is in this! The great and eternal principle of holy religion is this, as Jesus stated it, "That my joy may be in you, and that your joy may be full" (John 15:11). From one end to the other, the New Testament is a shout of joy. The angelic chorus sang it the night the Christ was born; and an angel of God declared to the shepherds; "Behold, I bring you tidings of great joy that shall be to all people" (Luke 2:10).

Regarding the Second Day of the Seventh Month

Verses 13-18, And on the second day were gathered together the heads of fathers' houses of all the people, the priests, and the Levites unto Ezra the scribe, even to give attention to the words of the law. 14 And they found written in the law, how that Jehovah had commanded by Moses, that the children of Israel should dwell in booths in the feast of the seventh month; 15 and that they should publish and proclaim it in all their cities, and in Jerusalem, saying, Go forth into the mount, and fetch olive branches, and branches of wild olive, and myrtle branches, and palm branches, and branches of thick trees to make booths, as it is written. 16 So the people went forth, and brought them, and made themselves booths, every one upon the roof of his house, and in their courts, and in the courts of the house of God, and in the broad place of the water gate, and in the broad place of the gate of Ephraim. 17 And all the

assembly of them that had come again out of the captivity
made booths, and dwelt in the booths: for since the days of
Jeshua the son of Nun unto that day had not the children
of Israel done so. And there was very great gladness. 18
Also day by day, from the first day unto the last day, he
read in the book of the law of God. And they kept the feast
seven days; and on the eighth day was a solemn assembly,
according unto the ordinance.

The prominent thing in this paragraph is the
thirst of the people to hear the word of God. "Once let
the sweetness of the Divine word be tasted, and there
springs up in the heart instantly a desire for more, like
that feeling of the Psalmist who wrote, 'Oh, how love I
thy law! It is my meditation all the day' (Psalm 119:
97)."[17] Not only did the people come to hear Ezra read
the law on that following day, but also on every day
throughout the Feast of Tabernacles (v. 18).

Leviticus 23:42 had commanded the children of
Israel to dwell in booths during this celebration.
However, some scholars seem to be perturbed over the
fact that some of the instructions mentioned here "are
not found in any existing Scripture";[18] but that is no
problem whatever. The words, "As it is written" (v. 15),
and the statement that all was done, 'According to the
ordinance" (v. 18) leave no room to doubt that at that
time such instructions were available. The fact that
imperfections in the text, or even the loss of portions of

---

[17] PC, op. cit., p. 89.
[18] Ibid.

God's word in that period, might indeed have left us ignorant of some things should neither surprise nor distress us. We can trust what Nehemiah wrote here.

Since the days of Jeshua (Joshua) the son of Nun unto that day had not the children of Israel done so (v. 17). This statement may be an interrogative; and if so, it is a declaration that the children of Israel had observed the Feast of Tabernacles (also called the Feast of Booths) from the days of Joshua till the occasion in this chapter, the Scriptural citings of celebrations in the days of both Solomon and Zerubbabel being proof enough of the truth of the sentence read as an interrogative; but, the critics find it much more delightful to read it as a dogmatic declaration to be cited at once as 'a contradiction,' 'an error,' 'an oversight' or some other euphemism for a falsehood. Oesterley, for example, noted that, "These words are not in accordance with other passages of Scripture; for this feast had been observed by Solomon (2C 7:8, 8:13) and by Zerubabel (Ezra 3:4). It is an 'oversight' of the chronicler's."[19]

Even if the sentence is accurately understood as declarative, the meaning then would be as stated by Rawlinson: "This cannot mean that there had been no celebration of this feast since the days of Joshua, nor even that there had been no occasion of it marked by their dwelling in booths, but only that there had not been *so joyous and general a celebration of it.* A similar statement is made of Josiah's celebration of the

---

[19] ASP, p. 333.

Passover."[20]

A number of other very able scholars are in full agreement with Rawlinson. "It is not the intention of the writer to state that the Feast of Tabernacles had not been kept since the days of Joshua until this occasion, but that there had been *no such celebration as this* since the times of Joshua."[21] Likewise, Keil wrote that, "The text only states that since the days of Joshua, the whole community had not *so* celebrated it."[22]

xxx

_____

[20] PC, op. cit., p. 89.
[21] FCC, op. cit., p. 473.
[22] CFK, op.cit., p. 234.

CHAPTER 9
Israel's Confession of Their Sins and Their Oath of Allegience to the God of Their Fathers

This chapter seems rather long, but no chapter could be long enough for an adequate record of the repeated apostasies of God's Chosen People. Nevertheless, this abbreviation of them, along with the earnest confession of all the people, appears as one of the redeeming moments in the history of Israel, and as one of the stars in their crown of glory.

Despite all the wretched sins and shortcomings of Israel, there was indeed a *righteous remnant* that included the blessed apostles and prophets of the New Testament who were able, through the grace and blessing of God, to resist and effectually defy the brutal godlessness of the Three False Shepherds (Zechariah chapter 11) and the hapless majority of racial Israel, led by the Pharisees, Sadducees and Herodians, and to welcome the Dayspring from on High. That glorious *Righteous Remnant* of Israel ushered in the Kingdom of God on the first Pentecost after the resurrection of Jesus Christ. In this wonderful chapter, we doubtless have some of the ancestors of that *Righteous Remnant.*

The Levites Lead Israel in Confessing Their Sins

Verses 1-4, Now in the twenty and fourth day of this month the children of Israel were assembled with fasting, and with sackcloth, and earth upon them. 2 And the seed of Israel separated themselves from all foreigners, and stood and confessed their sins, and the iniquities of their fathers. 3 And they stood up in their place, and read in the book of the law of Jehovah their God a fourth part of the day; and another fourth part they confessed, and worshipped Jehovah their God. 4 Then stood up upon the stairs of the Levites Jeshua, and Bani, Kadmiel, Shebaniah, Bunni, Sherebiah, Bani, and Chenani, and cried with a loud voice unto Jehovah their God.

All of this great outpouring of grief and confession took place as a result of reading God's law. "They had clearly desired to do this earlier (8:9); but it would have been inappropriate during the feast."[1] Therefore, they rallied for that purpose on the twenty fourth day of that same seventh month, the next month after the wall was built; and "This was only the second day after the conclusion of the Feast of Tabernacles."[2]

A very important revelation of this chapter is that it was the Levites, and not the priests, who led Israel in this penitential prayer of confession and praise of God. From the book of Malachi, we learn of the near total apostasy of the Jewish priesthood; and in Zechariah, they are clearly revealed as the false shepherds who destroyed the nation. There is not a word in this chapter that even hints of any priestly participation in this great repentance, confession and prayer. Some of them were even traitors in the employ of Tobiah and had even conspired to murder Nehemiah.

---

[1] ASP, p. 333.
[2] Ibid.

The seed of Israel separated themselves from all foreigners (v. 2). Keil noted that, "This is not primarily a reference to the dissolution of illegal marriages, but it is rather a voluntary renunciation of all connection with the heathen and of heathen customs."[3]

Then stood up upon the stairs ... Levites (v. 4). "The stairs mentioned here are those leading up to the platform or podium, which had been used for the reading of the Law."[4]

There follows at this point in the chapter a rather long prayer, ending in the solemn commitment of the people to be faithful to the God of Israel.

Rehearsal of God's Great Promise to Abraham

Verses 5-8, Then the Levites, Jeshua, and Kadmiel, Bani, Hashabneiah, Sherebiah, Hodiah, Shebaniah, and Pethahiah, said, Stand up, and bless Jehovah your God from everlasting to everlasting; and blessed be thy glorious name, which is exalted above all blessing and praise. 6 Thou art Jehovah, even thou alone; thou hast made heaven, the heaven of heavens, and all their host, the earth and all the things that are thereon, the seas and all that is in them, and thou preservest them all; and the host of heaven worshippeth thee. 7 Thou art Jehovah the God, who didst choose Abram, and broughtest him forth out of Ur of the Chaldees, and gavest him the name of Abraham, 8 and foundest his heart faithful before thee, and madest a

---

[3] CFK, Vol. 3c, p. 236.

[4] FCC, *Nehemiah*, p. 473.

covenant with him to give the land of the Canaanite, the Hittite, the Amorite, and the Perezzite, and the Jebusite, and the Girgashite, to give it unto his seed, and hast performed thy words; for thou art righteous.

A profitable and acceptable feature of any prayer is a rehearsal of God's promises and heartfelt praise for his fulfilment of them.   All of the things mentioned here have been the subject of our extensive comments upon the Pentateuch, particularly in Genesis. It appears that   during the whole history of ancient Israel that they seemed never to appreciate, nor even to remember, the *reason why* God called Abraham.   That reason: *"THAT IN THEE AND IN THY SEED (SINGULAR) ALL THE FAMILIES OF THE EARTH SHALL BE BLESSED"* (Genesis 12:3, 26:4).

Rehearsal of God's Deliverance of Israel from Egypt and his Guidance of them in the Wilderness

Verses 9-15, And thou sawest the affliction of our fathers in Egypt, and heardest their cry by the Red Sea, 10 and showedst signs and wonders upon Pharaoh, and on all his servants, and all the people of his land; for thou knewest that they dealt proudly against them, and didst get thee a name, as it is this day. 11 And thou didst divide the sea before them, so that they went through the midst of the sea on the dry land; and their pursuers thou didst cast into the depths, as a stone into the mighty waters. 12 Moreover in a pillar of cloud thou leddest them by day; and in a pillar of fire by night, to give them light in the way wherein

*they should go. 13 Thou camest down also upon mount
Sinai, and spakest with them from heaven, and gavest them
right ordinances and true laws, good statutes and
commandments, 14 and madest known unto them thy holy
sabbath, and commandedst them commandments, and
statutes, and a law, by Moses thy servant, 15 and gavest
them bread from heaven for their hunger, and broughtest
forth water for them out of the rock for their thirst, and
commandest them that they should go in to possess the
land which thou hadst sworn to give them.*

We submit as our commentary on these verses
Volume II (Exodus) in our series of works on the
Pentateuch.

God's Mercy Upon Israel in the Wilderness; His
Rejection of That Generation, and His
Bringing their Children Into
the Promised Land

*Verses 16-25, But they and their fathers dealt
proudly, and hardened their neck, and hearkened not to thy
commandments, 17 and refused to obey, neither were
mindful of thy wonders that thou didst among them, but
hardened their neck, and in their rebellion appointed a
captain to return to their bondage. But thou art a God
ready to pardon, gracious and merciful, slow to anger,
abundant in lovingkindness. amd forsookest them not. 18
Yea, when they had made them a molten calf, and said,
This is thy God that brought thee up out of Egypt, and had
wrought great provocations; 19 yet thou in thy manifold*

mercies forsookest them not in the wilderness: the pillar of cloud departed not from over them by day, to lead them in the way; neither the pillar of fire by night, to show them light, and the way wherein they should go. 20 Thou gavest also thy good Spirit to instruct them, and withheldest not thy manna from their mouth, and gavest them water for their thirst. 21 Yea, forty years didst thou sustain them in the wilderness, and they lacked nothing; their clothes waxed not old, and their feet swelled not. 22 Moreover thou gavest them kingdoms and peoples, which thou didst allot after their portions: so they possessed the land of Sihon, even the land of the king of Heshbon, and the land of Og king of Bashan. 23 Their children also multipliedst thou as the stars of heaven, and broughtest them into the land concerning which thou didst say to their fathers, that they should go in to possess it. 24 So the children went in and possessed the land, and thou subduedst before them the inhabitants of the land, the Canaanites, and gavest them into their hands, with their kings, and the peoples of the land, that they might do with them as they would. 25 And they took fortified cities, and a fat land, and possessed houses full of all good things, cisterns hewn out, vineyards, and oliveyards, and fruit-trees in abundance: so they did eat and were filled, and became fat, and delighted themselves in thy great goodness.

For our comment on the history of Israel as mentioned in these verses, see our commentaries on the Pentateuch, especially on Exodus, Leviticus, Numbers, and Deuteronomy. There is practically no additional information provided by this chapter. An exeption is the revelation that Israel actually appointed a captain to lead them back to Egypt. Numbers 14:1-4 has the information that such a move was suggested and recommended by some of the Israelites; but this is the only statement to the effect that they really appointed a captain to take them back to Egypt. Also, this writer does not recall any mention of the fact that their feet did not swell.

The Continued Disobedience of the People and Their Multiple Rebellions Against God

Verses 26-31, Nevertheless they were disobedient, and rebelled against thee, and cast thy law behind their back, and slew thy prophets that testified against them to turn them again unto thee, and they wrought great provocations. 27 Therefore thou deliveredst them into the hand of their adversaries, who distressed them: and in the time of their trouble, when they cried unto thee, thou heardest from heaven; and according to thy manifold mercies thou gavest them saviours who saved them out of the hand of their adversaries. 28 But after they had rest, they did evil again before thee; therefore leftest thou them in the hand of their enemies, so that they had dominion over them: yet when they returned, and cried unto thee, thou heardest from heaven; and many times didst thou deliver them according to thy mercies, 29 and testifiedst against them, that thou mightest bring them again unto thy law. Yet they dealt proudly, and hearkened not unto thy commandments, but sinned against thine ordinances (which if a man do, he shall live in them), and withdrew

the shoulder, and hardened their neck, and would not hear.
30 Yet many years didst thou bear with them, and testifiedst
against them by thy Spirit through thy prophets: yet would
they not give ear: therefore gavest thou them into the hand
of the peoples of the lands. 31 Nevertheless in thy manifold
mercies thou didst not make a full end of them, nor forsake
them; for thou art a gracious and merciful God.

These verses are an abbreviated but sufficiently specific elaboration of the multiple apostasies of the Chosen People, which in the aggregate constitute the entire record of the Old Testament. Wonderful indeed are the mercies of the gracious God who found a way to forgive Israel over and over again. An apostle has told us that these things were "written for admonition" (1 Cor. 10:11); and the great lesson for Christians is centered right here in this willingness of the heavenly Father to forgive the sins of his people, if only they will love God and be faithful to his word

In the final section of this prayer, Israel pleads their phenomenal sufferings as the basis of their plea for mercy, confessing at the same time that they fully deserved the punishments God had laid upon them. Still, despite their sufferings, they made a solemn covenant (of obedience) and sealed it.

Israel Had Indeed Returned; But They Were Still Servants of the Kings of Persia

Verses 32-38, Now therefore, our God, the great,
the mighty, and the terrible God, who keepest covenant and

lovingkindness, let not all the travail seem little before thee, that hath come upon us, upon our kings, on our princes, and on our priests, and on our prophets, and on our fathers, and on all thy people, since the time of the kings of Assyria unto this day. 33 Howbeit thou art just in all that has come upon us; for thou hast dealt truly, but we have done wickedly; 34 neither have our kings, our princes, our priests, nor our fathers, kept thy law, nor hearkened unto thy commandmnets and thy testimonies wherewith thou didst testify against them. 35 For they have not served thee in their kingdom, and in thy great goodness that thou gavest them, and in the large and fat land which thou gavest before them, neither turned they from their wicked works. 36 Behold, we are servants this day, and as for the land that thou gavest unto our fathers to eat the fruit thereof and the good thereof, behold, we are servants in it. 37 And it yieldeth much increase unto the kings whom thou hast set over us because of our sins: also they have power over our bodies, and over our cattle, at their pleasure, and we are in great distress. 38 And yet for all this we make a sure covenant, and write it; and our princes, our Levites, and our priests, seal unto it.

Alas, for Israel, their sinful kingdom would never be restored. Their nation would continue to be subject to the Persians, to the Greeks, and then to the Romans, until the promised Messiah would suddenly appear.

God's prophets, whom they had despised and murdered and whose words they scornfully rejected, would come no more. With Zechariah and Malachi, who were contemporaries of Nehemiah, the age of the prophets terminated. They were the last of the prophets until John the Baptist, in the spirit and power of Elijah, would thunder the message from the wilderness, "Repent ye, for the kingdom of God is at hand,"

Their priesthood became more and more reprobate; and God even cursed it; and, by the times of Christ, the Temple itself had become a "den of thieves and robbers." There is no tragedy like that of Israel; and something of the infinite pathos of their judicial hardening, of their rejection and murder of the Son of God, and of God's destruction of their nation in just retribution of their wickedness ---something of the pathos and tragedy of racial Israel, as distinguished from the true Israel, appears in this pitiful prayer of the Levites who tried in vain to bring the racial Israel back to God.

xxx

CHAPTER 10
Those Who Sealed the Covenant;
Terms of the Covenant

This writer finds it impossible to believe the flat declaration of Bowman that, "Verses 1-27 are interpolated,"[1] there being no historical evidence whatever of such a thing. The critical scholars seek to connect those verses with the book of Ezra, but that notion is refuted absolutely by the fact that, of the familes who returned (in the book of Ezra), only fourteen of them are found in the list here of those who sealed the covenant; therefore these twenty seven verses belong exactly where they are in the book of Nehemiah. We have already noted the defense of Y. Kaufmann who maintained that this chapter is a unit with chapters 8 and 9, and that it belongs exactly where it is.[2]

The last verse of chapter 9 states that, "Our princes, our Levites, and our priests seal unto it" (9:38); and some scholars state that the list of these appears in reverse order;[3] but the principle difference is that in chapter 10 (1) the princes are first (Nehemiah the governor), (2) then the priests, and (3) then the Levites. Thus the principal difference is the reversal of the position of the priests and Levites, which is explained by the fact that in chapter 9 the Levites are clearly the religious leaders of the confession and prayer, whereas

---

[1] IB, Vol. 3, p. 761.

[2] Y, Kaufmann, *History of the Religion of Israel, Vol. IV* (New York: KTAV, 1977).

[3] NLBC, p. 542.

in chapter 10, where the sealing of the document takes place, the priests, who ranked higher than the Levites, naturally had preference in the order of their signing. The actual signing of the covenant was apparently made by various groups, heads of houses, and officials, including some individuals, who affixed their seal instead of writing a signature. "The large number of such seals uncovered in recent excavations in Palestine shows that there is nothing improbable about this."[4]

We have noted already the reluctance of the priesthood, and even the treachery of some of them; but it is not surprising that they, seeing the popularity of the covenant, and following the lead of the governor Nehemiah, readily affixed their seals to it.

The Names of Those Who Sealed

Verses 1-27, Now those that sealed were Nehemiah, the governor, the son of Hacaliah, and Zedekiah,   2 Seraiah, Azariah, Jeremiah,   3 Pashhur, Amariah, Malchijah,   4 Hattasuh, Shebaniah, Malluch,   5 Harim, Maremoth, Obadiah,   6 Daniel, Ginnethon, Baruch,   7 Meshullam, Abijah, Mijamin,   8 Maaziah, Bilgai, Shemaiah: these were the priests.   9 And the Levites: namely, Jeshua the son of Azaniah, Binnui of the son of Henadad, Kadmiel;   10 and their brethren, Shebaniah, Hodiah, Kelita, Pelaiah, Hanan,   11 Micah, Rehob, Hashabiah,   12 Zaccur, Sherebiah, Shebaniah,   13

---

4 ASP, p. 334.

*Hodiah, Bani, Beninu.   14 The chiefs of the people:
Parosh, Pahath-moab, Elam, Zattu, Bani,   15 Bunni,
Azgad, Bebai,   16 Adonijah, Bigvai, Adin,   17 Ater,
Hezekiah, Azzur, 18 Hodiah, Hashum, Bezai,   19 Hariph,
Anathoth, Nobai, 20 Magpiash, Meshullam, Hezir,   21
Meshezabel, Zadok, Jaddua, 22 Pelatiah, Hanan, Anaiah,
23 Hoshea, Hananiah, Hasshub,   24 Hallohesh, Pilha,
Shobek,   25 Rehum, Hashabnah, Maaseiah,   26 and
Ahiah, Hanan, Anan, 27 Malluch, Harim, Baanah.*

Zedekiah (v. 1). The identity of this person is not
known.   Some have supposed him to have been the
same as Zadok (but Zadok is found in v. 21); others
have imagined that he must have been the governor's
secretary, which is as good a guess as any.

For all who wonder where the name of Ezra may
be in this list, Cook's opinion offers the solution that,
"The seal of the highpriestly house of Seraiah was
probably appended, either by Ezra personally, or by
Eliashib, both of whom were members of that house,"[5]

General Acceptance of the Covenant and
Terms Thereof

*Verses 28-31, And the rest of the people, the priests,
the Levites, the porters, the singers, the Nethinim, and all
they that had separated themselves from the peoples of the
lands unto the law of God, their wives, their sons, and their*

---

5 FCC, *Nehemiah*, p. 476.

daughters, every one that had knowledge and understanding; 29 they clave to their brethren, their nobles, and entered into a curse, and into an oath, to walk in God's law, which was given by Moses the servant of God, and to observe and do all the commandments of Jehovah our Lord, and his ordinances and his statutes; 30 and that we would not give our daughters unto the peoples of the land, nor take their daughters for our sons; 31 and if the peoples of the land bring wares or any grain on the sabbath day to sell, that we would not buy of them on the sabbath, or a holy day; and that we would forego the seventh year, and the exaction of every debt.

In this paragraph, four provisions of the covenant are given: (1) A strict promise to abide by all the divine commandments as revealed in the Law of Moses (v. 29); (2) the prohibition against mixed marriages with the pagans (v. 30); (3) strict observance of the sabbath day (v. 31); and (4) the honoring of the seventh year and its requirement of forgiving all debts (v. 31).

Restriction against marriage with pagans. Ezra had dealt with this problem (Chs. 9, 10); but the problem persisted, and there was constant need to address it.

Keeping the sabbaths. "Jeremiah 17:21, 22, and Amos 8:5 indicate clearly that trading on the sabbath day was prohibited."[6]

The sabbatical year a time of release of debts.

---

[6] NBCR, p. 409.

Deuteronomy 15:ff required that all debts (among Israelites) be cancelled, although that release did not apply to foreigners. Also, the fields were to lie fallow and remain uncultivated on the seventh year (Leviticus 25:2-7). "Such provisions would have greatly alleviated the distress in Jerusalem and all Judea (described in 5:1-4); but these regulations had apparently not been observed in Israel until this point."[7]

Further Provisions of the Covenant

Verses 32-33, Also we made ordinances for us to charge ourselves yearly with the third part of a shekel for the service of the house of God; 33 for the showbread, and for the continual meal-offering, and for the continual burnt-offering, for the sabbaths, for the new moons, for the set feasts, and for the holy things, and for the sin-offerings to make atonement for Israel, and for all the work of the house of God.

Also we made ordinances for ourselves (v. 33). "This was merely a revival of a charge levied by Moses upon every Israelite twenty years old and upward to pay a half shekel (Exodus 30:13),"[8] the only difference being in their reduction of it to one third of a shekel.

This *one third of a shekel* annual tax was levied against every Israelite and continued in force till the

---

[7] Ibid.

[8] CFK, *Nehemiah,* p. 253.

Roman destruction of Jerusalem in A. D. 70. Of course, through the years, the tax increased to the original half a shekel. Jesus Christ himself paid this tax for himself and the apostle Peter, in spite of our Lord's being exempt from it. This he did by sending Peter to take up the fish out of the sea of Galilee with a whole shekel in its mouth (Matthew 17:24-27). By this action, the Christ endorsed and approved the ordinance mentioned here. It was God's ordinance, despite the statement in v. 33 that "we made it." They only renewed an old duty.

The mention here of the showbread and of various kinds of sacrifices is only a detailed way of saying that the tax was for *everything* connected with the work in the house of God. For comments on the various things mentioned here, see our commentaries on the Pentateuch where all these things are first mentioned..

The Wood-Offering, the First-fruits, and the Tithes

Verses 34-39, And we cast lots, the priests, the Levites, and the people, for the wood-offering, to bring it into the house of our God, according to our fathers' houses, at times appointed, year by year, to burn upon the altar of Jehovah our God, as it is written in the law; 35 and to bring the first-fruits of our ground, and the first-fruits of all fruit of all manner of trees, year by year, unto the house of Jehovah; 36 also the first-born of our sons, and of our cattle, as it is written in the law, and the firstlings of our herds and of our flocks, to bring to the house of our God,

unto the priests that minister in the house of our God; 37
and that we should bring the first-fruits of our dough, and
our heave-offerings, and the fruit of all manner of trees, the
new wine, and the oil, unto the priests, to the chambers of
the house of our God; and the tithes of our ground unto the
Levites; for they, the Levites take the tithes in all the cities
of our tillage. 38 And the priest the son of Aaron shall be
with the Levites when the Levites take tithes: and the
Levites shall bring up the tithe of the tithes unto the house
of our God, to the chambers, into the treasure-house. 39
For the children of Israel and the children of Levi shall
bring the heave-offering of the grain, of the new wine, and
of the oil, unto the chambers, where are the vessels of the
sanctuary, and the priests that minister, and the porters,
and the singers: and we will not forsake the house of our
God.

This paragrph merely spells out, very briefly, the
obligations which had existed from the times of Moses
in the Pentateuch; and for comments on these various
kinds of gifts and offerings, our writings on all of these
are somewhat extensive in our commentaries on the
Pentateuch. There is no need whatever to rehearse
such comments here.

The only thing new here is the casting of lots to
determine who would bring the wood for use in the
temple, and when they would bring it. Wood was
probably much more plentiful in the early years of the
monarchy; but, "The times had changed. Judah had
been stripped of her forests; the Temple was relatively

poor, and some permanent arrangement for the supply of wood was necessary. Lots were cast to determine who would bring it, and when they would do it."[9]

Another arrangement, which this writer does not remember from the Pentateuch is that of requiring the Levite to take the tithe in the presence of a priest. That, of course, was to prevent the Levite from cheating on the tithe of the tithe he paid to the priesthood!

xxx

---

[9] PC, Vol. 7, *Nehemiah,* p. 111.

CHAPTER 11
Increasing the Population of Jerusalem

Several scholars link this chapter with chapter 7, viewing the intervening three chapters as a unit; and it is true that 7:4 speaks of the fact that Jerusalem was a large area compared with the few people that lived in it. However, the unity of the book of Nehemiah is apparent in the fact that every word of it pertains to the *safety* of the city of Jerusalem. The reading of the Mosaic law (ch. 7), the extended confession and prayers of the people (ch. 9), and the covenant of the people determined to obey God, ratified by an oath and a curse, and sealed by the leaders of the whole community (ch. 10) ---all of that was as intimately connected with the safety of Jerusalem as was the building of the wall itself, in fact, even more so.

Nehemiah was getting ready to dedicate the wall; and, in all probability, he had invited Ezra to be present for that occasion. Both Nehemiah and Ezra, were fully aware that all of Israel's disastrous sorrows and defeats had come about solely because of their shameful neglect of the very things covered in these three chapters (8-10). Those great leaders, seeing that the physical wall was built, sponsored and ordered the rebuilding of Israel's spiritual wall as well. That was done in these intervening three chapters; and the dedication was very properly delayed till that was done. The book of Nehemiah is a unity, logically and skilfully put together.

But what about differences in style, language,

vocabulary, and other oddities in those intervening chapters? The widespread disagreement of scholars and their conflicting views regarding what they are pleased to call "the sources" of these chapters exhibit, "A diversity that may seem bewildering and lead to skepticism with regard to a critical approach itself."[1] Indeed, indeed! The simple truth is that by far the most rational and satisfactory understanding of the book of Nehemiah is that of accepting it, first and last, and everything in between, as the production of Nehemiah.

That he included lists and events, words and sayings, that may have been originally derived from other sources than his own pen is obviously true; but so what? Is it not true with all authors? And, as we have often stressed, twentieth century scholars are simply too late, by entire millenniums of time, to be entrusted with their presumed prerogative of revising the Bible.

This chapter 11 fits in perfectly with what precedes it. (1) the physical wall was built; (2) the spiritual basis of Israel's safety was strengthened; and (3) now the population of Jerusalem needed to be increased as an additional element of their safety. Some of the critics would have proceeded differently; but this is the way Nehemiah did it.

"The artificial enlargement of capital cities by transferring inhabitants into them was common in ancient times. Tradition ascribed the greatness of Rome, in part, to this plan; and in 500 BC, Syracuse

---

1 WBC, Vol. 16, p.275.

became a great city in this way."² Rawlinson cited, "Megalopolis, Tigranocerta and Athens,"³ as other cities made great by this procedure. In this chapter, Nehemiah proceeded to build up the strength of Jerusalem in the same manner.

Casting Lots to See Who Would Move Into the City

Verses 1-2, And the princes of the people dwelt in Jerusalem: the rest of the people also cast lots, to bring one in ten to dwell in Jerusalem the holy city, and nine parts in the other cities. 2 And the people blessed all the men that willingly offered themselves to dwell in Jerusalem,

"The circuit of the wall of Jerusalem at this time was about four miles,"⁴ and there were simply not enough people living in the city to defend a wall of that length. The unwillingness of the people to live inside an unwalled city had brought about this situation; but now that the wall was built, some volunteered to live there. That it was still considered dangerous, however, was indicated by the "blessing" of those who volunteered. Also, it could have been no secret, that their primary duty would be to defend the walls against any attack.

Jerusalem the holy city (v. 1). Jerusalem was called the holy city because the temple was located therein.

---

2 FCC, *Nehemiah,* p. 477.

3 PC, Vol. 7c, *Nehemiah,* p. 116.

4 Ibid.

The rest of the people cast lots (v. 1). "The lot is
cast into the lap; but the whole disposing thereof is of
the Lord" (Proverbs 16:33). "In the course of Jewish
history, they cast lots in the selection of persons (Joshua
7:16-18), for the distribution of lands (Numbers 26:25-
26), and for determining the order in which persons
should execute an office (1C 24:5)";[5] and, in the
previous chapter of Nehemiah, it is written that they
cast lots to decide who would bring the wood for the
temple, and when they would do so. And even in the
NT, they cast lots to determine who would be numbered
among the twelve apostles to take the place of Judas
(Acts 1:26).

Chiefs of the Province that Dwelt in Jerusalem

*Verses 3-6, Now these are the chiefs of the province
that dwelt in Jerusalem: but in the cities of Judah dwelt
every one in his possession in their cities, to wit, Israel, the
priests, and the Levites, and the Nethinim, and the children
of Solomon's servants. 4 And in Jerusalem dwelt certain of
the children of Judah, and of the children of Benjamin. Of
the children of Judah, Athaiah the son of Uzziah, the son
of Zechariah, the son of Amariah, the son of Shephatiah,
the son of Mahalalel, of the children of Perez: 5 and
Maaseiah the son of Baruch, the son of Colhozeh, the son
of Hazaiah, the son of Adaiah, the son of Joiarib, the son
of Zechariah, the son of Shilonite. 6 All the sons of Perez
that dwelt in Jerusalem were four hundred threescore and*

---

5 Ibid.

eight valiant men.

The emphasis among the Jews continued to be upon genealogy. In this enumeration of the children of Judah, they were all traced back to Perez, one of the twin sons of Judah by his daughter-in-law Tamar. All of those mentioned in verses 3-9, according to Cundall, "Were the rulers of the people (the chiefs) already living in Jerusalem."[6] Significantly, the descendants of Judah and of Benjamin are named separately.

Conclusion of the List of Chiefs

Verses 7-9, And these are the sons of Benjamin: Salu the son of Meshullam, the son of Joed, the son of Pedaiah, the son of Kolaiah, the son of Maaseiah, the son of Ithiel, the son of Jeshaiah. 8 And after him Gabbai, Sallai, nine hundred twenty and eight. 9 And Joel the son of Zichri was their overseer; and Judah the son of Hassenuah was second over the city.

This concludes the list of the princes (chiefs) who were already living in Jerusalem. There were 1,396 of these.

The List of the Priests

Verses 10-14, Of the priests: Jedaiah the son of Joiarib, Jachin, 11 Seraiah the son of Hilkiah, the son of

---

6 NBCR, p. 409.

Meshullam, the son of Zadok, the son of Meraioth, the son of Ahitub, the ruler of the house of God, 12 and their brethren that did the work of the house, eight hundred twenty and two; and Adaiah the son of Jeroham, the son of Pelatiah, the son of Amzi, the son of Zechariah, the son of Pashhur, the son of Malchjah, 13 and his brethren, chiefs of fathers' houses, two hundred forty and two; and Amashsai the son of Azarel, the son of Ahzai, the son of Meshillemoth, the son of Immer, 14 and their brethren, mighty men of valor, a hundred twenty and eight. And their overseer was Zabdiel, the son of Heggedolim.

This list of the priests numbered 1,192.

The List of the Levites Numbered 284

Verses 15-18, And of the Levites: Shemaiah the son of Hasshub, the son of Azrikam, the son of Hashabiah, the son of Bunni; 16 And Shabbethiah and Jozabad, of the chiefs of the Levites, who had the oversight of the outward business of the house of God; 17 and Mattaniah the son of Mica, the son of Zabdi, the son of Asaph, who was the chief to begin the thanksgiving in prayer, and Bakbukiah the second among his brethren; and Abda the son of Shammua, the son of Galal, the son of Jeduthun. 18 And all the Levites in the holy city were two hundred fourscore and four.

The Porters and Gatekeepers Numbered 172

Verse 19-21, Moreover the porters, Akkub, Talmon, and their brethren, that kept watch at the gates were a hundred seventy and two. 20 And the residue of Israel, of the priests, the Levites, were in all the cities of Judah, every one in his inheritance. 21 But the Nethinim dwelt in Ophel: and Ziha and Gishpa were over the Nethinim.

The total number of the men living in the holy city is thus numbered at 3,044, not including women and children, nor the Nethinim. Whitcomb also gave this number as 3,044.[7] Ophel was indeed part of the holy city, having a wall of its own; and it was sometimes counted in, sometimes counted out of the city, as here. "These were augmented by a 10% levy drawn fom the surrounding areas, and an unspecified number of volunteers (v. 2)."[8]

Scholars disagree on the exact meaning of verse 1. Some take it, as did Whitcomb, to mean that the population was readjusted, so that ten per cent of the returnees lived in the city, and ninety percent in the outlying areas. If so interpreted, it would mean that, "The population of Judea had increased considerably during the previous century; because the 50,000 who returned with Zerubbabel from Babylon included

---

7 WYC, p. 443
8 NBCR, p. 409.

women and children."[9] The approximately 3,000 men in Jerusalem before this adjustment took place would mean that there were 30,000 Jewish men then living in Palestine, besides women and children. At a ratio of four to one, this would make the number of Israelites then in Judea about 120,000. Keil, however, wrote that, "The passage can have no other meaning, but that the population of Jerusalem was increased by a 10% fraction of the population living outside the city."[10] He admitted, however, that, "The statement, taken by itself, is very brief, and its connection with 7:5 not very evident."[11]

Artaxerxes Supported the Levites

Verses 22-24, The overseer also of the Levites in Jerusalem was Uzzi, the son of Bani, the son of Hashabiah, the son of Mattaniah, the son of Mica, of the sons of Asaph, the singers, over the business of the house of God. 23 For there was a commandment from the king concerning them, and a settled provision for the singers, as every day required. 24 And Pethahiah the son of Meshezabel, of the children of Zerah the son of Judah, was at the king's hand in all matters concerning the people.

Artaxerxes was indeed a friend of Israel; and here we find that he had allotted a regular payment for

---

[9] WYC, p. 443.

[10] CFK, *Nehemiah*, p. 267.

[11] Ibid.

the Levites and singers. He had already exempted them from all tolls, tribute, custom and taxes of every kind (Ezra 7:24); and his cooperation with both Ezra and Nehemiah in all of the things done for the Chosen People is the *sine qua non* of everything in both of these biblical books. "Now he had even gone further and assigned an allotment from the royal revenue for the support of the persons mentioned here."[12]   It is also of interest that the king showed in this action a definite preference for the Levites, as compared with the priests. Artaxerxes was probably aware of the general corruption of the priesthood, a corruption that merited and received a curse from Almighty God himself (Malachi 2:2) because of their detestable immorality. The king must have been aware that, if any prayers were to be offered for, "the king and his sons" (Ezra 6:10), the Levites, not the priests, would be the ones who did it.

A Roster of Towns And Villages Near Jerusalem

Verses 25-36,   And as for the villages, with their fields, some of the children of Judah dwelt in Kireath-arba and the towns thereof, and in Dihon and the towns thereof, and in Jekabzeel and the villages thereof,   26 and in Jeshua, Moladah, and Beth-pelet,   27 and in Hazar-shual and in Beer-sheba and the towns thereof,   28 and in Ziklag and in Meconah and in the towns thereof,   29 and in En-rimmon, and in Zorah, and in Jarmuth,   30 Zanoah,

---

12 FCC, **Nehemiah**, p. 479

Adullam, and their villages, Lachish and the fields thereof, Azekah and the towns thereof. So they encamped from Beer-sheba unto the valley of Hinnom. 31 The children of Benjamin also dwelt from Geba onward, at Michmash and Aija, and at Beth-el and the towns thereof, 32 at Anathoth, Nob, Ananiah, 33 Hazer, Ramah, Gittaim, 34 Hadid, Zeboim, Neballat, 35 Lod, and Ono, the valley of craftsmen. 35 And of the Levites, certain courses in Judah were joined to Bethlehem.

There is hardly a place-name in this list that is not loaded with many associations concerning events and persons mentioned in the long history of Israel; and it is impossible to note all of such connections here. Kiriath-arba, for example is Hebron; but during the long absence of Israel, it had again become known by its ancient name. As Hebron, it was one of the cities of Refuge; Ziklag is the city that the king of Gath gave to David; Anathoth was the home of Jeremiah; Nob is where Saul murdered the priests; Adullam was noted for a nearby cave where David was a fugitive from Saul; Lachish, the second largest city of Judea was taken by Sennacherib; the valley of Ono was the place to which Sanballat and Tobiah sought to lure Nehemiah to his death; Beer-sheba, the southernmost place in ancient Israel was frequently mentioned; Ramah featured prominently in the history of Ahab; "Lod, now Ludd, is the Lydda of Acts of Apostles; it was on the eastern edge of the Shephelah, about nine miles SE of Joppa."[13]

---

[13] PC, Vol. 7c, p. 120.

Bethel, another famous town, was where Jeroboam I installed one of his golden calves. "It is strange that Gibeon, Mizpah and Jericho are not mentioned, although they are listed in Nehemiah 3."[14] Perhaps this should alert us to the truth that this record is abbreviated.

This brings us near to the dedication of the wall, related in the next chapter; but Nehemiah was by no means finished with providing security and safety for Jerusalem. There yet remained the treacherous infiltration of the holy city itself by the godless Tobiah, aided and abetted by the high priest himself; and that would be the subject of the final chapter.

xxx

---

[14] WYC, p. 443

CHAPTER 12
Dedication of the Completed Wall of Jerusalem

(Note: in this chapter, we shall use the text of the RSV, *which has returned to the order of verses in the* KJV*).*

This chapter exhibits two separate parts: (1) certain lists of priests, high priests and Levites (vv. 1-16); and (2) the elaborate ceremonies of the dedication. Cook classified the lists thus: (1) the chief priestly and Levitical familes who returned with Zerubbabel (vv. 1-9); (2) the first six of the post-exilic high priests from Jesuha to Jaddua (vv. 10-11); (3) the actual heads of the priestly families in the times of the high priest Joiakim (vv. 12-21); and (4) the chief Levitical familes of Nehemiah's time (vv. 22-26). Cook wrote that all of these lists were probably compiled by Nehemiah, except the second;[1] he supposed that list might have been far later due to the mention of Jaddua, mentioned by Josephus as high priest in the times of Alexander the Great (330 BC). This writer rejects that supposition altogether.

Regarding the Problem of Jaddua (v. 22)

This is as good a place as any to dispose of the problem centered around the name Jaddua.

(1) There might easily have been several high priests named Jaddua. If there's anything about all these Jewish names we have been studying that stands

---

[1] FCC, *Nehemiah,* p. 479.

out above everyting else, it is that the same names appear again, and again, generation after generation. "For example there were twenty-seven Zechariahs"![2] And even among the Twelve Apostles there were two Simons and two James. Nehemiah mentions a Jaddua here (vv. 11, 22), apparently in his times; and Josephus mentions another one more than a century later. The critics will have to come up with something a lot better than this in order to late-date Nehemiah. We simply will not receive any such thing on the premise that *only one* high priest was named Jaddua!

(2) We believe that Josephus' identification of Jaddua as the high priest in the times of Alexander the Great is an error by Josephus. There's not a scholar on earth who has not questioned Josephus' reliability on many things.

(3). It is altogether possible that Jaddua lived to be over a hundred years old and might have been high priest in the times of both Nehemiah and Alexander. Whitcomb stressed this, pointing out that one of the high priests, "Jehoiada died at the age of 130 (2C 24:15)."[3] That possibility is supported by the fact that Jaddua died very soon after his meeting with Alexander the Great, indicating that he might indeed have been a very old man when that happened.

(4) Then there is the very definite possibility that the word Jaddua here is an interpolation. It is this writer's opinion that overwhelming odds favor this

---

[2] AMOB, p. 343.
[3] WYC, p. 443.

possibility. Williamson admitted that these lists are "defective," due to copyist's errors, etc. We appreciate Hamrick, a very recent scholar, and his elaboration of this very point. "Jaddua in verse 22 (ch. 12) may have been added by a subsequent editor. In the Hebrew, it reads, 'and Johanan, and Jaddua' (cf. KJV), as though the latter name had been inserted by a later hand."[4]

All of these four options may be defended, and indeed have been defended, by able scholars; so one may take his choice. Until the critics effectively refute all four of these options, we shall stick to our conviction that the appearance of the name of Jaddua in this chapter is no adequate basis whatever for late-dating Nehemiah.

There isn't anything that betrays the enthusiastic bias of critics in favor of late-dating Bible books any better that their ridiculous seizure of *one single word in a defective list of names* as their sole basis for denying the word of God, which ascribes this book to Nehemiah, and not to some mythical 'chronicler' living a hundred years later in the times of Alexander the Great. Such an action goes much further in discrediting the critics than it does toward late-dating Nehemiah.

Counting the list of the inhabitants of the province given in chapter 11, the four we have here in chapter 12 make five lists in all. "They are all connected with the genealogical register of the Israelite population of the whole province, taken by Nehemiah for the purpose of enlarging the population of

---

[4] BBC, Vol. 3. 499.

Jerusalem."[5]

We shall not discuss these lists in detail. It is sufficient to remember that they served their purpose as far as Nehemiah was concerned. The discrepancies, questions, problems and variations in all of these are insoluble at this period of time, twenty five centuries afterwards.

One of the first problems regarding the two lists in chapters 10 and 12 is that they do not coincide. "This difference is due to the time elapsed between the taking of the two lists; and also because, the names in chapter 10 are not the names of orders nor houses, but the names of heads of families."[6]

Priests and Levites Who Came Up With Zerubbabel

Verses 1-11, Now these are the priests and Levites who went up with Zerubbabel the son of Shealtiel, and Jeshua: Seraiah. Jeremiah, Ezra, 2 Amariah, Malluch, Hattush, 3 Shechaniah, Rehum, Meremoth, 4 Iddo, Ginnethoi, Abijah, 5 Mijamin, Maadiah, Bilgah, 6 Shemiah, Joiarib, Jedaiah, 7 Sallu, Amok, Hilkiah, Jedaiah. These were the chiefs and of their brethren in the days of Jeshua. 8 And the Levites: Jeshua, Binnui, Kadmiel, Sherebiah, Judah and Mattaniah, who with his brethren was in charge of the songs of thanksgiving. 9 And Bakbukiah and Unno their brethren stood opposite them in the service. 10 And Jeshua was the father of

---

5 CFK, *Nehemiah,* p. 265.

6 Ibid, pp. 268, 270.

Joiakim, Joiakim the father of Eliashib, Eliashib the father of Joiada, 11 Joiada the father of Jonathan, and Jonathan the father of Jaddua.

Verses 10 and 11 are a parenthesis thrown in at this point as an aid in the chronology. The names are those of the first six high priests in the period after the exile.

List of Priests When Joiakim was High Priest

Verses 12-21, And in the days of Joiakim were priests, heads of fathers' houses: of Seraiah, Meraiah; of Jeremiah, Hananiah; 13 of Ezra, Meshullam; of Amariah, Jehohanan; 14 of Malluci, Jonathan; 15 of Shebaniah, Joseph; 15 of Harim, Adna; of Meraioth, Helkai; 16 of Iddo, Zechariah; of Ginnethon, Meshullam; 17 of Abijah, Zichri; of Miniamin, Moadiah, Piltai; 18 of Bilgai, Shammua; of Shemaiah, Jehonathan; 19 of Joiarib, Matteniah; of Jedaiah, Uzzi; 20 of Sallai, Kallai; of Amok, Eber; 21 of Hilkiah, Hashabai; of Jedaiah, Nethanel.

List of the Levites in the Days of the Last Four High Priests Mentioned in Verses 10, 11

Verses 22-26, As for the Levites in the days of Eliashib, Joiada, Johanan, and Jaddua, there were recorded the heads of fathers' houses; also the priests until the reign of Darius the Persian. 23 The sons of Levi, heads of fathers' houses, were written in the book of the Chronicles until the days of Johanan the son of Eliashib.

24 And the chiefs of the Levites: Hashabiah, Sherebiah, and Jeshua the son of Kadmiel, with their brethren over against them, to praise and to give thanks, according to the commandment of David the man of God, watch corresponding to watch. 25 Mattaniah, Bakbukiah, Obadiah, Meshullam, Talmon, and Akkub were gatekeepers standing guard at the storehouses of the gates. 26 These were in the days of Joiakim the son of Jeshua son of Jozadak, and in the days of Nehemiah the governor and of Ezra the priest the scribe.

In the days of Joiakim (v. 26). That entire list of six high priests in vv. 10, 11, raises the question of why four were named in v. 22, whereas, here (v. 26), all of the names in this paragraph are identified as those who lived in the days of Joiakim. This makes it a certainty that the Darius the Persian mentioned here was none other than, "Darius Nothus, the second Persian king of that name."[7]   "This is proved by the Elephantine papyri."[8] It appears that the best explanation of why four high priests are named in verse 21 is that all four generations of them were living at the same time, which would mean that Jaddua was indeed quite a young child at the time.   The text nowhere states that the names given were those of people living throughout the administrations of all four of those high priests.

---

[7] CFK, op. cit., p. 273.

[8] WYC, p. 443.

Preparation for the Dedication Ceremonies

Verses 27-30, And at the dedication of the wall of Jerusalem they sought the Levites in all their places, to bring them to Jerusalem to celebrate the dedication with gladness, with thanksgiving, and with singing, with cymbals, harps, and lyres. 28 And the sons of the singers gathered together from the circuit round Jerusalem and from the villages of the Netophathites; 30 also from Beth-gilgal and from the region of Geba and Azmaveth; for the singers had built for themselves villages around Jerusalem. 29 And the priests and the Levites purified themselves; and they purified the people and the gates and the wall.

The purification ceremonies probably included the offering of sacrifices and the strict observance of all the prohibitions of the Mosaic law.

The time of this dedication was not long after the completion of the wall, as should have been expected. This writer was astounded that several scholars placed the dedication a decade or so after the wall was completed. Rawlinson made the dedication "thirteen years after the wall was finished."[9] Cook wrote that, "The dedication was deferred for nearly twelve years."[10] Such errors are due solely to the scholarly emphasis upon that misplaced name of the high priest Jaddua in v. 22. Short got it right. "The dedication was only a few

---

[9] PC, *Nehemiah*, p. 132.
[10] FCC, **Nehemiah**, p. 481.

days after the completion of the wall."[11]

Although our text does not give us the exact date of the dedication, the historical note in, "Second Maccabees 1:18 gives the date of the dedication as the twenty fifth of the ninth month (Kislew), only three months after the completion of the wall."[12]

The Grand Procession Atop the Wall to the Temple

Verses 31-37, Then I brought up the princes of Judah upon the wall, and appointed two great companies which gave thanks and went in procession. One went to the right upon the wall to the Dung Gate; 32 and after them went Hosahaiah and half of the princes of Judah, 33 and Azariah, Ezra, Meshullam, 34 Judah, Benjamin, Shemaiah, Jeremiah, 35 and certain of the priests' sons with trumpets: Zechariah the son of Jonathan, son of Shemaiah, son of Mattaniah, son of Micaiah, son of Zaccur, son of Asaph; 36 and his kinsmen, Shemaiah, Azarel, Milalai, Gilalai, Maai, Nethanel, Judah, and Hanani, with musical instruments of David the man of God; and Ezra the scribe went before them. 37 At the Fountain Gate they went up straight before them by the stairs of the city of David, at the ascent of the wall, above the house of David, to the Water Gate on the east.

Upon the wall ... upon the wall (v. 31). Many of the older scholars thought that the grand processions,

---

[11] NLBC, p. 540.
[12] NBCR, p. 409.

one moving clockwise, the other counter clockwise, circled the wall around the city, walking on the ground; but the text here flatly declares that they marched atop the wall. This is to be trusted as the way it happened. Excavations by Kathleen Kenyon in Jerusalem have indicated that, "Nehemiah's wall was nine feet wide."[13] As Hamrick noted,   "That was ample room for a procession to move along the top of it."[14]   Our map, p. 138, will show how the processions proceeded.

These verses concern only half the procession; there were two, one led by Ezra the priest the scribe, and the other by the governor Nehemiah.   Both began in the area between the Dung Gate and the Valley Gate, Ezra moving northward around the eastern wall of the city, and Nehemiah and his procession heading northward around the western wall, both processions coming together in the vicinity of the temple.

Nehemiah Heads the Procession Around the Western Section of the Wall

Verses 38-43, The other company of those who gave thanks went to the left, and I followed them with half of the people, upon the wall, above the Tower of the Ovens, to the Broad Wall, 39 and above the Gate of Ephraim, and by the Old Gate, and by the Fish Gate; and the Tower of Hananel, and the Tower of the Hundred, to the Sheep Gate; and they

---

[13] Kathleen Kenyon, *Jerusalem, Excavating 3,000 Years of History* (New York: McGraw-Hill,1967), p. 111.

[14] BBC, Vol. 3, p. 502.

came to a halt at the Gate of the Guard. 40 So both companies of those who gave thanks stood in the house of God, and I and half the officials with me; 41 and the priests Eliakim, Maaseiah, Minamin, Micaiah, Elioenai, Zechariah, and Hananiah, with trumpets; 42 and Maaseiah, Shemiah, Eleazar, Uzzi, Jehohanan, Malchijah, Elam, and Ezer. And the singers sang with Jezrahiah as their leader. 43 And they offered great sacrifices that day and rejoiced, for God had made them rejoice with great joy; and the women and children also rejoiced. And the joy of Jerusalem was heard afar off.

Any way it may be considerd, this is a very remarkable narrative. The whole celebration is outlined in such a manner that one may visualize it even today. There was indeed a great joy in Jerusalem.

Regulations Regarding Religious Duties of the People

Verses 44-47, On that day, men were appointed over the chambers for the stores, the contributions, the first-fruits, and the tithes, to gather into them the portions required by the law for the priests and for the Levites according to the fields of the towns; for Judah rejoiced over the priests and the Levites who ministered. 45 And they performed the service of their God and the service of purification, as did the singers and gatekeepers according to the command of David and his son Solomon. 46 For as in the days of David and Asaph of old there was a chief of the singers, and there were songs of praise and thanksgiving to God. 47 And all Israel in the days of

Zerubbabel and in the days of Nehemiah gave the daily portions for the singers and the gatekeepers; and they set apart that which was for the Levites; and the Levites set apart that which was for the sons of Aaron.

Men were appointed over the chambers for the stores ... the tithes ... to gather them (v. 44). Bringing tithes into Jerusalem was no doubt an arduous and constant work; and it is no wonder the duty was neglected. Here we learn that men were appointed to collect them from outlying areas and to deliver them to the storehouses in the temple. This no doubt pleased the vast majority of the people.

Nehemiah, in this paragraph, used the third person; but that does not mean another author nor that mythical chronicler. "The solemnity was terminated with the offering of great sacrifices and a general festival of rejoicing. In all that sacrificing, Nehemiah, the civil governor, was naturally superceded as the man in charge by Ezra the priest; and therefore Nehemiah related the close of the proceedings objectively, using the third person, as he had done in describing the preparations (v. 27), only using the first person when speaking of what was appointed by himself or his position."[15]   Biblical authors (and other ancient historians) very often used the third person in their writings; even Paul did so (2 Cor. 12:2-4).

This last paragraph emphasizes the widespread cooperation of the people with the priests and the

---

[15] CFK, op. cit., p. 282.

Levites. Israel considered their national safety as dependent upon the faithful observance of all the religious ceremonies and ordinances by the priests and Levites. By stressing that fact that this was being done, "The author," according to Cook, "Is comparing the religious activity and strictness of Nehemiah's time with that which had prevailed under Zerubbabel (described in Ezra 6:16-22), with the implication that the intermediate period had been a time of laxity."[16]

xxx

---

[16] FCC, op. cit., p. 482.

CHAPTER 13
Wholesale Apostasy of Israel in Nehemiah's Brief Absence

This is one of the saddest chapters in the Bible, for it relates Israel's prompt rebellion against God's law as soon as Nehemiah's back was turned. Of course, Nehemiah once more attempted to get Israel back on the right track, as related in this chapter; but that great effort on his part may also be viewed as a total failure.

Israel obeyed God only so long as some powerful administrator compelled them to do so. The sadness of this tragic failure of the once Chosen People is emphasized by the fact Nehemiah was their last chance to get right in the sight of God.

After Nehemiah, there would be no more prophets till John the baptist; their king had been taken away from them by the Lord; and they would never have another; the whole racial nation, with the exception of a tiny "righteous remnant" sank rapidly and irrevocably into that state of 'judicial hardening' foretold by Isaiah. Israel had stopped their ears, closed their eyes, and hardened their hearts; and, from that state of spiritual oblivion, there could be no recovery until the Christ should come; and the vast majority of them failed to seize even that opportunity.

Reading of the Law Regarding the Exclusion of Ammonites from the Congregation

Verses 1-3, On that day they read in the book of Moses in the audience of the people; and therein was found

*written that an Ammonite and a Moabite should not enter
into the assembly of God for ever, 2 because they met not
the children of Israel with bread and with water, but hired
Balaam against them, to curse them: howbeit our God
turned the curse into a blessing. 3 And it came to pass
when they heard the law, that they separated from Israel
the mixed multitude.*

The book of Moses (v. 1). "This probably meant
the entire Pentateuch."[1]

It is not clear whether this was a special occasion
for reading God's law, or if it was connected with the
prescribed reading of it at the Feast of Tabernacles,
which might have coincided, almost, with Nehemiah's
return to Jerusalem, following his absence in Persia. To
this writer, it appears most likely to have been a special
reading of the law arranged at once by Nehemiah upon
his return.

We have already noted that every word of
Nehemiah is focused upon providing safety for
Jerusalem; and the big thing in this chapter is that of
Nehemiah's throwing Tobiah out of the temple; and it
could hardly have been an accident that this reading
from God's law was pointed squarely at that sinful
treatment of Tobiah, an Ammonite enemy of
Nehemiah, and of the Israel of God.

This little paragraph is somewhat of a prelude to
the chapter. Neither the reading of God's law, nor
Nehemiah's entreaties would suffice to correct this

---

[1] FCC, *Nehemiah*, p. 482.

abuse. "Judicial proceedings would have to be taken,
and the mixed multitude removed by authority."[2]

Tobiah, the Ammonite Enemy, Thrown out of the Temple Chambers

*Verses 4-9, Now before this, Eliashib the priest,
who was appointed over the chambers of the house of our
God, being allied with Tobiah, 5 had prepared for him a
great chamber, where aforetime they had laid the meal-
offerings, the frankincense, and the vessels, and the tithes of
the grain, the new wine, and the oil, which were given by
commandment to the Levites, and the singers, and the
porters; and the heave-offerings for the priests. 6 But in all
this time I was not at Jerusalem; for in the two and
thirtieth year of Artaxerxes the king of Babylon I went unto
the king: and after certain days asked I leave of the king, 7
and I came to Jerusalem, and understood the evil that
Eliashib had done for Tobiah, in preparing him a chamber
in the courts of the house of God. 8 And it grieved me sore:
therefore I cast forth all the household stuff of Tobiah out
of the chamber. 9 Then I commanded, and they cleansed
the chambers: and thither brought I again the vessels of the
house of God, with the meal-offerings and the frankincense.*

We find it hard to understand the claims of some
that they do not know whether or not Eliashib was high
priest, or whether or not Nehemiah returned as
governor.   Eliashib is listed as a high priest in 12:10;

---

[2] PC, *Nehemiah*, p. 139.

and, besides that, only the high priest had sufficient authority to have done for Tobiah what was done here. And, as for Nehemiah, of course, he returned as governor; how else could he have "commanded" as stated in v. 9? The high priest would not have obeyed him or permitted the disruption of that fancy nest he had made for Tobiah in the temple chambers, unless Nehemiah, indeed, was governor, backed up by the full authority of the king of Persia.

There is much diversity of scholarly opinion on how long Nehemiah had been gone from Jerusalem prior to his return to find wholesale rebellion against God's laws. Keil believed that, "Nehemiah's absence must have lasted longer than a year, because so many illegal acts by the people could not have occurred in so short a time."[3] Nevertheless, "Nehemiah probably went to the court in Babylon in 433 BC, and returned to Jerusalem in 432 BC."[4] Regarding such a sudden and complete apostasy by Israel, the scholars may scream, "Incredible,"[5] as did Oesterley; but a careful reading of this chapter supports the reality of it. If Nehemiah left early in 433 BC and returned in late 432 BC, he might have been gone as long as eighteen months or a little longer. "Artaxerxes died in 423 BC";[6] and the very longest that Nehemiah could have been absent was about eight or nine years. Israel did not need years to

---

[3] CFK, *Nehemiah,* p. 288.

[4] FCC, *Nehemiah,* p. 483.

[5] ASP, p. 334.

[6] WYCm, p. 445.

rebel against God; for they, in their hearts, were in a continual state of rebellion from the times of Hosea and afterwards. It is this writer's opinion that Nehemiah was not halfway on his way back to Babylon, when Elisashib and his evil followers were dismantling all of the reforms Nehemiah had made.

"It is possible that Malachi was prophesying during this period,"[7] and from him, we understand that the whole priesthood of Israel was wicked (Malachi 2:2).

The People Had Stopped Paying Tithes to the Levites

Verses 10-14, And I perceived that the portions of the Levites had not been given them; so the Levites, and the singers, that did the work, were fled every one to his field. 11 Then contended I with the rulers, and said, Why is the house of God forsaken? And I gathered them together and set them in their place. 12 Then brought all Judah the tithe of the grain and the new wine and the oil unto the treasuries. 13 And I made treasurers over the treasuries, Shelemiah the priest, and Zadok the scribe, and of the Levites Pedaiah: and next to them was Hanan the son of Zaccur, the son of Mattaniah; for they were counted faithful, and their business was to distribute unto their brethren. 14 Remember me, O my God, concerning this, and wipe not out my good deeds which I have done for the house of my God, and for the observances thereof.

---

7 Ibid.

The Levites ... were fled every one to his field (v. 10). The people, particularly the landowners, princes and rulers of the people, stopped paying tithes; and the Levites, left without support, fled at once to farms to make a living. Of course, the rulers (v. 11) had a financial interest in abolishing tithes; and that is why Nehemiah began by assembling them and demanding an answer as to why the temple was deserted.

I contended with the rulers (v. 11). "The sin of profaning the temple was principally charged against the priests; but the omission of the payment of tithes was due to the indifference or opposition of the rulers."[8]

Remember me, O my God, concerning this (v. 14). This pitiful plea on the part of Nehemiah is understandable. The sudden and almost unbelievable totality of the people's rejection of God's word and their wholesale violation of all his commandments surely must have alerted Nehemiah to the fact that all of his high hopes for the nation of Israel would never be realized. There are four similar prayers of this nature in this single concluding chapter.

Their Wanton Violation of the Sabbath Day

Verses 15-18, In those days saw I in Judah men treading winepresses on the sabbath, and bringing in sheaves, and lading asses therewith; as also with wine, grapes, figs, and all manner of burdens, which they brought into Jerusalem on the sabbath day: and I testified against

---

8 PC, op. cit., p. 140.

them in the day wherein they sold victuals. 16 There dwelt men of Tyre also therein, who brought in fish, and all manner of wares, and sold on the sabbath to the children of Judah, and in Jerusalem. 17 Then I contended with the nobles of Judah, and said unto them, What evil thing is this that ye do, and profane the sabbath day? 18 Did not your fathers thus, and did not our God bring all this evil upon us, and upon this city? yet ye bring more wrath upon Israel by profaning the sabbath.

There dwelt men of Tyre also therein (v. 16). It was not contrary to God's law for foreigners to live in Jerusalem; but, "This, however, was a new fact, and one pregnant with evil consequences."[9] Men of Tyre had established a colony in Jerusalem; they were not bound by God's laws, and they no doubt led the way in advocating and encouraging the profanation of the sabbath.

Nehemiah's Strong Measures Against Sabbath Breaking

Verses 19-22, And it came to pass that when the gates of Jerusalem began to be dark before the sabbath, I commanded that they should not be opened till after the sabbath; and some of my servants set I over the gates, that there should no burden be brought in on the sabbath day. 20 So the merchants and sellers of all kind of wares lodged without Jerusalem once or twice. 21 Then I testified against them, and said unto them, Why lodge ye about the

---

9 FCC, op. cit., p. 484.

*wall? if ye do so again, I will lay hands on you. From that
time forth came they no more on the sabbath. 22 And I
commanded the Levites that they should purify themselves,
and that they should come and keep the gates, to sanctify
the sabbath day. Remember unto me, O my God, this also,
and spare me, according to the greatness of thy
lovingkindness.*

*When the gates of Jerusalem began to be dark before
the sabbath (v. 19).* These words take account of the
Jewish custom of counting every day from sunset to
sunset; thus the sabbath, as we would reckon time,
actually began at sundown on the preceding day. "The
Jews grounded this practice on the Genesis account of
creation, where the successive days are listed after the
formula, 'There was evening and morning, one day,' etc.
(Genesis 1:5)."[10]

Nehemiah closed the gates on the sabbath and
threatened violence against those who camped outside
waiting for the end of it; and these stern measures were
effective, as long as Nehemiah was governor with
authority to enforce them; but the reform, in all
probability, did not last ten days after Nehemiah's
governorship was terminated.

*O my God ... spare me according to the greatness of
thy lovingkindness (22).* Again, we have one of
Nehemiah's spontaneous prayers. This one is of special
interest. "Here Nehemiah acknowledges that his
salvation is dependent upon the greatness of God's

---

[10] PC, op. cit., p. 141.

lovingkindness, and not upon the multiplicity of his good deeds. The doctrine of God's grace in the OT is often tragically overlooked."[11]

Nehemiah Faces the Recurrence of Sinful Marriages With Pagans

Verses 23-31, In those days also saw I the Jews that had married women of Ashdod, of Ammon, and of Moab: 24 and their children spake half in the speech of Ashdod, and could not speak in the language of Judah, but according to the language of each people. 25 And I contended with them, and cursed them, and smote certain of them, and plucked off their hair, and made them swear by God, saying, Ye shall not give your daughters unto their sons, nor take their daughters for your sons, nor for yourselves. 26 Did not Solomon king of Israel sin by these things? yet among many nations was there no king like him, and he was beloved of his God, and God made him king over all Israel: nevertheless, even him did foreign women cause to sin. 27 Shall we then hearken unto you to do all this great evil, to trespass against our God in marrying foreign women?

28 And one of the sons of Joiada, the son of Elisashib the high priest, was son-in-law to Sanballat the Horonite: therefore I chased him from me. 29 Remember them, O my God, because they have defiled the priesthood, and the covenant of the priesthood, and of the Levites.

30 Thus cleansed I them of all foreigners, and

---

[11] BBC, Vol. 3, p. 505.

appointed charges for the priests and for the Levites, every one in his work; 31 and for the wood-offering, at times appointed, and for the first-fruits. Remember me, O my God, for good.

Remember me, O my God, for good (v. 31) This is the fourth of these little prayers in this chapter; and this proliferation of Nehemiah's earnest appeals to God may be understood to indicate his recognition of the desperate extremity into which the Chosen People had fallen. Candidly, there was little that any human being, or that even God himself, could do for Israel that had not already been done, over and over again.

Not only had a son of the high priest married a pagan; but Eliashib the high priest himself was "allied with Tobiah," probably by marriage; and the profaning of the priesthood was by no means restricted to these two violations. Again, we refer to Malachi 2:2 as the verdict of God himself regarding Israel's priests. By the times of Christ, the party of the Sadducees (among the priests) were outright atheists, not believing in angels, spirits, the resurrection or anything else that the word of God teaches (Matthew 22:23); and they had preempted unto themselves alone the office of the high priest. They along with the Herodians and Pharisees were the false shepherds who seduced and destroyed the vast majority of the Chosen People (Zechariah 11).

xxx

COMMENTARY
on ESTHER

INTRODUCTION

The Book of Esther is one of the most beautiful narratives ever written; and in spite of the fact that the name of God does not appear anywhere in it, His presence is felt in every single line of it. Some have insisted that there is no spiritual significance in it; but, as we shall show, there are analogies in it that are indeed loaded with spiritual implications of the greatest import.

The book has been classified by biblical enemies as 'a historical romance,' 'fiction,' or a fabrication based upon some pagan myth; nevertheless Esther stands in the sacred canon, and all of the devices of Satan have been unable to remove it.

Historicity. Of course, Esther is history, accurate, reliable, true. The proof of this is the Jewish celebration of the feast of Purim, celebrated continuously since the times of Esther till the present day. The critical allegation that the book of Esther was written in order to justify the observance of Purim is as unreasonable as an allegation would be that attempted to explain the Declaration of Independence as having been written to justify the American celebration of the Fourth of July. Keil declared that, "The feast of Purim must have been founded upon an historical event ... any other notion is opposed to common sense."[1]

---

[1] CFK, Vol 3c, p. 305.

Authorship. The author is unknown. However, it is evident that he was a contemporary of the events related, one who had access to and personal contact with the principal characters in the book, and who was evidently an eyewitness of the whole pageantry of the Persian court. He may have been a close friend of Mordecai, or even a relative.

Date. "The events narrated in Esther occurred between the years 483-473 BC,"[2] during the reign of Ahashuerus, the Xerxes of secular history. The date when Esther was written could not have been any later than the lifetime of the author who was contemporary with the events narrated. Rawlinson accepted a date near 450-440 BC. [4]

[3] Cook placed the date between 444-434 BC. [4]

Purpose. The purpose of Esther, as stated by Cook, was, "Simply to give an account of the circumstances under which the Feast of Purim was instituted."[5]

The Names in Esther. This is of special interest. Ahashaerus the king is certainly the Xerxes of Greek history by Herodotus. "The name in our version *Ahasherus* is a Hebrew adaptation of the Persian word for that king, *Khshayarsha,* which the Greeks turned into *Xerxes.*"[6] Now Herodotus also changed the name of

[2] WYC, p. 448.
[3] PC, Vol. 7c, *Esther,* p. iv.
[4] FCC, *Esther,* p. 487.
[5] Ibid.
[6] PC, op. cit., p. iii.

Xerxes' queen from *Vashti* (as in our version) to
Amestris;[7] but the variation in these names in
Herodotus, as compared with the Bible, is no basis
whatever for doubting the truth of the biblical record.
"We concluded that Vashti is Amestri."[8]

Unity. That the book of Esther comes from the
pen of a single author is virtually certain. Some critics,
having been checkmated in other customary avenues of
attack on Bible books, attempt to make the last section
(9:20- 10:3) a later additon; but, "Their arguments are
not persuasive ... it is not true that the mention of Purim
is confined to this section, for it is anticipated in 3:7;
and indeed the story seems to have been written
expressly for the purpose of commending the
observance of Purim.   Such unity of purpose
presupposes one author."[9]

The MT Superior to All Others. There are many
manuscripts of Esther; and the LXX has much material
connected with the narrative; and a whole section of the
Apocrypha has a lot more material on Esther; but
absolutely none of these is of any value in shedding light
on what is written in the Bible. As Joyce G. Baldwin
wrote concerning all these additions to the Book of
Esther, "At the end of a very detailed consideration of
all the early texts and versions, L. D. Paton concluded
that the Massoretic text upon which our English version
is based is the purest form of the text that has come

---

7 NLBC, p. 547.
8 Ibid.
9 NBCR, p. 412.

down to us."[10]

Meaning of the Name _Purim_. "This name is one of the pledges that this book is based upon history. The origin of this name can be explained in no other way than is done in this book, viz., by the circumstances that lots were cast on the fate of the Jews by a Persian official."[11] From this we know that the Feast of Purim is not an adaptation of some previous pagan holiday, as some critics would like to believe, but that it is an authentic celebration of an ancient Providential Deliverance of the Jewish Race from extermination by powerful ememies.

Haman the Agagite. This book sheds light on God's order to King Saul regarding the extermination of the Amalekites, particularly king Agag, an order that Saul foolishly violated. Here in Esther, generations later, we find one of the descendants of that same Agag, namely, Haman, armed with all-powerful authority, determined to exterminate the entire Jewish race. What a remarkable vindication is this for the wisdom and justice of God's orders to Saul! If Saul had obeyed God, it would have saved innumerable lives that were lost in the fiasco reported here.

No Confirmation Needed. One more word needs to be said about the historical accuracy, dependability, and authenticity of the book of Esther. It is freely admitted that, "Although archaeology as yet cannot prove the actual historicity of this book (Esther), it

---

[10] Ibid.

[11] CFK, p. 305.

supplies ample illustrative evidence pointing to its genuineness."[12] It is this writer's conviction that "no proof" is needed. The Bible is its own verification. The findings of archaeology, although interesting enough, are not needed to confirm the Bible. It is a sinful fallacy indeed which supposes that some pagan inscription digged up from the mud of Mesopotamia is needed to *confirm* what is written in the Bible. There are entirely too many errors inscribed upon granite memorials of our own times to allow any notion that such archaeological findings are infallibly accurate. The marble monument at the foot of Wall Street, New York City, honors Robert Fulton as Inventor of the Steamboat; but that is a patent falsehood, contradicted by an even more elaborate monument erected by the Congress of the United States in Berea, Ky.[13]

Hatred of Biblical Books. The undying hatred of the Bible is evident in many of the attacks upon it. All other avenues of attack having been closed, critical enemies shout that the things in Esther are "unreasonable," "why should Vashti have refused"? "would any king have authorized the destruction of an entire race of his subjects"? "what a fool Haman would have been to publish his intention of slaughtering the Jews almost a whole year before the day set for their extermination"? etc. etc. In such critical allegations, we

---

[12] AAOT, pl. 308.

[13] This monument rightfully honors John Fitch as the inventor
    of the steamboat, exhibiting a letter from Robert Fulton
    honoring Fitch as the inventor.

may read, as Keil expressed it, "Only the unsupprted decisions of subjectivistic antipathy to the contents of Esther" (and of the whole Bible)."[14]

Unreasonable Behavior in Esther. Yes, there are indeed many things in Esther that strike one as fundamentally opposed to ordinary intelligence. Haman's eagerness to destroy all the Jews on earth because only one of them offended him, Vashti's refusal of her husband's request, the king's acceptance of his minister's idea of proper punishment, the king's allowing Haman to have his way regarding the Jews, Esther's going unbidden into the king's presence ---these and many other things in Esther do not fall into the category of what ordinary people with ordinary intelligence would have done.

Xerxes as Revealed by Herodotus. Xerxes and the other evil characters revealed in Esther were fully capable of doing everything that is attributed to them therein.   "Greek and Roman historians tell us that Xerxes was a luxurious, voluptuous, and extremely cruel tyrant. After his whole army of 1,040,000 men had been entertained on their march to Greece, and after an enormous sum had been contributed to help defray the cost of that expedition, by Pythius the rich Lydian, Xerxes was so enraged by a request of Pythius whose five sons were in Xerxes' army, that the eldest be released to aid the comfort of Pythius' declining years; after all that, Xerxes was so enraged by the request that he order Pythius' oldest son to be cut in two, and made

---

[14] CFK, op. cit., p. 312.

his whole army to pass between the pieces."[15] "He even beheaded the men who had built the famous bridge of boats across the Hellespont, because a storm had destroyed it; and he commanded the sea to be scourged, and to be chained by sinking fetters in it! Just imagine old Xerxes whipping the ocean! He was a debauchee who, after his return from Greece, sought to drive away his vexation at his shameful defeat by revelling in the sensual pleasures of his harem."[16] In the light of all this, is there anything unbelievable about what is related in Esther?

"The days of Xerxes (Ahashuerus) are so far removed from our times that, it is easy for objections to be raised regarding the book of Esther's historicity, based upon a subjective assessment of its credibility rather than upon any knowledge of Persian affairs in the fifth century BC."[17] The quotations from Herodotus, just cited, make such a subjective judgment ridiculous.

Esther. This book is quite properly named after her. There was no hero, male or female, in the history of Israel, save only the Messiah, who was entitled to any greater honor. "The name is Persian, meaning *star*; here Hebrew names was Hadassah meaning *myrtle* (2:7)."[18] "Esther became queen in 478 BC, and five years later in 473 BC she saved the Jews from massacre; she came upon the scene forty years

---

[15] Herodotus, as quoted by Keil, p. 306,7
[16] Herodotus, as quoted by Keil, p. 307.
[17] NBCR, p. 412.
[18] WYC, p. 447.

before the Temple was rebuilt and thirty years before
the wall was finished. Her influence was felt for
generations. The work of both Ezra and Nehemiah
benefitted from her influence. The attitude of
Artaxerxes I, who succeeded Xerxes was doubtless
influenced by Esther. Had it not been for Esther,
Jerusalem might never have been rebuilt."[19]

"If the Hebrew nation had been wiped out five
hundred years before Christ came, what a tragic
difference that might have made in the history of
mankind ---no Hebrew nation, no Messiah, a lost
world! The victory of Satan would have been total.
This beautiful Jewish girl of the long ago, though she
herself might not have known it, played a key role in
paving the way for the Savior of mankind to come into
the world."[20]

The Language and Vocabulary. Everything about
Esther is Persian; the book has no evidences whatever
of the Greek period, making it absolutley necessary to
date it in the Persian period.

Many other things might be written in an
introduction, but these are sufficient to show the validity
of our trust in the Holy Bible; and we shall now proceed
to enjoy this marvelous story of how God saved his
people from wholesale destruction.

xxx

[19] HHH, p. 222.
[20] Ibid.

CHAPTER 1
Half-drunken Xerxes Deposes his Queen Vashti (Amestris)

Xerxes Makes Preparations to Invade Greece

Verses 1-8, Now it came to pass in the days of Ahashuerus (this is Ahashuerus who reigned from India even unto Ethiopia, over a hundred and twenty and seven provinces), 2 that in those days when the king Ahashuerus sat on the throne of his kingdom, which was in Shushan the palace, 3 in the third year of his reign, he made a feast unto all his princes and his servants; the power of Persia and of Media, the nobles and princes of the provinces, being before him; 4 when he showed the riches of his glorious kingdom and the honor of his exellent majesty many days, even a hundred and fourscore days. 5 And when these days were fulfilled, the king made a feast unto all the people that were present in Shushan the palace, both great and small, seven days, in the court of the garden of the king's palace. 6 There were hangings of white cloth, of green, and of blue, fastened with cords of fine linen and purple to silver rings and pillars of marble; the couches were of gold and silver, upon a pavement of red, and white, and yellow, and black marble. 7 And they gave them drink in vessels of gold (the vessels being diverse one from another), and royal wine in abundance, according to the bounty of the king. 8 And the drinking was according to the law; none could compel: for so the king had appointed to all the officers of his house, that they should do according to every man's pleasure.

Although not apparent in our text, the very first

words in the MT (the Hebrew) are "and it came to pass," which is made the occasion by Duff to declare that, "The book of Esther is a truncated narrative";[1] but Keil pointed out that no such conclusion is justified.[2] Many of the biblical books begin with the word *and,* indicating their connection with the rest of the canonical books of the Bible. "Joshua, Judges, Ruth, First Samuel, Second Samuel, Ezekiel, and Jonah all begin with the word *and.*"[3]

What is revealed here is a six-months interval of intense preparations by Xerxes for the invasion of Greece. It was terminated by a big banquet that lasted a week. During this period all of the mighty princes of his extensive dominion were summoned to appear, probably in successive assignments, to be entertained and to see the king's exhibition of his power and riches, and also, most likely, to receive his assignment to them regarding the troops each would supply for that immense army which he gathered together for the invasion. Our text does not elaborate this; but we learn much about it from Herodotus

This is Ahasuerus that reigned, etc. (v. 1). In the time of these events, there were no less than three great men called Ahasuerus; the prophet Daniel mentioned one of them, but he was not a king; and there was another Ahasuerus (also a king, Xerxes II) mentioned by Ezra (4:6). "Here the author of Esther, who probably

---

[1] ASP, p. 336.

[2] CFK, Vol. 3, p. 319.

[3] NLBC, p. 551,

knew of the others, distinguished this Ahashuerus from the one named in Daniel as 'the Ahashuerus who reigns,' and from the king mentioned in Ezra by the enormous size of his dominion."[4]

Who reigned from India ... to Ethiopia (v. 1). "A foundation tablet has been recovered from Xerxes' palace at Persepolis which lists both India and Ethiopia as provinces of Xerxes' realm. Also Herodotus mentioned that both the Ethiopians and the Indians paid tribute to Xerxes."[5]

One Hundred twenty and seven provinces (v. 1). We learned from Ezra and Nehemiah that there were 27 satrapies in the Perisan empire; but these divisions were different. "The satrapies were taxation districts; but these provinces were racial or national units in the vast empire."[6]

In those days when Ahashuerus sat on his throne (v. 2). It is strange that Persian kings almost constantly sat on their throne. "Herodotus wrote that Xerxes watched the battle of Thermopylae (480 BC.) seated on a throne! And Plutarch wrote the same thing regarding the battle of Salamis, which came that same year."[7]

Upon his throne which was in Shushan the palace (v. 2). There were four capitals of Persia; and the king, at times, reigned in each of them. These were,

---

[4] PC, Vol. 7c, p. 1.
[5] NLBC, p. 551.
[6] NBCR, p. 415.
[7] CFK, op. cit., p. 321.

"Shushan, Babylon, Ecbatana, and Persepolis."[8]

In the third year of his reign (v. 3). As Xerxes came to his throne in the year 486 BC, this would have been 483, BC.[9]

The magnificent decorations, the luxurious surroundings and all the glory of the Persian palace are beautifully described in these verses. It is particularly interesting that drinking vessels of gold, each one of a different design, were features of that concluding banquet.

And the drinking was according to the law (v. 8). It is amusing to us that some of the scholars declare that there was not any such law regarding drinking; but the text flatly says there was, and furthermore, it relates what the law was, i.e., *"They should do according to every man's desire" (v. 8).* This was the law, tailor-made for that occasion by the king himself! We appreciate Keil's comment that, "While this law granted permission for any one to drink as *little* as he desired, it also allowed every one to drink as *much* as he desired! Drunkenness was almost a universal sin among the Gentiles. And rulers, especially, indulged in it. Even Alexander the Great drank himself to death. This great banquet given by Xerxes was by no means a beautiful party. It was an unqualified disaster.

---

8 NLBC, p. 551.
9 NBCR, p. 395.

Vashti Refuses to Honor The King's Call
to Display Her Beauty

Verses 9-12, Also Vashti the queen made a feast for the women in the royal house which belonged to king Ahashuerus. 10 On the seventh day, when the heart of the king was merry with wine, he commanded Mehuman, Biztha, Harbona, Bigtha, and Abagthar, Zethur, and Carcas, the seven chamberlains that ministered in the presence of Ahashuerus the king, 11 to bring Vashti the queen before the king with the crown royal, to show the peoples and the princes her beauty; for she was fair to look on. 12 But the queen Vashti refused to come at the king's commandment by the chamberlains: therefore was the king very wroth, and his anger burned in him.

When the heart of the king was merry with wine (v. 10). This appears to this writer as a euphemism with the meaning that the king was drunk. That this is true appears from the fact of the king's unreasonable request.

The seven chamberlains that ministered before the king (v. 10). The fact of these men having access to the king's harem indicates that all of them were eunuchs. Scholars usually suggest that this request of the king was reasonable; but this writer cannot believe that it was reasonable, else Vashti, knowing the outrageous nature of the king's ungovernable temper, would not have disobeyed him. She most certainly knew that death itself might be the penalty of her refusal.

But the queen refused to come (v. 12). Scholars have suggested a number of possible reasons why Vashti would not obey the king; but in all likelihood, Vashti was pregnant with Artaxerxes I. John Bendor-Samuel writes that, "This banquet probably took place just before the birth of Artaxerxes";[10] and her natural modesty rebelled against making a display of herself before the king and his well drunken banqueteers.

Vashti the Queen is Deposed and Dispossessed

What a heartless, evil wretch was Xerxes! "His design was to present Vashti unveiled before a multitude of semi-drunken revellers ... Xerxes' behavior here was a cruel outrage upon one whom he, above all men, was bound to respect and protect."[11] In a few days she would give birth to his son who would succeed him on the throne; but this half drunken old fool had no honor or respect for anyone on earth except himself.

Some small measure of appreciation for Xerxes may be found in the fact that he did not at once order the death and dismemberment of Vashti, as he would later do for the oldest son of Pythius; for he restraind his anger sufficiently that he took the matter up with his councillors.

Verses 13-22, Then the king said to the wise men, who knew the times (for so was the king's manner toward

---

[10] NLBC,, p. 551
[11] PC. op. cit., p.15.

all that knew law and judgment; 14 and next unto him were Carshena, Shethar, Admatha, Tarshish, Meshes, Marsena, and Memucan, the seven princes of Persia and Media, who saw the king's face, and sat first in the kingdom), 15 What shall we do unto the queen Vashti, according to law, because she hath not done the bidding of the king Ahashuerus by the chamberlains? 16 And Memucan answered before the king and the princes, Vashti the queen hath not done wrong to the king only, but also to all the princes, and to all the peoples that are in all the provinces of the king Ahashuerus. 17 For this deed of the queen will come abroad unto all women, to make their husbands contemptible in their eyes, when it shall be reported, The king Ahashuerus commanded Vashti the queen to be brought in before him, but she came not. 18 And this day will the princesses of Persia and Media who have heard of the deed of the queen say the like to all the king's princes. So will there arise much contempt and wrath. 19 If it please the king, let there go forth a royal commandment from him, and let it be written among the laws of the Persians and the Medes, that it be not altered, that Vashti come no more before the king Ahashuerus; and let the king give her royal estate unto another that is better than she. 20 And when the king's decree which he shall make shall be published throughout all his kingdom (for it is great), all the wives shall give to their husbands honor, both to great and small. 21 And the saying pleased the king and the princes; and the king did according to the word of Memucan: 22 for he sent letters into all the king's provinces, into every province according to the writing thereof, and to every people after their language, that every *man should bear rule in his own house, and should speak according to the language of his people.*

Nothing could demonstrate more forcefully the low estate of women in the ancient world than the brutal facts of this outrage against Vashti. In all the societies of mankind where women are unprotected by the teachings of the Son of God, women have invariably been reduced to the status so clearly visible in this chapter. Only in Jesus Christ are women elevated to the respected and honored status they deserve; and the great pity of our generation is that women are being wooed and persuaded by political promises of all kinds to give up their worship of the Christ. They are promised "equality" with men; but it is a specious 'equality,' like that which the women of Russsia got when they gave up even an imperfect Christianity for communism. It turned out to be "equality" to carry the bricks, sweep the streets, and work till they dropped dead in the fields. Let the women of America beware!

The seven princes of Persia and Media (v. 14). In the book of Daniel, one finds the expression, "The law of the Medes and the Persians"; but a little later in this chapter, it reads, "The law of the Persians and the Medes." Why the difference? In Daniel's day, the king was a Mede (Darius); so the Medes were mentioned first; but now Xerxes, a Persian, was the ruler; so the Persians came first!. The Medes and the Persians were the two principal races that formed the Medo-Persian Empire; but it was never two empires, only one.

It is of interest that Xerxes' letter to all the 127

ethnic groups in his empire was addressed to each one
of the groups in their native language. Also, there was
added that provision that every man should use only his
native language in his own house, which certainly
presented a problem in homes where there were mixed
marriages with the races. Such a law was
unenforceable. But as Keil noted, "Xerxes was the
author of many strange facts besides this."[12]

Halley and others held the opinion that one of
the last actions of Xerxes before he left on that four-
year campaign against Greece was the deposition of
Vashti, and that, "He did not marry Esther until four
years later in 478 BC, after he returned from the
Grecian campaign."[13] This accounts for the four year
gap between this chapter and the next one. This
conclusion is fully supported by the writings of
Herodotus.

xxx

---

[12] CFK, op. cit., p. 332.
[13] HHH, p. 222.

CHAPTER 2
Esther Becomes Queen Instead of Vashti

This chapter takes us into the seraglio of Xerxes, an ancient Persian ruler, most certainly one of the vilest cesspools of immorality, selfishness, greed, hatred, wickedness, lust and shame that existed in the ancient pagan world. In order to protect and preserve the Chosen People, God worked his will in the lives of the evil men who controlled and directed the affairs related in this chapter. It is somewhat distressing to this writer that there is almost no word of condemnation in the commentaries we have consulted regarding this festering Satanic ulcer on the body of the human race, called Shushan the palace. Yes, we know that Solomon did it also; but it was still sinful, a rebellion against God that cried to high heaven for vengeance.

Verse 16 tells us that Esther became queen in Xerxes' seventh year; and, as the great feast mentioned in the previous chapter was in his third year (1:3), we must understand a time lapse of some four years in between chapters 1 and 2. During this period, Xerxes fought the Grecian war.

Although the military expedition against Greece was principally concluded in the years 481-479 BC,[1] the greater portion of the entire four-years gap between the punishment of Vashti and the coronation of Esther were consumed by Xerxes' preparations for the

---

[1] WYC, p. 448

campaign, and by his efforts to cover some of his losses afterwards.

That Grecian campaign was an unqualified disaster for Xerxes. (1) At Thermopylae, a handful of Spartans under Leonidas checked and delayed his mighty army; and (2) later that same year Xerxes' navy of 1,400 ships was unable to overcome 380 ships of the Greeks in the Battle of Salamis. (3) In 479 BC, at Plataea, "The bulk of the Persian army was destroyed. Meanwhile the Greek fleet commanded by the king of Sparta drove the Persian fleet to the Asian mainland at Mycale. Leotychidas, the Spartan king, landed his sailors and marines farther up the coast, destroyed the Persian fleet and inflicted heavy casualties on a supporting army. The Ionians and the Aeolians at once rose in revolt, thus ending the Persian invasion of Greece in the final disaster for Persia."[2]

After Xerxes' return to Shushan, Herodotus tells us that he consoled himself over his shameful defeats by sensual indulgences with his harem.

The Search for a Replacement for Vashti

Verses 1-4, After these things, when the wrath of king Ahashuerus was pacified, he remembered Vashti, and what she had done, and what was decreed against her. 2 Then said the king's servants that ministered unto him, Let there be fair young virgins sought for the king: 3 and let the king appoint officers in all the provinces of his

---

[2] EnBr, Vol. 10, p. 765.

*kingdom, that they may gather together all the fair young
virgins unto Shushan the palace, unto the house of the
women, unto the custody of Hegai the king's chamberlain,
keeper of the women; and let their things for purification be
given them; 4 and let the maiden that pleases the king be
queen instead of Vashti.*

After these things ... he remembered Vashti. This
means after the Grecian campaign, and after Xerxes
had begun to seek a more normal pattern of living.
Anderson viewed the last clause here as, "A subtle
suggestion that the king desired to reinstate Vashti, but
he had signed an irrevocable decree against her."[3] This
is probably true, because his son, and heir, Artaxerxes I,
born during the Grecian campaign, or just prior to it,
was now, no doubt a charming child of three or four
years of age. The king found himself a victim of his own
drunken and extravagant decree against Vashti; but
there was nothing he could do about it.

Of course, he might have tried to reinstate
Vashti; but the king's advisors, in such a development,
might easily have fallen under the severe wrath and
punishment inflicted upon them by a restored Vashti;
therefore, they proposed this shameful rape of all the
pretty girls in Persia as a prerequisite for the choice of
Vashti's successor. Evil beast that he was, Xerxes liked
the idea, "and the king did so"!

And the king did so (v. 4). This means that they
searched throughout the vast domain of the Persian

---

[3] IB, Vol. 3, p. 839.

empire, and brought "all the fair young virgins to Shushan" (v. 3). "What unspeakable horror this must have caused among all the beautiful young women of Persia! They were forcibly taken from their homes, turned over to a eunuch in the house of the women, and secluded for life among the wretched company of the king's concubines."[4] The king would gratify his lust upon these girls, one each night, as they came to his bed. And then what happened? They were returned to the harem, henceforth and forever mere chattels, his property, having no more rights than one of the king's dogs.

Anderson wrote that, "Here the author ignored the Persian custom that stipulated that the king could marry only a Persian,"[5] insinuating that this account is founded, not on fact, but upon legend and folklore; but such opinions are in error, reflecting only anti-biblical bias. Yes, Herodotus states that there was such a custom; but it was not the sacred author of Esther who ignored it; it was the wicked Xerxes and his evil advisers. Xerxes' own father had married a foreigner; and any notion that Xerxes would have honored such a custom is ridiculous.

Before leaving this paragraph, it should be noted that the young women thus conscripted as subjects of the king's lust had no choice whatever in the matter. They were ordered into the king's harem, from which they would never be able to escape.

---

4 NBCR, p. 415,
5 IB, Vol. 3, p. 839.

The Introduction of Mordecai and Esther

Verses 5-7, There was a certain Jew in Shushan the palace whose name was Mordecai the son of Jair, the son of Shimei, the son of Kish, a Benjamite, 6 who had been carried away from Jerusalem with the captives that had been carried away with Jeconiah king of Judah, whom Nebuchadnezzar the king of Babylon had carried away. 7 And he brought up Hadassah, that is Esther, his uncle's daughter, for she had neither father nor mother, and the maiden was fair and beautiful; and when her father and mother were dead, Mordecai took her for his own daughter.

Mordecai (v. 5). This name is said to be derived from the pagan god Marduk, meaning "dedicated to Mars."[6]

Carried away from Jerusalem (by) Nebuchadnezzar (v. 6). That deportation of Jews was more than a century prior to the events of this chapter; and the meaning appears to be that Mordecai's parents or grandparents were the ones carried away. Mordecai's name suggests that he was born in Babylon, although the Babylonians generally changed the names of people whom they employed, as in the case of Daniel and others.

These three verses serve the purpose of introducing the persons around whom the rest of the narrative is woven.

---

[6] AMOB, p. 253.

Esther Taken Into the House of the King's Women

Verses 8-11, So it came to pass when the king's commandment and his decree was heard, and when many maidens were gathered unto Shushan the palace, to the custody of Hegai, that Esther was taken into the king's house, to the custody of Hegai, keeper of the women. 9 And the maiden pleased him, and she obtained kindness of him; and he speedily gave her the things for her purification, with her portions, and the seven maidens who were meet to be given her out of the king's house: and he removed her and her maidens to the best place of the house of the women. 10 And Esther had not made known her people nor her kindred; for Mordecai and charged her that she should not make it known. 11 And Mordecai walked every day before the court of the women's house, to know how Esther did, and what would become of her.

The key development here was Hegai's partiality to Esther. The words *speedily* and *the best place* (v. 9) show that Hegai probably shortened the one year stay in the house of women for Esther and that he moved her as quickly as possible into the rotation for the king's bed.

Esther's Turn to Go in to the King

Verses 12-15, Now when the turn of every maiden was come to go into king Ashuerus, after it had been done to her according to the law for the women twelve months (for so were the days of their purifications accomplished, to wit, six months with oil of myrrh, and six months with sweet odors and with the things for the purifying of women), 13 then in this wise came the maiden unto the king. Whatsoever she desired was given her to go with her out of the house of the women unto the king's house. 14 In the evening she went, and on the morrow she returned into the second house of the women, to the custody of Shaashgaz, the king's chamberlain who kept the concubines: she came in unto the king no more, except the king delighted in her, and she were called by name. 15 Now when the turn of Esther the daughter of Abihail the uncle of Mordecai, who had taken her for his daughter, was come to go in unto the king, she required nothing but what Hagai the king's chamberlain, the keeper of the women, appointed. And Esther obtained favor in the sight of all them that looked upon her.

In the evening she went; and on the morrow she returned (v. 14). Where are there any sadder words than these? One frightful night in the bed with Ahashuerus, and the next morning relegated to the status of a concubine, never more to see him, unless called by name; and the odds are that he did not even remember the names of half of them. The text states that there were *many* of these women.

Esther Becomes Queen of Persia

Verses 16-18, So Esther was taken unto king Ahashuerus into his house royal in the tenth month, which is the month Tebeth, in the seventh year of his reign. 17

And the king loved Esther above all the women, and she obtained favor and kindness in his sight more than all the virgins; so that he set the royal crown upon her head, and made her queen instead of Vashti. 18 Then the king made a great feast unto all his princes and his servants, even Esther's feast; and he made a release to the provinces, and gave gifts, according to the bounty of the king.

Only Almighty God could have brought to pass such a thing as this. "This humble Jewish maiden, an orphan, dependent for her living upon the charity of her cousin Mordecai ---this girl became the first woman in all Persia, the wife of the most powerful living monarch on earth, the queen of an empire comprised of more than half the world of that time."[7]

It was always thus when God in his infinite wisdom laid his plans to preserve the Chosen People from destruction. He sent Joseph to be seated next to the throne of Egypt; he brought up Moses in the palace of Pharaoh and made him an heir to the throne; in the land of their captivity, he made Daniel the third ruler in the kingdom; and now, when Satan would again make a move to destroy Israel, God placed Esther in a strategic position to prevent it; and it happened again with both Ezra and Nehemiah who had earned and received the respect of Artaxerxes; nor can we rule out the very great probability that it was the influence of Esther that, in part at least, had resulted in the honors that came to them.

---

[7] PC, Vol. 3c, p. 39.

He made a release to the provinces (v. 18). It is not known exactly what this was, but it may have been merely a holiday.

Mordecai Saves the King From Assassination

Verses 19-23, And when the virgins were gathered together the second time, then Mordecai was sitting in the king's gate. 20 Esther had not yet made known her kindred nor her people; as Mordecai had charged her: for Esther did the commandment of Mordecai, like as when she was brought up with him. 21 In those days, while Mordecai was sitting in the king's gate, two of the king's chamberlains, Bigthan and Teresh, of those that kept the threshold, were wroth, and sought to lay hands on the king Ahashuerus. 22 And the thing became known to Mordecai, who showed it unto Esther the queen; and Esther told the king thereof in Mordecai's name. 23 And when inquisition was made of the matter, and it was found to be so, they were both hanged on a tree: and it was written in the book of the chronicles before the king.

And when the virgins were gathered together the second time (v. 19). This indicates the time when Mordecai discovered that plot against Ahashuerus. There were two gatherings of virgins for the king, the one mentioned in v. 8, and a second one after that. "It was at that second collection of virgins that Mordecai had the good fortune to save the king's life."[8]

---

[8] FCC, *Esther*, p. 494.

It is incorrect to view any of these amazing events as mere coincidences. The hand of God is evident in every one of them. Esther's obedience of Mordecai reflects the Fifth Commandment of the Decalogue; and Mordecai's saving the life of the king reflected the Sixth Commandment. It would have been quite easy to agree with Bigthan and Teresh, for Ahashuerus certainly deserved to be murdered, a fate that he indeed suffered about thirteen years later. Who would have wanted to kill him? Any one of the fathers of those countless women the king had forced to leave their families might have killed the king if they had a chance.

Esther's continuing to conceal her identity as a Jewess was vital to what happened. If Haman had known she was Jewish, he could never have decided to kill all the Jews. Her making the plot known in Mordecai's name enrolled Mordecai's name in the chronicles of the king; and then the king forgot all about it ---all of these things were absolutely vital for God's saving his people from the wrath of Haman; and not one of them was a mere coincidence. God was at work in history.

xxx

*Ashamed to Kill Just One Man, Haman Decided to
Exterminate the Whole Israel of God*

Verses 1-6, *After these things did king Ahashuerus
promote Haman the son of Hammedatha the Agagite, and
advanced him, and set his seat above all the princes that
were with him. 2 And all the king's servants that were in
the king's gate, bowed down, and did reverence to Haman;
for the king had so commanded concerning him. But
Mordecai bowed not down, nor did him reverence. 3 Then
the king's servants, that were in the king's gate, said unto
Mordecai, Why transgressest thou the king's
commandment? 4 Now it came to pass, when they spake
daily unto him, and he hearkened not unto them, that they
told Haman, to see whether Mordecai's matters would
stand: for he had told them that he was a Jew. 5 And when
Haman saw that Mordecai bowed not down, nor did him
reverence, then was Haman full of wrath. 6 But he thought
scorn to lay hands on Mordecai alone; for they had made
known to him the people of Mordecai: wherefore Haman
sought to destroy all the Jews that were throughout the
whole kingdom of Ahashuerus, even the people of
Mordecai.*

    They told Haman (v. 4). Tale bearers in all
generations have deserved the contempt in which they
are generally held. These tale bearers were the cause of
many thousands of deaths which ultimately resulted
from Haman's hatred. Haman might never have
noticed Mordecai's refusal to bow down, had it not been

for the gossips.

The thing that stands out in this paragraph is the egotistical pride of Haman. Only one man in a multitude did not bow down to him; and he was at once angry enough to kill a whole race of people. Haman would have launched his evil plan at once; but first there was the necessity to get the king's permission to do so.

Haman the Agagite (v. 1). See our introduction to Esther for comment on this. This name of a remote ancestor of Haman should not be viewed as, "A mere epithet to indicate contempt and abhorrence."[1] Haman was indeed a descendant of King Agag, an ancient enemy of Israel in the days of King Saul. The Jewish historian Josephus agreed with this.

The reason why Mordecai would not bow down to Haman was probably due to the fact that, "Haman was demanding not mere allegiance but worship; and Mordecai refused it on the grounds of the First Commandment. Israelites were expected to prostrate themselves before their kings."[2]

Haman Receives the King's Permission to Destroy Israel

Verses 7-11, In the first month, which is the month Nisan, in the twelfth year of king Ahashuerus, they cast Pur, that is, the lot, from day to day, and from month to month, to the twelfth month, which is the month Adar. 8

[1] JRD, p. 286.
[2] NBCR, p. 416.

And Haman said unto king Ahashuerus, There is a certain
people scattered abroad and dispersed among the peoples in
all the provinces of thy kingdom; and their laws are diverse
from the laws of every people; neither keep they the king's
laws: therefore it is not for the king's profit to suffer them.
9 If it please the king, let it be written that they be
destroyed: and I will pay ten thousand talents of silver into
the hands of those that have charge of the king's business,
to bring it into the king's treasuries. 10 And the king took
his ring from his hand, and gave it unto Haman the son of
Hammedatha the Agagite, the Jews' enemy. 11 And the
king said unto Haman, the silver is given thee, and the
people also, to do with them as seemeth good to thee.

Critical enemies of the Bible, having no other
grounds upon which they may deny or object to the text,
sometimes must fall back upon their subjective
imaginations that this or that biblical statement is
"unrealistic, unreasonable, or unlikely to have
occurred." One may find plenty of such subjective
objections to what is written here.

Some ask, "Would any king have given blanket
permission to anyone to destroy a considerable
percentage of the people in his whole kingdom"? The
answer to that is that, "Xerxes certainly did so." And
even that was not any more unreasonable or stupid than
some other actions of that evil king as reported by
Herododtus.

Others have pointed out that it was a terribly
foolish thing for Haman to have published a whole year
in advance his intention of exterminating the Jews.

Archaeology, however, has uncovered dramatic information on how this happened. "Haman's method for fixing the date for the destruction of the Jews has been revealed by excavations at Susa (Shushan) by M. Dieulafoy, who actually recovered one of those quadrangular prisms engraved with the numbers 1, 2, 5 and 6. The word *pur* is derived from the Persian *puru,* that is, *lot;* and it is now known that *'they cast Pur' (3:7)* means that *they cast lots.*"[3] This fully explains why almost a year elapsed between Haman's decision to massacre the Jews, which he published at once, and the date set for the execution of his ruthless plan.

Significantly, Haman was so sure of receiving the king's permission, that he actually cast lots for the day he would do it before mentioning the matter to the king. Also, that tremendous promise of ten thousand talents of silver, which was well over $10,000,000.00, which Haman promised to pay into the king's treasury, was also most likely based upon the presumption by Haman that the king would not accept it.

The Day Set; the Decree Signed; the Massacre Announced

Verses 12-15, Then were the king's scribes called, in the first month, on the thirteenth day of the month; and there was written according to all that Haman commanded unto the king's satraps, and to the governors that were over every province, and to the princes of every people, to every province according to the writing thereof, and to every

---

[3] AAOT, p. 309.

people after their language, in the name of king
Ahashuerus was it written, and it was sealed with the king's
ring. 13 And the letters were sent by posts, into all the
king's provinces, to destroy, to slay, and to cause to perish,
all Jews, both young and old, little children and women, in
one day, even upon the thirteenth day of the twelfth month,
which is the month Adar, and to take the spoil of them for
a prey. 14 A copy of the writing, that the decree should be
given out in every province, was published unto all the
peoples, that they should be ready against that day. 15 The
posts went forth in haste by the king's commandment, and
the decree was given out in Shushan the palace. And the
king and Haman sat down to drink; but the city of Shushan
was perplexed.

God's people never faced a more terribile threat
than this one. The egomaniac Haman had engineered
that which might easily have destroyed the entire race
of the Chosen People; but there was no way that God
would have allowed such a thing to happen; because all
of the glorious promises of Messiah to redeem men
from their sins were contingent upon the preservation of
the Israel of God until that Messiah was born in
Bethlehem. God had foreseen this threat. He had
foreseen it when king Saul was ordered to destroy the
Amalekites. Saul failed to do so; but God did not
abandon his people.

God used the drunken request of Xerxes to
degrade Vashti the queen; he elevated an orphan
Jewish girl to take her place; he planted the name of
Mordecai in the chronicles of the king; and he would

remind Xerxes of that fact at precisely the proper instant. Oh yes, for all of his power and hatred, Haman had undertaken to do that which was impossible.

And the king and Haman sat down to drink (v. 15). A little later in this narrative, we shall read of the execution of Haman by what amounted to his crucifixion; but, sad as a thing like that surely is, it should be remembered that Haman was the kind of man who could condemn unnumbered thousands, perhaps even as many as a million people, to murder by wholesale massacre, and then sit down to drink liquor and enjoy himself. The fate encountered by this servant of the devil was fully deserved.

xxx

CHAPTER 4
The Israel of God in Sackcloth, Ashes, and Tears

The last verse of the previous chapter mentioned that the city of Susa was perplexed. "Although the Jews certainly had enemies in Susa, the majority of the Persians were Zoroastrians, and were likely to sympathize with the Jews. There might also have been other national groups in Persia who would have been alarmed and apprehensive at the king's decision to slaughter all the Jews."[1] Some might have been fearful that their group might be next. It must have been a major shock to the Persian capital when the king's decree became known.

The Jews throughout the whole Persian empire at once exhibited their grief, alarm, mourning and fear, in much the same manner as did Mordecai.

Mordecai Learns All that Was Done

Verses 1-3, Now when Mordecai knew all that was done, Mordecai rent his clothes, and put on sackcloth with ashes, and went out into the midst of the city, and cried with a loud and a bitter cry; 2 and he came even before the king's gate; for none might enter the king's gate clothed with sackcloth. 3 And in every province, whithersoever the king's commandment and his decree came, there was great mourning among the Jews, and fasting, and weeping, and wailing; and many lay in sackcloth and ashes.

---

[1] PC, Vol 7c, p. 74.

This great mourning prevailed in every province of the vast empire, including Jerusalem and Judaea of course. Although the name of God is not mentioned in Esther, this outpouring of grief on the part of the Chosen People was nothing at all unless it was an appeal for God's intervention to save his people from their threatened destruction. The sackcloth and ashes were universally recognized as signs of extreme grief and distress. "Either sackcloth or ashes was a sign of deep mourning; but both together were indications of the most distressing grief possible."[2]

"All the Jews throughout Persia broke out into mourning, weeping, and lamentations, while many of them exhibited their mourning as did Mordecai."[3] Mordecai's purpose for such a visible demonstration of his mourning was to alert Esther that something was terribly wrong and to get the truth of the situation and its seriousness to Esther.

Esther the Queen Gets a Full Report From Mordecai

Verses 4-8,   And Esther's maidens and her chamberlains came and told it her; and the queen was exceedingly grieved; and she sent raiment to clothe Mordecai, and to take his sackcloth from off him; but he received it not. 5 Then called Esther for Hathach, one of the king's chamberlains, whom he had appointed, to attend upon her, and charged him to go to Mordecai, to know

---

[2] Ibid, p. 83.
[3] CFK, Vol 3c, p. 350.

what this was, and why it was. 6 So Hathach went forth to Mordecai in the broad place of the city, which was before the king's gate, 7 And Mordecai told him all that had happened to him, and the exact sum of the money, that Haman had promised to pay to the king's treasuries for the Jews, to destroy them. 8 Also he gave him the copy of the writing of the decree that was given out in Shushan to destroy them, and to show it unto Esther, and to declare it unto her, and to charge her that she should go in unto the king, to make supplication unto him, and to make request before him, for her people.

Esther sent raiment to clothe Mordecai ... but he received it not (v. 4). "Mordecai's refusal to accept the clothing was evidence to Esther that his actions were not caused by personal sorrow, but by an unusually dire public caalamity."[4]

The exact sum of money that Haman agreed to pay (v. 7). Throughout the book of Esther, it is evident that Mordecai had access to any information that he requested; and this mention of that ten thousand talents of silver Haman agreed to pay the king indicates, that regardless of the king's seeming refusal of it, that it became finally a binding part of the agreement. "The most natural interpretation of this is that the king's acceptance of the blood money was part of the transaction."[5]

The copy (v. 8). "*A copy* is the way this reads in

---

[4] IB, Vol. 3, p. 853.

[5] Ibid.

the Hebrew, which is correct. Mordecai had made a copy in order to send it to Esther."[6]

To declare it unto her (v. 8). This means that Hathach was probably intended to read it to the queen; she might not have known the Persian language.

Charge her ... to make request, for her people (v. 8). This means that Hathach, at least, and probably all of Esther's maidens and servants knew that she was a Jewess. Even if she had not told it to them, they would soon have known it through her concern for and interest in Mordecai. The king, however, probably did not learn of it till Esther told him.

Mordecai's Request of Esther Loaded With Danger

Verses 9-12, And Hathach came and told Esther the words of Mordecai. 10 Then Esther spake unto Hathach, and gave him a message unto Mordecai, saying 11 All the king's servants, and the people of the king's provinces, do know, that whosoever, whether man or woman, shall come unto the king in the inner court, who is not called, there is one law for him, that he be put to death, except those to whom the king shall hold out the golden sceptre, that he might live: but I have not been called to come in to the king these thirty days. 12 and they told to Moredecai Esther's words.

The golden sceptre (v. 11). "In all of the numerous representations of Persian kings (by sculptors

---

[6] PC, op. cit., p. 84.

and inscriptions recovered by archaeologists), the king
holds a long tapering staff (the sceptre of Esther)."[7]
Death was the penalty for any person who came
unbidden into the private area of a Persian king.

Esther did not by this reply refuse to accept
Mordecai's charge; she merely apprised him of the
extreme danger to herself in such a request. Esther was
also apprehensive that the king had not invited her into
his presence in a month, indicating that his love for her
had cooled, and that at that time the king might have
been sensually involved with someone else. There was
certainly no guarantee that the king would be pleased
by her coming uninvited into his presence.

Mordecai Charged Esther to Take the Risk; See the King

*Verses 13-17,   Then Mordecai bade them return
answer unto Esther, Think not with thyself that thou shalt
escape in the king's house, more than all Jews. 14 For if
thou altogether holdest thy peace at this time, then will
relief and deliverance arise to the Jews from another place,
but thou and thy father's house will perish: and who
knoweth whether thou art come to the kingdom for such a
time as this? 15 Then Esther bade them return answer
unto Mordecai, 16 Go gather together all the Jews that are
in Shushan, and fast ye for me, and neither eat nor drink
three days, night or day; I also and my maidens will fast in
like manner; and so will I go in unto the king, which is not*

---

[7] FCC, *Esther*, p. 496.

according to the law: and if I perish, I perish. 17 So
Mordecai went his way, and did according to all that
Esther had commanded him.

For sheer courage, for faithful acceptance of an
assignment fraught with mortal danger, for filial
obedience to her beloved foster-father Mordecai, for
her patriotic zeal and determination to rescue her
people from massacre, yes, and for evident trust in God,
and confidence in his blessing, Esther's action here
equals or surpasses anything ascribed in the literature of
all nations to the the greatest heroes of the human race.
What a marvel was Esther!

If thou holdest thy peace ... thou and thy father's
house will perish (v. 14). "Mordecai's argument here was
brutal in its clarity. Death awaited Esther whether or
not she went in to the king. She had nothing to lose. If
she failed, deliverance would come from some other
place; but maybe, who knows, maybe God had made
her queen just for the purpose of rescuing his people."[8]

Some scholars make a big thing out of there
being no mention of God's name in the book of Esther;
nevertheless a most vital and living faith in God is
evident in every line of it. Why all that fasting (and
prayer that always accompanied it)? Why? It was an
appeal for God's help.

Note here that Mordecai expected deliverance
from some other quarter, even if Esther failed. Why?
He believed in God's protection of the Chosen People.

---

[8] NBCR, p. 417.

"Esther was here invited by Mordecai to see that there was a divinely ordered pattern in her life, and that this was her moment of destiny."[9]

"Although Mordecai did not speak of God nor allude directly to his promises, he still grounded his hopes for the preservation of God's People upon the word and promises of God as revealed in the holy scriptures."[10] Yea, even more than his *hopes,* his utmost *confidence* in that preservation is revealed; note the words: "Relief and deliverance will arise from another place" (v. 14). This could be nothing other than faith and trust in God.

Fast ye for me ... I and my maidens will fast (v. 16). "Here we have more evidence of the religious element in Esther. Her fast could have had no object other than to obtain God's favor and protection in what she was resolved to do."[11] Speaking of Esther's fasting, Dummelow wrote that, "This was Esther's request for united prayer on her behalf."[12]

If I perish, I perish. (v. 26). Esther accepted her dreadfully dangerous mission, "In a spirit of resignation."[13]

xxx

---

[9] Ibid., p. 418.

[10] CFK, op. cit., p. 353.

[11] FCC, op. cit., p. 497.

[12] JRD, p. p. 287.

[13] Ibid.

CHAPTER 5
Haman Prepares to Execute Mordecai At Once

Verses 1-4, Now it came to pass on the third day, that Esther put on her royal apparel, and stood in the inner court of the king's house, over against the king's house: and the king sat upon his royal throne in the royal house, over against the entrance of the king's house. 2 And it was so, when the king saw Esther the queen standing in the court, that she obtained favor in his sight; and the king held out to Esther the golden sceptre that was in his hand. So Esther drew near, and touched the top of the sceptre. 3 Then said the king unto her, What wilt thou queen Esther? and what is thy request? it shall be given thee even to the half of my kingdom. 4 And Esther said, If it seem good unto the king, let the king and Haman come this day unto the banquet which I have prepared for him.

On the third day ... Esther put on her royal apparel. (v. 1). This was the third day of her fasting, during which she had not worn her royal apparel; perhaps she had even been clad in sackcloth.

The king sat on his royal throne (v. 1). D. J. Wiseman tells us of, "A limestone palace relief recovered from Susa (which) shows Darius I sitting upon an elaborate throne, holding a long sceptre (five or six feet in length) in his hand." [1]

Esther the queen standing in the court (v. 2). This was the moment of truth for Esther. If the king had merely refrained from noticing her appearance, she

---

[1] NBD, p. 294.

would have been dragged out of the court and slaughtered. One can only imagine her excitement and fear, as she stood there, facing either her death or the king's forgiveness of her intrusion, "Her thoughts wavering between hope and fear."[2]

Then said the king, What wilt thou, queen Esther? (v. 3). The king received her with honor. So far so good. The victory belonged to Esther and her people; but only *IF* (and what an *IF* that was!) Esther's request, when made known to the king, would actually be granted.

It shall be given thee, even to the half of my kingdom (v. 3). Such a kingly oath was hyperbole, of course; nevertheless it was a mighty promise indeed. See Mark 6:23 where such an oath resulted in the murder of John the baptist.

"The LXX has an addition to the scene described here. The king kissed his wife tenderly and restored her when she fainted through excitement."[3] In spite of the fact that the MT omits that, there is certainly nothing unreasonable in what was stated. "The king must have known that she desperately wanted something, or else she would not have risked death by her appearance before him."[4]

Let the king and Haman come this day to the banquet I have prepared (v. 4). This is a surprise to the reader, who naturally might have expected an

---

2 MH, Vol. 2, p. 1135.
3 ASP, p. 338.
4 NLBC, p. 555.

immediate petition from Esther for the salvation of the Jews. "But Esther was too cautious, too wary of the dangerous ground upon which she stood, to risk it all at once. She would wait; she would gain time; she would be sure that she had the king's affection before she makes that appeal upon which all depended."[5]

Here in the attitude of the king we find an example of of the great truth that, "The king's heart is in the hand of Jehovah as the watercourses" (Proverbs 21:1). The fate of ancient Israel turned upon the whim of this all-powerful monarch; but that response, in this situation, moved in perfect harmony with God's will.

Esther Delays Her Request Until A Second Banquet

Verses 5-8, Then the king said, Cause Haman to make haste, that it may be done as Esther hath said. So the king and Haman came to the banquet that Esther had prepared. 6 And the king said to Esther at the banquet of wine, What is thy petition, and it shall be granted thee: and what is thy request? and even to the half of the kingdom it shall be performed. 7 Then answered Esther and said, My petition and my request is: 8 If I have found favor in the sight of the king, and if it please the king to grant my petition, and to perform my request, let the king and Haman come to the banquet that I shall prepare for them, and I will do tomorrow as the king hath said.

Why was Esther so reluctant to make her request

---

5 PC, Vol 7c, p. 102.

known? Matthew Henry suggested that it might have been due, (1) "To her prudence as she sought more time to ingratiate herself with the king, (2) or that her heart failed her as she did not find sufficient courage to make it known without further time for prayer, or (3) that it was due to God's overruling providence which would use the intervening time prior to that second banquet to make the granting of Esther's petition absolutely certain."[6] It might very well have been a combination of all these things. "She wisely concluded that the king would understand that there was indeed a real petition in the background; which, of course, he did."[7]

Joyce Baldwin thought that Esther's intuition told her that the strategic moment had not yet come. "Although she could not have foreseen it, that second invitation played an essential part in bringing about her opportunity."[8] "This, of course, was providential. The intervening events, as recorded in chapter 6, provided the necessary background for her accusation, and the king's appropriate response to it."[9]

I will do tomorrow as the king hath said (v. 8). "This meant that, 'Tomorrow, I will reveal my request.'"[10]

---

[6] MH, op. cit., p. 1136.
[7] FCC, *Esther*, p. 497.
[8] NBCR, p. 418.
[9] WYC, p. 453.
[10] CFK, Vol. 3c, p. 356.

Haman Prepares For the Execution of Mordecai

Verses 9-14,   Then went Haman forth that day joyful and glad of heart; but when Haman saw Mordecai in the king's gate, that he stood not up, nor moved for him, he was filled with wrath against Mordecai. 10 Nevertheless Haman refrained himself, and went home; and he went and fetched his friends and Zeresh his wife. 11 And Haman recounted unto them the glory of his riches, and the multitude of his children, and all the things wherein the king had promoted him, and how he had advanced him above the princes and servants of the king. 12 Haman said moreover, Yea, Esther the queen did let no man come in with the king unto the banquet which she had prepared but myself; and tomorrow also am I invited by her together with the king. 13 Yet all this availeth me nothing, so long as I see Mordecai the Jew sitting at the king's gate. 14 Then said Zeresh his wife and all his friends unto him, Let a gallows be made fifty cubits high, and in the morning speak thou unto the king that Mordecai may be hanged thereon; then go thou in merrily with the king unto the banquet. And the thing pleased Haman, and he caused the gallows to be built.

The picture of Haman that emerges here is a good example of, "The deceived sinner, glorying in himself, hating God, and God's people."[11] "Although Esther's maids and other attendants knew of her Jewish race, Haman obviously did not; and that ignorance was

---

[11] WYC, p. 453.

his undoing."[12]

Some critics have found fault with the height of the gallows mentioned here, making it either imaginative, untrue, or ridiculous; but they overlook the key fact that the text does not say how high the gallows was. The text only states that Haman's advisers recommended a gallows that high. As a matter of fact, the Hebrew here is not 'gallows' at all, but 'tree.'[13] Crucifixion was the usual form of punishment in Persia. It was Zeresh, Haman's wife, who mentioned that the gallows should be fifty cubits high (some eighty or ninety feet); but that was nothing more than such a remark as that once heard in the old west that, "So and so should be hanged as high as heaven"!

Archibald Duff has an excellent explanation of how this was probably done. "This stake would have been some ten feet high, but set aloft upon a citadel (or the city wall), as in the case of Nicanor (2 Mac. 15:35)."[14]

It is hard to understand why the mother of ten sons would have desired to see any man crucified; and her unwomanly suggestion found its terrible retribution when she saw her husband and ten sons all crucified on the same day.[15]

"Although God's name was not mentioned in Esther, probably because the narrative might have been

---

[12] Ibod.
[13] ASV margin.
[14] ASP, p. 338.
[15] EOTB, p. 365.

copied from Persian court records; yet God's providential care of his children is nowhere more visible than here."[16]

The shameful character of Haman is featured in this verse. In spite of innumerable blessings and preferments above all others except the king, he was an egomaniac. "He was a coarse, undisciplined man, little better than a savage; and yet he was the chief minister of the greatest monarch in the world at that time. Worldly prominence and power are no proof of goodness or greatness of soul."[17]

"Haman's unhappiness because of Mordecai's refusal to honor him is true to the type; for it is lesser men who magnify and exaggerate slights; the great are able to overlook them."[18]

xxx

---

[16] HHH, p. 223.
[17] PC, op. cit., p. 110.
[18] NBCR, p. 418.

CHAPTER 6
Haman Gets the Shock of His Life;
The Higher They Are the Farther They Fall

There is hardly anything in the literature of mankind that presents a more dramatic contrast of the highest status and the lowest ever attained by a man on one single day than that which is here revealed in the person of Haman the great Prime Minister of the Persian Empire under Xerxes.

On the morning of that crucial day, he was at the very pinnacle of his power and glory, anticipating that within that day he would execute his most hated enemy, enjoy a banquet along with the king himself in the apartment of the queen of Persia, supposing, as his advisers had suggested, that he would hang Mordecai and then "go merrily with the king unto the banquet" (5:14).

However, during the previous night, God had been at work to frustrate the purpose of this evil genius of the devil, whose purpose was to destroy the Israel of God from the face of the earth. Before the sun went down, Haman would be hanged on his own gallows, his hated enemy Mordecai the Jew would be appointed in his place, and his posterity of ten sons would be destroyed. Zeresh would see a crucifixion all right, but not that of Mordecai.

Where in the literature of all nations is there anything else that compares with such a dramatic reversal of one's status as that which is here recorded?

Haman knew that Mordecai was a Jew, of

course; but considering it beneath his dignity to gratify his spirit of hatred upon a single individual, he had determined to destroy the whole Jewish race. Several things the fool did not know. He did not know that the foolish edict he had maneuvered Xerxes into sending forth would also result in the murder of the queen. He might have been able to bring that about, however, if he had refrained from his lust to murder Mordecai at once.

He did not know that Mordecai had saved the king's life, nor that the record was written in the chronicles of the king, nor that the king had encountered a sleepless night, nor that the king would be interested in rewarding Mordecai at the very moment when he would appear for the purpose of asking the king's permission to hang Mordecai. Speaking of surprises, where was there ever anything that matched the one that confronted Haman on his way to "go merrily with the king unto the banquet"?

The King's Decision to Reward Mordecai

Verses 1-3, On that night could not the king sleep; and he commanded to bring the book of records of the chronicles, and they were read before the king. 2 And it was found written that Mordecai had told of Bigthana and Teresh, two of the king's chamberlains of those that kept the threshold, who had sought to lay hands on the king Ahasuerus. 3 And the king said, What honor and dignity hath been bestowed on Mordecai for this? Then said the king's servants that ministered unto him, There is nothing done for him.

The king was resolved to reward Mordecai; but even before he had time to announce his decision, Haman had arrived for the purpose of asking the king's permission to hang Mordecai! What an inopportune moment for Haman's request!

The King Asked Haman's Suggestion on How to Reward the Man Whom the King Delighted to Honor

Verses 4-6, And the king said, Who is in the court? Now Haman was come into the outward court of the king's house, to speak unto the king to hang Mordecai on the gallows he had prepared for him. 5 And the king's servants said unto him, Behold, Haman standeth in the court. And the king said, Let him come in. 6 So Haman came in. And the king said unto him, What shall be done unto the man whom the king delighteth to honor?   Now   Haman said in his heart, To whom would the king delight to do honor more than to myself.

As a consequence of Haman's egotism in thinking that his suggestions would be applied to himself, he really went all out with what he proposed.

Haman's Advice on How to Honor the Man

Verses 7-9, And Haman said unto the king, For the man whom the king delighteth to honor, 8 let royal apparel be brought which the king useth to wear, and the horse that

the king rideth upon, and on the head of which a crown
royal is set: 9 and let the apparel and the horse be
delivered to the hand of one of the king's most noble
princes, that they may array the man therewith whom the
king delighteth to honor, and cause him to ride on
horseback through the street of the city, and proclaim
before him, Thus shall it be done to the man whom the king
delighteth to honor.

None of the writers we have consulted has dealt
with the possibility that Ahasuerus might have discerned
Haman's supposition that such honors would be done to
himself, and that he detected in that egocentric minister
the ambition to sieze the crown itself.   Certainly, a
man's riding on a horse with a royal crown on his head
was a very powerful symbol of royal authority.   Such
would most certainly have been an effective way of
reminding Haman that   he was not **the** **most noble**
prince, but **one of the most** noble princes.

On the head of which a crown royal is set (v. 8).
"The practice of setting crown-like head-dresses on
horses is attested by Assyrian reliefs."[1]

Only the king seems to have been ignorant of the
feud between Mordecai and Haman; certainly
everybody in Shushan must have been aware of it.
"Thus the king had no idea of the irony of the situation
in which he placed his favorite minister."[2] However, the
whole city of Shushan would have been astounded at

---

[1] NBCR, p. 418.
[2] Ibid.

this development.

Haman Ordered to Honor Mordecai the Jew

Verses 10-11, Then the king said to Haman, Make haste, and take the apparel and the horse, and do even so to Mordecai the Jew, that sitteth at the king's gate: let nothing fail of all that thou hast spoken. 11 Then took Haman the apparel and the horse, and arrayed Mordecai, and caused him to ride through the street of the city, and proclaimed before him, Thus shall it be done unto the man whom the king delighteth to honor.

The most significant words in this paragraph are the words. "Mordecai the Jew" on the lips of the king. There is no evidence whatever that the king knew that Mordecai was a Jew prior to that sleepless night and his hearing the reading of the record of the chronicles. With that information in hand, the king might also have become aware that Esther was a Jewess, her connection with Mordecai would have guaranteed that. Therefore, we believe that, contrary to what some writers have written, Ahasuerus had already made up his mind to put the hook in the nose of Haman, even prior to that second banquet. His order for Haman to honor Mordecai certainly did that very thing.

The Reaction of the People to Mordecai's Honor at the Hands of Haman

Verses 12-14, And Mordecai came again to the king's gate. But Haman hasted to his house, mourning and having his head covered. 13 And Haman recounted unto Zeresh his wife and all his friends everything that had befallen him. Then said his wise men and Zeresh his wife unto him, If Mordecai before whom that hast begun to fall, be of the seed of the Jews, thou shalt not prevail against him, but shalt surely fall before him. 14 While they were yet talking with him, came the king's chamberlains, and hasted to bring Haman unto the banquet that Esther had prepared.

Haman's mourning and covering his head indicated that he fully understood the horrible demotion he had already received at the hands of the king.   We attribute that demotion to the fact of the king's recognition of Haman's secret desire to take the crown.

Everyone in Susa knew the providential blessing of the Jews, beginning with Cyrus' edict for their return to Jerusalem; and the people, including Haman's 'wise men,' were aware of the hand of God in Jewish history.

Joyce Baldwin's remark that, "Most commentators, other than Jews, see all of the coincidences in this narrative as more characteristic of fiction than of real life,"[3] should be rejected as

---

[3] Ibid.

incorrect. *All Christians* see the hand of God in every line of this remarkable history.

The historical proof of everything written here is seen in the influence of Esther which prevailed in the Persian Empire throughout the times of Ezra and Nehemiah, whose work, in both instances was doubtless made possible by the influence of this great queen. In a very real sense, the book of Esther appears here, following Ezra and Nehemiah as an explanation of *how* their ministries came to be possible.

The historicity of Esther receives presumptive proof in the very fact of God's name being omitted. That means that no Jew could possibly have written it. Then who did write it? Someone who had access to Persian court records; and it is impossible to imagine any kind of motivation that could have led to writing a fictitious yarn with the cosmic dimensions of the book of Esther. It therefore is most certainly history, not fiction.

Verse 14 here relates that the chamberlains came to take Haman away to the banquet. "Haman went to Esther's second banquet like a sheep to the slaughter."[4]

xxx

---

[4] WYC, p. 454.

CHAPTER 7
Esther Makes Her Request Which the King Granted, and Identified Haman as Her Enemy, Whom the King Executed

This second banquet was the climax of the episode. Esther made her petition for her life and for the life of all her people, identified Haman as the author of the plot to murder them, and was rewarded by the king's favorable reception of her plea.

Esther's Petition for Her Life

Verses 1-4, So the king and Haman came to the banquet with Esther the queen. 2 And the king said again to Esther on the second day at the banquet of wine, What is thy petition, queen Esther? and it shall be granted thee: and what is thy request? even to the half of the kingdom it shall be performed. 3 Then Esther the queen answered and said, If I have found favor in thy sight, O king, and if it please the king, let my life be given me at my petition, and my people at my request: 4 for we are sold, I and my people, to be destroyed, to be slain, and to perish. But if we had been sold for bondmen and bondwomen, I had held my peace, although the adversary could not have compensated for the king's damage.

What an incredible shock that request must have been to Haman! At this point, he no doubt began to understand that Esther was pleading for the life of all the Jews whom Haman had determined to destroy, and that she herself was among the number. This request was most skilfully presented.

(1) Esther protested that if the Jews had merely been sold as slaves, she would have held her peace.

(2) She protested that Haman had lied about being able to compensate the king for the damage done.

(3) She displayed perfect knowledge of Haman's immense bribe, noting that she and her people had been "sold."

(4) She placed all the blame on Haman, ignoring the king's own responsibility for that evil decree.

The King's Request for the Adversary's Identity

Verses 5-7, Then spake the king Ahasuerus and said unto Esther the queen, Who is he, and where is he, that durst presume in his heart to do so? 6 And Esther said, An adversary and an enemy, even this wicked Haman. Then Haman was afraid before the king and the queen. 7 And the king arose in his wrath from the banquet of wine and went into the palace garden: and Haman stood up to make request for his life to Esther the queen; for he saw that there was evil determined against him by the king.

At this juncture, the king began to get the whole picture. Indeed it had been Haman who had concocted that evil story about the Jews, had advised their destruction, and with the king's ring had himself mailed out the decree calling for their slaughter. In his anger, the king arose and left the banquet; and Haman was astute enough to know that his goose was indeed cooked. Naturally, Haman pleaded with Esther to spare his life; and when it became apparent that she would not help him, he fell at her feet imploring her. "He was still prostrate before the reclining queen, probably clasping her feet as a suppliant, when the furious king returned from his walk in the garden."[1] "Like the Greeks and Romans, the Persians reclined at their meals on sofas or couches."[2]

We have no agreement with, "Some commentators (who) have criticized Esther for not interceding for Haman."[3] However, such writers forget that as long as Haman lived, he was a deadly threat to the Jewish people. Esther was wise enough to see that although Haman was at the moment defeated; if he had survived, he might have found a way to achieve his purpose.

The King Returned and Ordered Haman's Execution

Verses 8-10, Then the king returned out of the palace garden into the place of the banquet of wine, and Haman was fallen upon the couch where Esther was. Then said the king, Will he even force the queen before me in this house? As the word went out of the king's mouth, they covered Haman's face. 9 Then said Harbonah, one of the king's chamberlains that went before the king, Behold also, the gallows fifty cubits high, which Haman hath made for

---

[1] NBCR, p. 418.

[2] FCC, *Esther,* p. 499.

[3] NLBC, p. 356.

Mordecai, who spake good for the king, standeth in the
house of Haman. And the king said, Hang him thereon.
10 So they hanged Haman on the gallows that he had
prepared for Mordecai. Then was the king's wrath pacified.

Will he even force the queen before me (v. 8)? The
furious king was placing the worst possible construction
upon Haman's prostrate position before Esther,
suggesting by these words that Haman was attempting
to rape the queen. That was certainly not the case at
all; but it is a matter of history that Xerxes was capable
of doing nearly anything, and that he was unstable,
unreasonable and capricious. It was the knowledge of
all this that had fueled Esther's fear when she went
unbidden into his presence.

As the word went out of the king's mouth (v. 8).
The singular rendition of *WORD* in this place is correct;
"For it is singular in the Hebrew."[4] Furthermore, "That
Hebrew word may also be rendered *JUDGMENT,* being
therefore a statement that the king immediately
pronounced the judgment of death against Haman."[5]
The fact that they immediately, "covered Haman's face,"
supports that understanding of the passage.

Then said Harbonah ... Behold also, the gallows
fifty cubits high in the house of Haman (v. 9). This sheds
further light on that gallows. Its being *in the house of*
Haman forbids the notion that it was really that tall.
How then was it "fifty cubits high"? The answer appears

---

4 NBCR, p. 418.
5 Ibid.

to be that it had been placed at that altitude on the city wall, where, in all probability Haman's house was located; and in that position, it could be seen from the place where the banquet of wine was being held. The meaning then would be that the gallows was that high, in the sense of being erected at that elevation. Our analysis of this has some element of speculation in it; but it is difficult to suppose that any kind of structure nearly a hundred feet in height could have been constructed over night. Also, the word *behold* indicates that it was visible from the palace.

Then the king's wrath was pacified (v. 10). Very well, so far, so good! But the danger was far from being averted. That evil decree sent forth in the authority of the "Law of the Medes and Persians that altereth not," was still out there, in every province of the Empire (Daniel 6:9). The great danger of a wholesale slaughter of the Jews still persisted.

xxx

CHAPTER 8

The Practical Reversal of that Irrevocable Decree

This chapter deals with the danger that yet remained. Yes, Haman was dead, but that decree which he had devised was still in force, backed up by the power of that "Law of the Medes and Persians that altereth not." This meant that all the Jews in the Persian empire were still subject to general slaughter and the confiscation of their property on the thirteenth of Adar. Something had to be done about that.

Consequences of Haman's Execution

Verses 1-2, On that day did the king Ahasuerus give the house of Haman unto Esther the queen. And Mordecai came before the king; for Esther had told what he was unto her. 2 And the king took off his ring, which he had taken from Haman, and gave it to Mordecai. And Esther set Mordecai over the house of Haman.

The house of Haman (v. 1). "Confiscation of goods and properties of the condemned accompanied executions in Persia, as in other Oriental countries."[1] The house of Haman included not merely the castle and its furnishings but also the host of servants, retainers, and attendants that went along with it.

The king gave this vast estate to Esther; and she might well have desired to give it to Mordecai; but what she did was even better. She placed him in absolute

---

[1] FCC, *Esther,* p. 500.

control over it, thus providing him with a residence and dignity that were appropriate to his new office as Prime Minister.

Summarizing the consequences in evidence here: (1) Haman's vast properties were conferred upon Esther; (2) Mordecai was given the management and control of them; (3) Ahasuerus bestowed the office of Prime Minister upon Mordecai when he gave him the ring that had been worn by Haman. (4) The ring gave Mordecai the power to seal documents and to convey with them the authority of law.

"It was perfectly natural for the king to confer this great authority upon Mordecai. The king had already delighted to honor him for exposing the plot against the king's life."[2]   Also, he had learned that Mordecai was the foster father of the queen.

Esther Entreats the King To Cancel Haman's Edict

Verses 3-6, And Esther spake yet again before the king, and fell down at his feet, and besought him with tears to put away the mischief of Haman the Agagite, and his device that he had devised against the Jews. 4 Then the king held out to Esther the golden sceptre. So Esther arose, and stood before the king. 5 And she said, If it please the king, and if I have found favor in his sight, and the thing seem right before the king, and if I be pleasing in his eyes, let it be written to reverse the letters devised by Haman, the son of Hammedatha the Agagite, which he wrote to destroy

---

[2] WYC, p. 455.

*the Jews that are in all the king's provinces: 6 for how can
I endure to see the evil that shall come upon my people? or
how can I endure to see the destruction of my kindred?*

It is of interest that Mordecai does not carry this
urgent request to the king.   He was the new First
Minister of the empire; but he might have felt that
Esther would be more likely to have a favorable reply
from the king. At any rate, Esther did it.

*And the king held out to Esther the golden sceptre
(v. 4).*   "This seems to imply that Esther had again
approached the king unbidden."[3]

And (if) I be pleasing in his eyes (v. 5).   Esther's
appeal was prefaced with the usual stereotyped phrases
used by petitioners; but these words stress Esther's
personal attractiveness to the king.   This was indeed a
delicate feminine touch.

Reverse the letters devised by Haman (v. 5).   This
was indeed exactly what should have been done; and
this exceedingly intelligent and tactful queen here gave
Ahasuerus a valid reason why he should have done so;
but that silly rule about the "Law of the Medes and
Persians that altereth not," prevented the king from
taking such action.   Note the tact of Esther here.   "She
was careful not to put any blame on the king for
Haman's wicked letters."[4]

"Many have accused Esther and her race of
cruelty because of their slaughter of their enemies, but

3 JRD, p. 288.
4 WYC, p. 455.

without justification. She implored for the bloody edict of Haman to be reversed (v. 5); and if she had been heard, no blood at all would have been shed; but the Gentile mind was not of the kindly sort. Oh no. The king likes to see blood; he is a sportsman. Blood must flow. You Jews defend yourselves. Fight!"[5]

Unable to Reverse the Decree, the King
Did the Next Best Thing

Verses 7-8, Then the king Ahasuerus said unto Esther the queen and to Mordecai the Jew. Behold, I have given Esther the house of Haman, and him they have hanged upon the gallows, because he laid his hand upon the Jews. 8 Write ye also to the Jews, as it pleaseth you, in the king's name, and seal it with the king's ring; for the writing which is written in the king's name, and sealed with the king's ring, may no man reverse.

I have given Esther the house of Haman, and him they have hanged (v. 7). "Ahasuerus, anxious to show Esther that he did indeed love her, here recounted the favors already bestowed upon her; but he added that no one, not even the king of Persia, had the right to reverse a decree signed and sealed with the king's ring."[6] "The king was saying that his refusal to reverse the decree was not due to his lack of desire, but to his lack of

---

[5] ASP, p. 339.
[6] WYC, p. 455.

ability."[7]

Nevertheless, as Cook stated it, "Ahasuerus did, in fact, practically reverse the wicked decree."[8] This he accomplished by allowing Mordecai to write whatever letters he pleased to the Jews, giving them full authority to unite, gather together, arm themselves, and defend themselves against all attacks.

A Counter Edict Sent Forth by Mordecai

Verses 9-14, Then were the king's scribes called at that time, in the third month, which is the month Sivan, on the three and twentieth day thereof; and it was written according to all that Mordecai commanded unto the Jews, and to the satraps, and the governors and princes of the provinces which are from India unto Ethiopia, a hundred twenty and seven provinces, unto every province according to the writing thereof, and unto every people after their language, and to the Jews according to their writing, and according to their language. 10 And he wrote in the name of king Ahasuerus, and sealed it with the king's ring, and sent letters by posts on horseback, riding on swift steeds that were used in the king's service, bred of the stud: 11 wherein the king granted the Jews that were in every city to gather themselves together, and to stand for their life, to destroy, to slay, and to cause to perish, all the power of the people and province that would assault them, their little ones and women, and to take the spoil of them for a prey,

---

[7] JRD, p. 288.
[8] FCC, op. cit., p. 500.

*12 upon one day in all the provinces of king Ahasuerus,
namely, upon the thirteenth day of the twelfth month,
which is the month Adar. 13 A copy of the writing, that the
decree should be given out in every province, was published
unto all the peoples, and that the Jews should be ready
against that day to avenge themslves on their enemies. 14
So the posts that rode upon swift steeds that were used in
the king's service went out, being hastened and pressed on
by the king's commandment; and the decree was given out
in Shushan the palace.*

      **In the third month, which is the month Sivan (v.
9).** "The name Sivan is another Babylonian name, the
third month being sacred to the moon god.   It
corresponded to our May-June."[9] "The date was June
25, 474 BC, a little over two months after the first
decree was issued,"[10] thus allowing over eight months
for the Jews to prepare their defenses.
      To destroy, to slay, and to cause to perish (v. 11).
This decree followed very closely the language of the
edict of Haman (3:13) in order to nullify it to the fullest
extent possible. "The exact treatment intended for the
Jews was to be meted out for their enemies."[11] "The
irrevocability of Haman's decree made it necessary for
Mordecai to duplicate in reverse all of its provisions,
thus inevitably giving the impression of a very harsh
decree. When the day came, it stressed that the Jews

---

9 PC, Vol. 7c, p. 142
10 WYC, p. 455.
11 NBCR, p. 419.

did not plunder their enemies."[12]

The Jews were authorized to take the property of their attackers, but when the time came they waived that right.

All the power of the people and province (v. 11). "This is a reference to the military forces."[13]

The Great Rejoicing of the Jews Everywhere

Verses 15-17, And Mordecai went forth from the presence of the king in royal apparel of blue and white, and with a great crown of gold, and with a robe of fine linen and purple: and the city of Shushan shouted and was glad. 16 The Jews had light and gladness, and joy and honor. 17 And in every province, and in every city, whithersoever the king's commandment and his decree came, the Jews had gladness and joy, a feast and a good day. And many from among the peoples of the land became Jews; for the fear of the Jews was fallen upon them.

Mordecai went forth ... with a great crown of gold (v. 15). "The Hebrew has two different words for crown, namely, **KETHER** which referred to the type of crown worn by the monarch, and **ATARAH,** a crown of an inferior kind frequently worn by nobles."[14] Mordecai's crown was the latter. His great authority, symbolized here by his apparel and the crown, was, however, one of

---

[12] NLBC, p. pp. 556,557.

[13] WYC, p. 455.

[14] PC, op. cit., p. 142.

the primary reasons for the Jews' rejoicing.

"The Jews ... had a feast and a good day (v. 16).
"This celebration was in anticipation of the feast of
Purim, which was first celebrated eight months later
(9:17-19)."[15]

*And many among the peoples of the land became
Jews (v. 17).* "Such a providential outworking of events
in favor of the Jews convinced many of the power of
God, and caused them to become proselytes."[16]

Some scholars have interpreted this acceptance
of Judaism as merely a political maneuver, not based
upon any sincere belief in God; but Keil wrote that,
"This might have been true of some of the inhabitants of
Shushan, but the majority certainly acted from more
honorable motives."[17]

xxx

---

[15] WYC, p. 455.

[16] NBCR, p. 419.

[17] CFK, Vol. 3c, p. 371.

CHAPTERS 9
Institution and Observance of the Feast of Purim, Celebrating the Great Victory of Israel on the Thirteenth of Adar

On That Fateful Day, Thirteenth of Adar

Verses 1-10, *Now in the twelfth month, which is the month Adar, on the thirteenth day of the same, when the king's commandment and his decree drew near to be put in execution, on the day that the enemies of the Jews hoped to have rule over them (whereas it was turned to the contrary, that the Jews had rule over them that hated them), 2 the Jews gathered themselves together in their cities throughout all the provinces of the king Ahasuerus, to lay hands on such as sought their hurt: and no man could withstand them; for the fear of them was fallen upon all the peoples. 3 And all the princes of the provinces, and the satraps, and the governors, and they that did the king's business, helped the Jews, because the fear of Mordecai was fallen upon them. 4 For Mordecai was great in the king's house, and his fame went forth throughout all the provinces; for the man Mordecai waxed greater and greater. 5 And the Jews smote all their enemies with the stroke of the sword, and with slaughter and destruction, and did what they would to them that hated them. 6 And in Shushan the palace the Jews slew and destroyed five hundred men. 7 And Parshandatha, and Dalphon, and Aspatha, 8 and Poratha, and Adalia, and Aridatha, 9 and Parmashta, and Arisai, and Aridai, and Vaizatha, 10 the ten sons of Haman the son of Hammedatha, the Jews' enemy, slew they; but on the spoil they laid not their hand.*

The Jews gathered themselves together in their cities (v. 2). "This does not mean exclusively Jewish cities, but cities where the Jews constituted an element in the population."[1] At this point in history, there were no exclusively Jewish cities outside of Judaea.

On such as sought their hurt (v. 2). "Retaliation was limited to those who actively sought to kill the Jews."[2]

All the princes, etc. ... helped the Jews (v. 3). Rawlinson believed that this did not include military help, but only moral support;[3] but Dummelow wrote that, "The great massacre (v. 16) was, in part, the work of Persian authorities and their military forces."[4] The latter viewpoint seems more reasonable to this writer. F. C. Cook also agreed with this.[5]

The fear of Mordecai had fallen upon them (v. 3). "It was clear to all the Persian authorities that both the king and Mordecai favored the Jews, and those who attacked the Jews would surely have brought wrath upon themselves."[6]

And the Jews smote all their enemies (v. 5). "There were many Persian citizens who took full advantage of the first decree and attacked their hated Jewish

---

[1] PC, Vol. 7c, p. 156.
[2] NLBC, p. 557.
[3] PC, op. cit., p. 156.
[4] JRD, p. 288.
[5] FCC, *Esther,* p. 502.
[6] WYC, p. 456.

neighbors; but, deprived of government support, and faced by a newly encouraged people, they were totally defeated."[7]

Parshandatha, etc ... the ten sons of Haman (vv. 7-10). "These names are Persian and traceable to old Persian roots."[8] This fact alone makes it impossible to accept the unsupported allegation of critics that, "The book of Esther is fiction."[9] Such critics attempt to identify Esther as a fiction written in the times of the Maccabees; but who, on earth, three hundred years after the events related would have remembered, or could have invented, ten authentic Persian names for the sons of Haman?

But on the spoil they laid not their hand (v. 10). This statement occurs no less than three times in this chapter, appearing also in vv. 15 and 16. "The Jews had a right to take the spoil, but they waived it, because they were fighting for survival, not for material gain. They were not the aggressors in this conflict, but they were defending themselves from their enemies who sought to slay them."[10]

Summary of Casualties in Shushan and the Provinces

Verses 11-16, On that day the number of those slain in Shushan the palace was brought before the king.

---

[7] Ibid.

[8] FCC, op. cit., p. 502.

[9] ASP, p. 340.

[10] NLBC, p. 557.

12 And the king said unto Esther the queen, The Jews have slain and destroyed five hundred men in Shushan the palace, and the ten sons of Haman; what then have they done in the rest of the king's provinces! Now what is thy petition? and it shall be granted thee: or what is thy request further? and it shall be done. 13 Then said Esther, If it please the king, let it be granted to the Jews that are in Shushan to do tomorrow also according to this day's decree, and let Haman's ten sons be hanged upon the gallows. 14 And the king commanded it so to be done: and a decree was given out in Shushan; and they hanged Haman's ten sons. 15 And the Jews that were in Shushan gathered themslves together on the fourteenth day also of the month Adar, and slew three hundred men in Shushan; but on the spoil they laid not their hand. 16 And the other Jews that were in the king's provinces gathered themslves together, and stood for their lives, and had rest from their enemies, and slew of them that hated them seventy and five thousand; but on the spoil they laid not their hand.

Let Haman's ten sons be hanged upon the gallows (v. 13). These had been slain on the previous day; "This is a request that their dead bodies be exposed, such exposure being a mark of infamy."[11]

And a decree was given out in Shushan (v. 14). This decree did not regard the exposure of the bodies of Haman's sons. "It granted permission to the Jews to fight against their enemies on the morrow also."[12]

---

[11] JRD, p. 288.
[12] CFK, op. cit., p. 374.

This continuation of the conflict for an extra day in Shushan resulted in two different days being celebrated by the Jews. "In the capital, they celebrated the 15th of Adar, and in the provinces they celebrated the 14th."[13] It is not known exactly why there were two days of fighting in Shushan. Evidently, a strong band of Jewish enemies had not been defeated that first day; and therefore the king granted an extra day in which three hundred more Jewish enemies were destroyed.

Explanation of the Two Different Celebrations

Verses 17-19, This was done on the thirteenth day of the month Adar; and on the fourteenth day of the same they rested, and made it a day of feasting and gladness. 18 But the Jews that were in Shushan assembled themselves together on the thirteenth day thereof, and on the fourteenth thereof; and on the fifteenth day of the same they rested, and made it a day of feasting and gladness. 19 Therefore do the Jews of the villages and the unwalled towns, make the fourteenth day of the month Adar a day of gladness and feasting, and a good day, and of sending portions to one another.

Mordecai Recommended the Annual Celebration of the Fourteenth and Fifteenth Days of Adar

Verses 20-25, And Mordecai wrote these things, and sent letters unto all the Jews that were in all the

---

[13] PC, op. cit., p. 157.

*provinces of the king Ahasuerus, both nigh and far, 21 to
enjoin them that they should keep the fourteenth day of the
month Adar, and the fifteenth day of the same, yearly, 22
as the days wherein the Jews had rest from their enemies,
and the month which was turned unto them from sorrow
to gladness, and from mourning into a good day; that they
should make them days of feasting and gladness, and of
sending portions one to another, and gifts to the poor. 23
And the Jews undertook to do as they had begun, and as
Mordecai had written unto them; 24 because Haman the
son of Hammedatha, the Agagite, the enemy of all the Jews,
had plotted against the Jews to destroy them, and had cast
Pur, that is, the lot, to consume them, and to destroy them;
25 But when the matter came before the king, he
commanded by letters that his wicked device, which he had
devised against the Jews, should return upon his own head,
and that he and his sons should be hanged on the gallows.*

This letter marked the beginning of the Jewish
feast of Purim. "Here he wrote to the provincial Jews
suggesting that they observe two days, namely, the 14th
and 15th days of Adar, annually, with an explanation of
why he thought that should be done, but without issuing
any order to that effect."[14] Later, when Mordecai's
suggestion was favorably received, he issued an order
enjoining its observance.

*The month which was turned unto them from
sorrow to joy (v. 23).* This is the theme of Purim.
"Sorrow turned into joy, mourning into dancing, utter

---

[14] PC, op. cit., p. 158.

destruction into glorious triumph ---this is the dominant idea of Purim, to which all else was secondary and subordinate."[15]

The Origin of the Name for the Feast of Purim

Verses 26-28,   Wherefore they called these days Purim, after the name of Pur.   Therefore because of all the words of this letter, and of that which they had seen concerning this matter, and that which had come unto them,   27 the Jews ordained, and took upon them, and upon their seed, and upon all such as joined themselves unto them, so that it should not fail, that they would keep these two days according to the writing thereof, and according to the appointed time thereof, every year;   28 and that these days should be remembered and kept throughout every generation, every family, every province, and every city; and that these days of Purim should not fail from among the Jews, nor the remembrance of them perish from their seed.

The feast of Purim is today observed by the Jews; and it has been continually observed throughout history, from the times of Xerxes (who was assassinated in the year 465 BC) until the present day, for almost twenty-five centuries; and, to this writer, it appears as an absolute impossiblity that such a sequence of observances could have been initiated, or kicked off, by some unknown writer's fictitious yarn. It takes twenty

---

[15] Ibid.

times as much faith to believe that allegation as it takes
to believe the Bible.

    They called these days Purim, after the name of Pur
(v. 26). The word **Pur** is the Persian word for **lot.** which
is a reference to Haman's casting lots to decide the day
when the Jews would be destroyed. "The Jews took the
Persian word **Pur,** and gave it a Hebrew plural **Purim,**
either because the Persian method of casting involved
several lots, or because Haman cast **Pur** several times
(3:7)."[16]

The Second Letter Establishing the Feast of Purim

    Verses 29-32, Then Esther the queen, the daughter
of Abihail, and Mordecai the Jew, wrote with all authority
to confirm this second letter of Purim. 30 And he sent
letters unto all the Jews, to the hundred and twenty and
seven provinces of the kingdom of Ahasuerus, with words of
peace and truth, 31 to confirm these days of Purim in their
apppointed times, according as Mordecai the Jew and
Esther the queen had enjoined them, and as they had
ordained for themselves and for their seed, in the matter of
their fastings and their cry. 32 And the commandment of
Esther confirmed these matters of Purim; and it was
written in the book.

    The queen ... and Mordecai ... wrote with all
authority (v. 29). The teaching here is that the feast of
Purim was established in Israel, not by religious

---

[16] Ibid.

authority, but by civil authority; and there is no way that such a thing could have been allowed in Israel, except as a consequence of such events as are related in Esther and at a time closely associated with those events. *This second letter of Purim (v. 29).* "This was a new letter, not the one mentioned in v. 20; and this one included a period of fasting (v. 31)."[17] "That first letter was merely a recommendation; but its favorable reception prompted Esther and Mordecai to make the feast official."[18] Evidently the incorporation of a day of fasting into the feast of Purim was due to suggestions from the provinces upon their reception of that first letter.

Quite appropriately, the day of fasting was called the Fast of Esther, stressing the anxiety and danger that existed when, after three days of fasting, she went unbidden into the presence of Ahasuerus. That fast is observed on Adar 13th, and the two days of feasting on the succeeding two days. "The Jews still keep this day as Esther's fast, prior to the Purim celebrations proper, marked by the reading of the roll of Esther in its original chant, accompanied by blessings and hymns."[19]

And it was written in the book (v. 32). Keil understood this as a reference to, "Some book which has not come down to us";[20] and despite our reluctance to disagree with Keil, we cannot accept this. Only one

---

[17] WYC, p. 456.
[18] FCC, p. 503.
[19] NBCR, p. 420.
[20] CFK, op. cit., p. 378.

book is mentioned in Esther and that is the "Book of the Chronicles of the kings of the Medes and Persians" (2:23, 10:2). In fact, the implication throughout Esther is that practically all of it is documented in that book. Certainly, "The author of Esther drew on written sources."[21]

xxx

---

[21] NLBC, p. 557.

CHAPTER 10
Final Note on the Greatness of Mordecai

Verses 1-3, And the king Ahasuerus laid a tribute upon the land, and upon the isles of the sea. 2 And all the acts of his power and of his might, and the full account of the greatness of Mordecai, whereunto the king advanced him, are they not written in the book of the chronicles of the kings of Media and Persia? 3 For Mordecai the Jew was next unto king Ahasuerus, and great among the Jews, and accepted of the multitude of the brethren, seeking the good of his people, and speaking peace to all his seed.

The purpose of the author in this very short chapter is that of stressing the greatness of Mordecai, the key word being that, in all the world, no one was any greater than Mordecai except the king. "Mordecai was next unto king Ahasuerus"! This required a preliminary note on how great was Ahasuerus. He was the ruler of most of the world as it was known then, from India to Ethiopia, with one hundred twenty-seven provinces, and here is added a note that he laid tribute upon the land and the isles of the sea. After the Grecian campaign, in which Xerxes suffered defeat, his dominion over the isles of the sea was reduced, but still existed. "Cyprus and Aradus were among the isles he still ruled."[1]

Not only was Mordecai next to king Ahasuerus; but his mighty deeds were written in the book of the chronicles of the Medo-Persian empire, along with that of their mighty kings. Incidentally, we have here the

---

[1] FCC, *Esther,* p. 503.

most conspicuous evidence that the Medo-Persian Empire was never two empires, but only one; the record of all their kings was in the same book!

"The author of Esther here emphasized the great power and wealth of Xerxes in order to show the marvelous providence of God in elevating a despised Jew to a position of honor and trust in such an empire."[2]

Many things we would like to know. For example, how long did Esther remain on the throne as queen? How many years did Mordecai continue as Prime Minister? "But Esther was not written to record the lives of emperors, queens, or prime ministers, but to preserve the record of a great national deliverance of God's people, a deliverance which would bring comfort and hope to millions of Jews through millenniums of time."[3]

Seeking the good of his people, and speaking peace to all his seed (v. 3). "The meaning of these two phrases is that Mordecai procured both by word and deed the good and prosperity of his people. This is the way in which honor and fortune are attained, the way indicated in the 34th Psalm (vv. 13-15), when teaching the fear of the Lord."[4]

Joyce Baldwin pointed out that, "These three verses are couched in thoroughly biblical terms. Zechariah 9:10 speaks of the Messiah that, 'He shall speak peace to the nations (9:10)'; and no earthly ruler

---

[2] WYC, p. 456.
[3] NLBC, p. 557.
[4] CFK, Vol. 3c, p. 380.

could have done more than to speak peace to his people."[5]

Speaking peace to all his seed (v. 3). In all probability Mordecai was a eunuch, and therefore we understand 'his seed' here to be a reference to God's Israel.

xxx

---

[5] NBCR, p. 420.

BIBLIOGRAPHY
Bibliography for Commentary on Ezra, Nehemiah and Esther

VERSIONS OF THE BIBLE CONSULTED

American Standard Version, 1901 (Ft. Worth: Star Bible Publi-
    cations, Inc.).
Authorized Version (King James Bible) (New York: Collins Clear
    Type Press).
Cross-Reference Bible with Various Readings (New York: Cross-
    Reference Bible Company, 1910).
Douay Version of the OT (New York: Catholic Book Publishing
    Company, 1948).
Good News Bible (New York: American Bible Society, 1974).
La Biblia, Dios Habla Hoy (Spanish Bible) (New York: American
    Bible Society 1979).
New International Version (Grand Rapids: Zondervan Publishing
    House, 1982).
New Standard Revised Version (Nashville: Holman Bible Pub-
    lishers, 1989).
NIV Interlinear Hebrew-English OT (Grand Rapids: Zondervan
    Publishing House, 1979).
Revised Standard Version (New York: Thomas Nelson and Sons,
    1946).
Bible in Modern English by James Moffatt, 1929.

DICTIONARIES AND ENCYCLOPEDIAS

Britannica World Language Dictionary (Chicago: William Benton,
    Publisher, 1961).
Encyclopaedia Britannica (Chicago: William Benton, Publisher,
    1961).
Encyclopedia of Ancient Egypt (New York & Oxford: Facts
    on File, 1991).
International Standard Bible Encyclopedia (Chicago: Howard-
    Severance Company, 1915).
New Bible Dictionary (Grand Rapids: William B. Eerdmans
    Publishing Company, 1965).

Peloubet's Bible Dictionary (Chicago: The John C. Winston, 1926).
Webster Dictionary, Complete and Unabridged, International
    Edition (New York: J. J. Little and Ives, 1957).
Wycliffe's Bible Encyclopedia (Chicago: Moody Press, 1974).

AUTHORS QUOTED

Anderson, Bernard W., in *Interpreter's Bible, Vol. 3,* (New York:
    Abingdon Press, 1986).

Baldwin, Joyce G. in *New Bible Commentary Revised* (Grand
    Rapids: Wm. B. Eerdmans Publishing Company, 1967).
Barker, P. C. in *Pulpit Commentary Vol. 6* (Grand Rapids: Wm. B.
    Eerdmans Publishing Company, 1950).
Barker, William P. , *Everyone in the Bible* (Westwood, N. J.:
    Fleming H. Revell, 1966).
Batten as quoted by A. E. Cundall in NBCR.
Bendor-Samuel, John, in *New Laymans Bible Commentary* (Grand
    Rapids: Zondervan Publishing House, 1979).
Bowman, Raymond A. in Interpreter's Bible, Vol. 3, (New York:
    Abingdon Press, 1956).

Clarke, Adam, *Commentary on Whole Bible, Vol. 2* (London: T.
    Mason & G. Lane, 1837).
Cook, F. C., *The Bible Commentary , Kings and Chronicles* (Grand
    Rapids: Baker Book House, 1953).
Cundall, A. E, in NBCR.

DeHoff, George W., *DeHoff's Commentary, Vol. 2* (Murfreesboro,
    TN: DeHoff Publications, 1977).
Delitzsch, F. in *Keil-Delitzsch Old Testament Commentary* (Grand
    Rapids: Wm. B. Eerdmans Publishing Company)
Dilday, Russell H., Jr., in *Teacher's Bible Commentary* (Nashville;
    Broadman Press, 1972)

Duff, Archibald, in *Arthur S. Peake's Bible Commentary* (Edinburgh: T. C. & E. C. Jack, Ltd., 1924).

Dummelow, J. R., *Commentary on the Holy Bible* (New York: The Macmillan Company, 1937).

Gilkey, Charles W., in *Interpreter's Bible, Vol. 3* (New York: Abingdon Press, 1956).

Halley, Henry H., *Bible Handbook* (Grand Rapids: Zondervan Publishing House).

Hamrick, Emmett Willard, in *Broadman Bible Commentary, Vol. 3*

Henry, Matthew in *Matthew Henry's Commentary, Vo. 2.*

Herodotus, as quoted by C. F. Keil.

Jamieson, Robert, in *Jamieson Fausset and Brown Commentary.*

Josephus, Flavius, *Life and Works of*, translated by William Whiston (New York: Holt, Rinehart and Winston).

Kaufmann, Y, *History of the Religion of Israel, Vol. IV* (New York: KTAV, 1977)

Keil. C. F., *Commentary on the Old Testament, Vol. 3* (Grand Rapids: Wm. B. Eerdmans Publishing Company).

Kenyon, Kathleen, *Jerusalem: Excavating 3,000 Years of History* (New York: McGraw-Hill, Publishers, 1967).

Kenyon, Sir Frederick, *The Bible and Archaeology* (New York, 1940).

Lockyer, Herbert, *All the Men of the Bible* (Grand Rapids: Zondervan Publishing House, 1938).

Oesterley, W. O. E., *First and Second Chronicles* in A . S. Peake's Commentary (London: T. C. & E. C. Jack, Ltd., 1924).

Porter, H. , in *International Bible Encycolpedia* (Chicago: The Howard-Severance Company, 1915).

Rawlinson, G., in *Pulpit Commentary, Vol. 7* (Grand Rapids: Wm. B. Eerdmans Publishing Company, 1950).

Short, Stephen S., in New Laymans Bible Commentary (Grand Rapids: Zondervan Publishing House, 1979).

Simmons, Billy E. *First and Second Chronicles* in Teacher's Bible Commentary (Nashville: Broadman Press, 1972).

Thompson, J. A. , *The Bible and Archaeology* (Grand Rapids: Wm. B. Eerdmans Publishing Company, 1982).

Unger, Merrill F., *Archeology and the Old Testament* (Grand Rapids: Zondervan Publishing House, 1960).

Whitcomb, John C. in Wycliffe Bible Commentary (Chicago: Moody Press, 1962).

Whiston, William, *Josephus, Life and Works of* in JOSA (New York: Holt, Rinehart and Winston).

Williamson, H. G. M., in *Word Bible Commentary, Vol. 16* (Waco: Word Publishing Company, 1985).

Wilson, R. Dick, in ISBE.

Woodhouse, Christopher Montague. in *EnBr., Vol. 10*

xxx

INDEX
For Vol. VIII of Historical Books